MARY TUDOR
ENGLAND'S FIRST QUEEN REGNANT

I am a Catholic man and a priest. In that faith have I lived and in that faith do I intend to die, and if you esteem my religion treason, then I am guilty. As for any other treason, I never committed any. I stand condemned for nothing but the saying of Mass, hearing confessions, preaching and such like duties and functions of priesthood.

St Edmund Campion. Extract of his speech delivered at his execution. He was charged and found guilty of treason by the Elizabethan regime in 1581. Campion was hanged, drawn and quartered as one of nearly two hundred Catholics executed in England by Elizabeth I for their faith.

Mary Tudor

England's First Queen Regnant

Truth is the Daughter of Time

Gregory Slysz

GRACEWING

First published in England in 2015

by

Gracewing
2 Southern Avenue
Leominster
Herefordshire HR6 0QF
United Kingdom

www.gracewing.co.uk

ISBN 978 085244 856 4

Typeset by Word and Page, Chester

Cover design by Bernardita Peña Hurtado

CONTENTS

List of Illustrations   vi

Abbreviations   vii

Introduction   1

I. THE MAKING AND UNMAKING OF BLOODY MARY

1. Initial Uncertainty over the Marian Legacy   9

2. The Catholic Fifth Column and the Consolidation of the British Nation-State   18

3. Catholic Apologia and Attempts to Buck the Anti-Catholic Trend   33

4. Continuity and Revision   44

II. PAWN AND VICTIM

5. Mary's Earliest Years: A Childhood Blighted by Parental Discord   59

6. Mary in Limbo   78

7. From Troublesome Daughter to Troublesome Sister   92

8. Mary the Politician   103

III. CREATIVE RECONSTRUCTION RATHER THAN BLIND REACTION

9. The Challenges of the Restoration and the Nature of Later-Medieval and Early Tudor Religion   127

10. The Nature of Mary's Personal Faith   143

11. Cardinal Pole and the Programme of Restoration   153

12. Defending the Indefensible   174

Conclusion   199

Bibliography   207

Index   219

ILLUSTRATIONS

Fig. 1. *O the Roast Beef of Old Englan*d (*The Gate of Calais*),
 1748, William Hogarth (1697–1764)   28

Fig. 2. Posthumous Portrait of Henry VIII with Queen Mary
 and Will Somers the Jester. Artist unknown, 16th century.   86

Fig. 3. The tomb of Elizabeth I (and Mary I)   200

Fig. 4. Artist's impression of Queen Mary's place of rest, 1558–1606,
 based on a description by Henry Machyn. Sketch by Stephen
 Grant.   201

ABBREVIATIONS

Acts	John Foxe's *Acts and Monuments* online: http://www.johnfoxe.org/
APCE	Acts of the Privy Council of England: http://www.british-history.ac.uk/catalogue.aspx?type=3&gid=156
CSPS	Calendar of State Papers, Spain: http://www.british-history.ac.uk/catalogue.aspx?gid=136
CSPV	Calendar of State Papers relating to English Affairs in the Archives of Venice: http://www.britishhistory.ac.uk/catalogue.aspx?gid=140
LPFD	Letters and Papers, Foreign and Domestic, Henry VIII: http://www.british-history.ac.uk/catalogue.aspx?gid=126
Original Letters	*Original Letters Relative to the English Reformation Written during the Reigns of King Henry VIII, King Edward VI and Queen Mary, Chiefly from Authenticated Copies of the Autographs and Edited for the Rev. Hasting Robinson.* Cambridge: Cambridge University Press, 1846.

To my mother, in gratitude for everything

INTRODUCTION

OVER THE PAST FEW DECADES, the reign of Mary I has received much scholarly attention. Hitherto dominant assumptions about the nature of the reign, its policies, its achievements, its power-brokers, their motives and above all Mary herself have undergone extensive reassessment. The task, however, has had to overcome centuries of misinformation and anti-Catholic propaganda that conspired to depict the English Reformation as an inevitable popular revolt against a corrupt and detested Church, and Queen Mary as one who attempted to stop this process with extreme cruelty. This imagery became an important component of a political-national ideology that underpinned 'liberal' England/Britain until quite recently.

A reader who has been raised on the Whig idea that a national ideology was something practised by Continentals may baulk at the suggestion that politically sober Britain was founded on a prejudicial ideology which viewed the Catholic religious outlook as essentially evil and those who espoused it as traitors. Yet not only was Britain founded on an ideology, but on one that was largely based on myth and prejudice. The architects of all this were powerful confessional and political interests which emerged in the wake of Henry VIII's break with Rome during the early 1530s and which have come to reinforce one another ever since out of mutual self-interest. With the national Church came a new national identity. Its custodians were powerful stakeholders whose personal interests were tied to the new order. The brief Catholic interregnum under Mary saw their interests wane somewhat, only for them to recover with the succession of Mary's half-sister Elizabeth. Henceforth the tide against the old, Catholic order was to turn decisively. The nation at large would eventually accept the new order, having been subjected to intense anti-Catholic propaganda as well as intimidated by draconian legislation that sought to leave no doubt in people's minds about how to think and act.

The mythology surrounding Mary was fostered by centuries of political conditioning, which skewed opinion against her. Notwithstanding Mary's methods in suppressing Protestantism, which as a reaction to heresy was not atypical for Protestant and Catholic rulers alike at the time, her politics and religion were incompatible with those favoured by her successors. The more England, and later Britain, distanced itself from the old religion and political commitments, the more its rulers had to denigrate those who were associated with them. As such, Mary, as the last Catholic monarch of

England, whose brief reign was sandwiched between two 'great' Protestant rulers, Henry VIII and Elizabeth I, was a key target. Britain's unity and very idea of nationhood was mostly built on Protestantism. In ruling the waves and regularly confronting Catholic foes, Britain would accommodate little goodwill for those whose religion automatically rendered them alien and as such a security hazard for the realm. In time, Mary would acquire the sobriquet 'Bloody', her reign and policies would be maligned and her sanity questioned. Children would learn from nursery rhymes of her contrariness, cruelty and infertility[1] and how she blinded 'mice'[2] who opposed her, while adolescent girls, wishing to catch sight of their future husband, were encouraged to practise a grotesque ritual involving the use of mirrors and candles in darkened rooms.[3]

By contrast, history has treated the founders and consolidators of England's Protestantism much more benignly. Had history writing on the period been governed by objective criteria, it would have applied any number of fitting sobriquets to Henry VIII to reflect the cruelty and disasters of his reign – Henry the Adulterer, Henry the Fornicator, Henry the Cruel, Henry the Vandal, Henry the Bigamist, Henry the Merciless, Bloody Henry. But of course it did not. The occasional accusation of tyranny, perhaps, but nothing approaching lasting opprobrium. If anything, his ebullient, unsavoury temperament that could decide the fate of a person on a whim has been reduced to that of the kind of cantankerousness associated with old men[4] and his dictatorship to that of a necessary evil supported by the people who were 'conscious of the fact that Henry was their only bulwark against the recurrence of civil strife'.[5] His daughter Elizabeth, the off-spring of Henry's marriage to Anne Boleyn, has similarly escaped the kind of misrepresentations and smears that her half-sister has had to endure. 'Perhaps no ruler', noted Kevin Sharpe, 'has left so enduring an impression on the English memory or the nation's past as Elizabeth Tudor'.[6] That is not to say that both she and her administration have not been subject to much critical analysis. Accusations of political indecisiveness, mismanagement of religious policy, ineptitude in the face of parliamentary and courtly factionalism, financial mismanagement, foreign policy confusion and governmental sterility have all been levelled against her.[7] Least complimentary of all is Christopher Haigh's stinging indictment of the Elizabethan reign as being '30 years of illusion followed by 15 years of delusion'.[8] But all that said and done, criticism of Elizabeth has been drowned out by an inordinate amount of praise of both her and her administration that frequently has morphed into absurd sycophancy towards 'Good Queen Bess', the Virgin Queen who, it was said, sacrificed herself on the altar of national duty. Her human frailties have been air-brushed out of vision and her policy errors have been eclipsed by alleged successes, while her execution of Catholics, including 146 priests, as well as many monks in Ireland, who were executed without trial by her troops,[9] has been depicted as a mark of strength in turbulent and dangerous times.

Governing Elizabeth's image has been the cult of Gloriana, initiated during her reign and nurtured ever since. 'From her first chronicler, William Camden', writes Sharpe, 'to the classic biographer of modern times, Sir John Neale, (largely male) historians have fallen in love with Elizabeth and approached the queen, as she endeavoured to present herself during her life, as an object of desire, as well as a focus of impartial study.'[10] With the advent of gender history, feminist historians, who largely shunned Mary for her 'reactionary' religious views, portrayed Elizabeth 'as a champion of women's rights in a patriarchal world'.[11] From contemporary portraiture to modern television and cinematic portrayals, the myth of the Virgin Queen, tied to her realm, the English Deborah, the strong-willed champion of Protestantism,[12] has served the national story well. No negative sobriquets here either.

The historiography of these themes offers crucial insight into the motives behind the manner in which they have been treated. The dominant trend for most of the four centuries since Henry VIII broke from Rome was of course Protestant triumphalism and most of the literature that was on offer for at least the first two centuries of this time was not history at all, but embittered polemic, highlighted by the sixteenth-century offerings of the austere Scottish Presbyterian John Knox and his English counterpart John Foxe. Here Catholicism and the work of its key devotees were essentially equated with satanic machinations against what was hailed as divinely inspired religious purification. Even when writing on the subject became more 'reasoned' with the likes of eighteenth-century Enlightenment writer David Hume and the nineteenth-century Whig historian Thomas Babington Macaulay, its core retained the erstwhile polemic: the Reformation may have been unpleasant, at times driven by greedy and objectionable individuals, but ultimately it brought forth salvation from superstition, and set England on the course to prosperity and modernity. Catholics attempted to redress the balance with their own confessional polemic, Nicholas Sanders (also spelt Sander), for instance, in the late Elizabethan era and Hugh Tootell, writing under the pseudonym Charles Dodd, in the mid-eighteenth century. However, the pariah status of these writers would ensure that their work would have limited success in influencing wider audiences. Even the more accommodating atmosphere of the nineteenth century changed things little for Catholic writers like John Lingard and Aidan Gasquet. The continuing marginalisation of Catholicism ensured that their revisions of erstwhile Protestant orthodoxy were to have limited public exposure.

It was ironic that some of the first breakthroughs in moderating public opinion towards Mary came from outside Catholic circles, most notably from the Anglicans, Elizabeth and Agnes Strickland, whose *The Lives of the Queens of England*, published during the 1840s,[13] dispelled many myths about both Mary's character and the nature of her government. But such revision too would find it difficult to compete with either prevailing Whig haughtiness or British messianism during a particularly triumphalist age. And in any case it was not without faults. While it may have slain some myths it promoted others to fit the prevailing Victorian preconceptions about the fairer sex. The Stricklands may have let Mary off the hook regarding the persecutions of Protestants, for which they blamed others, but they saddled her with a reputation of emotional instability. An emotionally unstable Mary could in turn explain her disposition to be so easily influenced by her wicked ministers. This aspect of the revision, essentially a re-hash of Foxian martyrology, was consolidated in the nineteenth century by James Anthony Froude, and picked up in the twentieth by Albert Fredrick Pollard. Mary herself may not have been cruel, but her administration was, and she herself was mad and incompetent. With some minor modifications, this caricature was to hold sway over both popular and scholarly imaginations for over a century until it was finally challenged, and then dismantled, by the end of the twentieth century under a different set of political conditions.

It has only been relatively recently that there has been a concerted effort to challenge the legends that have sullied both Mary's character and her reign, though, as Linda Porter noted, the 'tendency to depict her as a sad little woman who would have been better off as the Tudor equivalent of a housewife' persists.[14] Generally, however, the harsh edges of the verdict on her reign have been greatly blunted. Although there remains resistance in some quarters to exonerate totally 'this religious fanatic'[15] or to view Mary's reign in any way as 'creative',[16] it is being broken. Views that continue to look at Mary's reign as being totally 'sterile'[17] are no longer taken seriously. As the misrepresentations and prejudices are peeled away what remains is a reign like any other – successes, failures, unfulfilled goals, personal tragedies, exultation and crises, nuances that the vilification of her by her detractors obscured for so long.

*

This particular study has an overriding purpose, namely to offer an introduction to the key themes of Marian history in an accessible single volume. It is both biography and study of the policies of one of the most controversial monarchs of British history. For ease of access to the subject, the text is organised into three parts. The first focuses on the historiography on the Marian period, and seeks to highlight the reasons behind the misrepresentation of the Marian reign. Only when the motives of chroniclers and historians of the period have been analysed can one have hope of making any sense of the legends and fantasies that have surrounded the image of Mary down the centuries. The second part focuses on the years of her childhood, adolescence and early adulthood, tracing her long journey from a pampered child to England's first queen regnant. Then it re-evaluates Marian political and economic policies, hoping to dispel the myth that the administration was sterile and plagued by incompetence. The final part of the study traces the restoration of Catholicism to England as well as discussing the suppression of Protestantism, the most contentious policy with which the Marian administration has been associated. Here the long-standing assumption that Marian religious policy was a failure will be challenged.

It is always difficult in studies of this nature to try to strike a balance between detail and generalisation. I have attempted not to labour points or to inundate the text with excessive biographical detail. If readers require further information about a particular point they are directed to specialist texts in the bibliography. I hope that the sought-after balance between depth and breadth has been struck and a coherent introduction to the period has been produced. I of course leave final judgement to the reader.

NOTES

[1] 'Mary, Mary Quite Contrary, How does your garden grow? With silver bells and cockle shells, And pretty maids all in a row.' Although the anti-Catholic and derogatory content of this popular eighteenth-century nursery rhyme has some connection with Mary, Queen of Scots, it is more likely to have been associated with Mary Tudor. There are several interpretations of its content, all, however, being consistent with the negative view of Mary which had developed by the time of its first publication in 1744. The garden, for instance, could be an allusion either to graveyards, in reference to the growing number of Protestant victims or to Mary's infertility and phantom pregnancies. There are three colloquial references to torture instruments, silver bells being a type of thumb screw, cockle shells, an implement placed on genitals and maids, the type of guillotine called the Maiden. Reference to 'Pretty maids all in a row', could conversely be an allusion to 'rows' of executed Protestants or even to Mary's several miscarriages, while cockleshells could conceivably also be a reference to the reluctance of her husband, Philip, to engage in sexual relations with her, preferring instead affairs with other women (cuckolding).

[2] 'Three blind mice, three blind mice, See how they run, see how they run, They all ran after the farmer's wife, Who cut off their tails with a carving knife, Did you ever see such a thing in your life, As three blind mice?' Mary here is depicted as the 'farmer's wife', which alludes to her possession of vast estates across England and who proceeds to act against three noblemen who opposed her.

[3] The ritual involved chanting repeatedly 'I stole your baby Bloody Mary' while gazing into a mirror and holding a candle in a darkened room. An apparition of Mary, they were told, would presage premature death.

[4] Most notably in the classic 1933 cinematographic biography of the Henry, *The Private Life of Henry VIII* with Charles Laughton in the leading role.

⁵ See for instance A. F. Pollard, *Henry VIII* (London: Longman, Green and Co., 1919), p. 429.

⁶ K. Sharpe, *Selling the Tudor Monarchy: Authority and Image in Sixteenth Century England* (New Haven and London: Yale University Press, 2009), p. 319.

⁷ For a succinct discussion of historians' views on Elizabeth and her regime see J. Guy, 'Elizabeth I and Politics: The Views of Historians', http://www.tudors.org/asa2-level/59-elizabeth-i-and-politics-the-views-of-historians.html, accessed 12 June 2012. See also A. G. R. Smith, *The Emergence of a Nation State: The Commonwealth of England 1529–1660* (London: Longman, 1997), pp. 111–250.

⁸ C. Haigh, *Elizabeth I* (London: Longman, 2001), p. 202.

⁹ B. S. Gregory, *Salvation at Stake Christian Martyrdom in Early Modern Europe* (Cambridge, Mass.: Harvard University Press, 1999), p. 6

¹⁰ Sharpe, *Selling the Tudor Monarchy*, p. 319.

¹¹ Ibid.

¹² J. Guy, *Tudor England* (Oxford: Oxford University Press, 1998), pp. 250-289.

¹³ A. Strickland (and E. Strickland), *Lives of the Queens of England: From the Norman Conquest*, 8 vols. (London: Colburn & Co., 1851–2). Although the authorship is credited only to Agnes, many of the biographies were actually written by her sister Elizabeth, who insisted on anonymity.

¹⁴ L. Porter, *Mary Tudor, The First Queen* (London: Piatkus, 2009), p. 418.

¹⁵ F. Wilson, 'The Sunday Times Christmas Books', *The Sunday Times* (29 November 2009), http://www.thesundaytimes.co.uk/sto/culture/books/non_fiction/article191236.ece, accessed 23 August 2013.

¹⁶ Guy, *Tudor England*, p. 226.

¹⁷ A. F. Pollard, *The History of England: From the Accession of Edward VI to the Death of Elizabeth* (London: Longman, Green and Co., 1910), p. 172.

I

The Making and Unmaking
of Bloody Mary

Initial Uncertainty
over the Marian Legacy

A STUDY OF MARIAN HISTORIOGRAPHY raises several important issues. For one, it reveals that Britain's national story is not immune to gross ideological manipulation. Constructed by politically and religiously motivated chroniclers, the anti-Marian narrative was reiterated well into the modern era by historians at the top of their profession despite the existence of alternative perspectives. The search for the historical Mary, however, should not ignore some of the unsavoury aspects of her reign for to do so would not only inhibit the enquiry but also attract accusations of scholarly sleight of hand. Any historiographical survey will ultimately have limitations. Compromises need to be made in the pursuit of a balance between depth and breadth, which unfortunately does leave gaps. The gaps in the following survey, of which there are many, are not due to any favouritism towards one writer over another, but merely to a conscious effort to avoid repetition that inevitably leads to excessive length that does not necessarily bring any additional benefit. The purpose of the survey, therefore, is to offer an overview of the key determinants of Marian historiography, details of which readers can acquire from the scholarship of the highlighted writers themselves.

Elizabeth's choice in 1558 to opt for a Protestant religious settlement set in motion a process that would see England dramatically transform its politics and the nature of its society. What had led to this was the reformation that Elizabeth's father, Henry VIII, had pursued during the 1530s.

The Henrician Reformation, however, was never primarily about religion. Rather, it was sparked by Henry's capricious attempt to resolve his marital affairs. He may have revived religious heresies that had been long marginalised, not least by the young king himself for his own political purposes, but he was never a radical religious reformer. Many of the religious reforms that he pursued, which in due course led to a break from Rome, in fact were not so different from those which renowned Catholic reformers like Desideriius Erasmus and Thomas More had flirted with for some time.

But once the schism happened, political opportunities emerged for Henry that outweighed any anxieties he may have harboured about the dangers of religious reform to doctrinal orthodoxy. He could have opted to return to the Roman fold after the death of Anne Boleyn, his adulterous 'marriage' having come to an end; he chose not to do so. Supported by elites that had significantly profited from the subversion of papal authority, Henry had become the supreme ruler of both Church and state and he was determined that no pope was ever going to take this away from him. Moreover, the capital that had been diverted from the Church to the Treasury, together with the free-for-all during the Dissolution of the monasteries, rendered reformist religion too profitable to be abandoned.

Self-interest by the country's political elites was even more at the heart of the reformation that Henry's son Edward and his regents were to pursue. It is worth contrasting here the relative ease with which Mary was able to overturn in Parliament Edward's religious settlement with her inability to restore to the Church the land that had been appropriated by secular authorities during the Dissolution. The newly enriched placed a far greater premium on their loot than they did on their religious preferences.

The reversal by Elizabeth of papal supremacy that had been briefly re-established by Mary allowed England again to turn away from the Catholic mainstream. Although the 1559 settlement was not particularly radical, it was sufficient to keep the peace, and probably reflected Elizabeth's own religious outlook. More importantly for the secular elites, it was to guarantee their interests that they had garnered over the past few decades. Protestantism was not so much the end (though no further settlements would follow) as the constitutional means by which the new economic and political reality would come about and be maintained, independent of any outside interference, papal or otherwise.

But this was not going to be straightforward. England was not the military superpower that it would become later. Elizabeth faced the prospect of both invasions by continental Catholic powers and domestic Catholic plots. Catholicism thus came to be seen as a common denominator that underpinned the dangers that confronted England and so much of the battle against it was to be a propagandist one. It was a task made easier by Pope Pius V's bull of 1570 which not only excommunicated Elizabeth but also declared her to be 'the pretended queen of England and the servant of crime'. What is more, by charging and commanding 'all and singular the nobles, subjects, peoples and others [...] not [to] dare obey her orders, mandates and laws',[1] Pope Pius effectively declared war on her. Elizabethan propagandists and historians (though often it was difficult to distinguish one from the other) went to task to portray Catholicism as a threat to everything that was holy and worthy. Above all, the subsequent Catholic domestic plots, in the wake of the papal bull, ensured that Catholicism would not only come to be associated with foreign threats but also with treason.

The elevation of Elizabeth's cult of personality was the product of national and patriotic assertiveness of the English state over the Roman Church. Tensions between the Church and the state were already present in early-medieval times, notably in the dispute between Thomas Becket and King Henry II during the late twelfth century and which henceforth would simmer beneath the surface and occasionally emerge. But there was nothing in any of this to presage the impending Church–state schism. Henry VII's triumph over the English episcopate in 1486, for instance, over whether or not the Church was entitled to offer sanctuary to indicted traitors was no dress rehearsal for the turmoil of the 1530s.[2] Even the initial salvos of the Reformation Parliament, which ended up sitting from 1529 to 1535, offered few insights into the scenario that was to come. But as Henry's Great Matter, as his marital crisis came to be called, progressed, the context of Church–state relations was to change for ever. Thomas Cromwell, who by 1532 had become Henry VIII's principal secretary, adapted the theories of parliamentary sovereignty that had been developed by lawyers like Christopher St Germain and Simon Fish, which enabled him to dress the reformation in patriotic garb. Cromwell knew that the pope would sooner or later threaten Henry with excommunication. If the king was to win the battle he would need to deploy something similarly threatening. His weapon of choice would be patriotism, a relatively new political concept which in turn required the country 'to be aroused to a new sense of its sovereignty and potency' and as such 'Rome had to be demonised as "the foreigner" and "the enemy"'.[3] Consequently, a new religious order, purged of outside interference, would be forged. It was to be based on an appeal to national sovereignty that claimed that England had always been independent except for papal usurpations that corrupted its faith. Parliament, the nominal voice of the people, would be used to facilitate this new order, compliance to which would be ensured by the state coercive machine. By the Act in Restraint of Appeals of 1533 England was declared 'an empire [. . .] governed by one supreme head and king', who a year later, by virtue of the Act of Supremacy, became 'the supreme head of the Church of England'. With this legislation began the process of the marginalisation of Roman Catholicism.

*

The campaign to blacken Mary's reputation started immediately after her death and originated at the very top of the Elizabethan administration and long before any disputes over religion emerged. On 21 November 1558, merely four days after Mary died, Count Feria, Spain's ambassador to England, wrote to Mary's husband, King Philip, to express his concerns regarding the publication by Mary's 'scurvy' Lord Privy Seal, Sir Edward

Hastings, of the smears of 'wagging tongues', that untruthfully accused the late queen of 'having sent great sums of money to your Majesty' and even himself of having 'sent [your Majesty] 200,000 ducats' during his tenure as ambassador.[4] A new sense of confidence gripped 'the heretics', reported Feria, who 'are more free than ever, the heretics thinking that they will be able to persecute the Catholics'.[5]

The initial delight among Protestant circles about Mary's premature death released a burst of inflammatory polemic against both her and her administration. Pamphleteers and hothead preachers were quick off the mark to slander Mary as the foreigner who had come close to ruining the country and subordinating it to Spanish interests. The firebrand Scottish preacher, John Knox, combined a profound abhorrence towards the Marian reign with revulsion towards female rule in general. Mary, 'that horrible monster Jezebel of England', offered a good example, together with other female rulers, notably Mary, Queen of Scots, of 'how abominable before God is the Empire or Rule of a wicked woman, yea, of a traiteresse and bastard'.[6] His polemical pamphlet *The first blast of the trumpet against the monstruous regiment of women*, published in 1559, was so brazen in its abhorrence of female rule that it struck a negative chord with Elizabeth, who condemned it by royal proclamation. For John Aylmer, however, a bishop returning from Marian exile, to associate wickedness and incompetence with Mary's gender rather than only with her character was to let the Catholic queen off the hook. She was cruel and incompetent, he noted in his *An Harbour for faithful and true subjects*, published in 1559 as a reply to Knox, not because she was a woman but because of what she was.

For some, pouring scorn on the Marian reign offered an opportunity to express contempt for what they saw as a betrayal of the Edwardian Reformation. Robert Crowley, for instance, publisher, chronicler and evangelical polemicist, and another returnee from Marian exile, argued that Edward's reforms had been despoiled by self-interested men who had replaced one corrupt system with another.[7] Crowley's polemic was induced to a large extent by concerns over who would succeed Elizabeth, a common theme among evangelical writers, uneasy about the possible return of a Catholic monarch.[8] For Crowley, as well as other contemporary evangelicals, disillusioned with the outcome of the Edwardian Reformation, the ill-fated Jane Grey had represented the epitome of Protestant virtue. But there was no question of having endorsed Jane's claim to the throne as to have done so would have, by implication, denied Elizabeth's right of succession. Elizabeth's legitimacy in turn could not have been recognised without the simultaneous recognition of that of Mary, given that the legitimacy of both stemmed from their father's last testament. Jane's claim, conversely, was based on nothing more than a conspiracy to exclude Mary from the throne. Crowley's begrudging acceptance of Mary's legitimacy, however, was coupled with a robust condemnation of her malevolent reign which he claimed had been God's punishment for England's infidelity to His Word.[9]

Anti-Marian polemic was taken to uncharted levels by John Foxe in his highly celebrated *Actes and Monuments of these Latter and Perillous Days, Touching Matters of the Church*, popularly known as the 'Book of Martyrs', first published in 1563. The focal point of Foxe's work was not so much Mary as her ministers and clerics, especially the bishop of London, Edmund Bonner, who Foxe claimed had compelled Mary to endorse the cruelties of her administration. Mary's faith was of course abhorrent and her sins numerous, having also been responsible for her personal unhappiness and purported bitterness, but she herself was not primarily responsible for the deeds of her administration. By making a distinction between the queen and her ministers, Foxe was able to condemn the Marian government as evil without excessively impugning Mary's reputation that could have reflected negatively on Elizabeth herself. Moreover, by singling out her minister priests and the rest of the clergy, he could attack the Catholic Church as the main culprit of the malaise that he accused the Marian administration of having caused. Ultimately, it was his graphic imagery of burning 'martyrs' that ensured that his martyrology endured for centuries, fitting in well with the political requirements of subsequent generations.

Knox and Foxe, however, represented the extremities of the polemic. Generally, the Marian period and Mary herself were as yet spared the universal opprobrium that they would be subjected to later. Although Elizabethan chroniclers, preachers, poets and politicians were in agreement that Edward VI's premature death and Mary's accession came as divine retribution for England's sins,[10] they tempered their providential assessment of the Marian reign with rational provisos that exonerated Mary from its worst excesses. Most Elizabethan chroniclers adopted a much more temperate tone than that of Knox and Foxe. Yes, they would not only lay blame for the cruelties of Mary's reign squarely on her clerics but they would also highlight the queen's virtues. Richard Bancroft, for instance, archbishop of Canterbury from 1604 to 1610, wrote of her 'mild and pitifull' disposition,[11] while John Clapham, an early biographer of Elizabeth, commented on Mary's 'noble' and 'bountiful' nature, that was 'inclined to pity and compassion'. He added, however, that 'much blood was shed in her time', for which he firmly apportioned blame to her bishops, especially Bonner.[12] Richard Grafton, Edward's chief printer, wrote even more flatteringly of Mary, in his *A Chronicle at Large*, published in 1568, her imprisonment of him for his evangelical zeal, seemingly not lessening his opinion of her. He was particularly taken by the fortitude she displayed during the Wyatt rebellion of 1554 against her which had as its aim to place Elizabeth on the throne (see chapter 8).[13]

The practice of praising Mary's virtues, and casting her as a victim of others continued up to the end of Elizabeth's reign. In *Albion's England*, a lengthy history of England in verse, first published in 1586, the poet William Warner acknowledged Mary's courage and fortitude. Like Crowley earlier in the reign, Warner was caught up in ongoing questions over succession and similarly praised the virtues of Jane Grey, and as Crowley, he was compelled to concede Mary's legitimacy, and for similar reasons. Yet he was also keen to note that notwithstanding her 'most tyrannous Raigne', she endured much in her life, particularly at the hands of her unfaithful husband. 'Her death did many a good man's life from Tyranny redeeme', she was 'Neither blameless' nor 'all to blame' was his conclusion.[14]

Exaggerated praise of Mary, however, during the Elizabethan period, was 'impolitic at best',[15] as the celebrant at Mary's funeral Mass in Westminster Abbey, John White, the bishop of Winchester, discovered. A fervent supporter who had welcomed Mary and Philip as they entered Winchester to be married, White in his sermon expressed deep admiration and affection for the dead queen. Her virtues were many, he noted. 'She used singular mercy towards offenders [...] pity and compassion towards the poor and oppressed [and] clemency amongst her nobles.'[16] Impassionately, he wished the new queen 'a prosperous reign in peace and tranquillity, if it be God's will', adding, in reference to the Book of Ecclesiastes 9: 4, 'But whoever is joined with all the living has hope, for a living dog is better than a dead lion'.[17] It is uncertain what White precisely had in mind. Any *double entendre*, however, was not lost on Elizabeth: the lion was dead, the dog remained. White was immediately placed under house arrest, and subsequently deprived of his see, dying a year after his release in January 1559. Although Elizabeth herself may have baulked at any explicit criticism of Mary in public, she did her utmost to encourage undercover activity to sabotage her half-sister's reputation. 'She is highly indignant about what has been done to her during the queen's lifetime', reported Feria in his last interview with Elizabeth,[18] who, wrote Linda Porter, 'never forgot or forgave her treatment during her sister's reign [...] In her eyes she was always entirely blameless', rather than the focus of successive plots. 'She could not see how the pattern of her behaviour must have looked to her sister.'[19]

For Catholics, Mary was not a particularly strong card to play amidst the triumphalist Elizabethan anti-Spanish and anti-Catholic propaganda. After the vainly held hope that Elizabeth would restore Catholicism had been dashed following the new religious settlement of 1559, Catholics were faced with the stark choice of conformity, recusancy or exile. These choices were to forge a battleground between so-called Appellants and Exiles.

The former, having been incarcerated in appalling conditions in Wisbech prison, near Cambridge, would appeal to the Crown for a reconciliation, while the latter, by contrast, would pursue aggressive attempts to forge a restoration. The two would not see eye to eye, Appellants blaming the Jesuits in particular for provoking Elizabeth into reacting against their subversive activity with ever more draconian anti-Catholic measures and Exiles viewing Appellants as being too willing to compromise their faith. This battle would in fact continue until emancipation in 1829.[20]

Elizabethan Catholic chroniclers in any case were thin on the ground. The most prominent Marian apologist of the period, Nicholas Sanders, wrote from exile, having fled England in 1558. Ordained a priest in 1560, becoming consultant to Pope Gregory XIII on English affairs, Sanders, like his Protestant contemporaries, wrote from a confessional perspective. His most notable work, *De origine ac progressu scismatis Anglicani* ('The rise and growth of the Anglican schism') was first published in 1581, though it was later edited and augmented with new material by another exile, Edward Rishton, who published it in Cologne in 1585. Difficult to acquire and not translated into English until 1877,[21] its impact on the public was limited. Tracing the origins of the Reformation, Sanders cited malevolent motives for the break with Rome, which he argued, had brought the wrath of God upon England. In his view, Mary's premature death had only aggravated England's woes, exposing the country to ruin at the hands of heretics. Unfettered in its partisanship, the work did not even refer to the Marian burnings of Protestants, focusing instead on the illegitimacy of Elizabeth, a hostility that reflected Sanders's own involvement in futile plots to depose her and restore Catholicism to England.

The futility of the cause of Catholic restoration was symbolically reinforced by the death in 1585 of the last remaining Marian bishop, Thomas Goldwell. For a brief period the attention of England's Catholics turned to the succession claims of Mary, Queen of Scots. However, with the defeat of the Northern Earls' Rebellion in 1569 as well as the discovery of the subsequent Ridolfi, Throckmorton and Babington plots in 1570, 1583 and 1586 respectively, and with the execution of Mary herself in 1587, England's Catholic cause was all but lost. Notwithstanding the resilience and resistance of the post-Marian recusant Church to Elizabethan religious legislation, the growing severity of the anti-Catholic measures, as well as the desacralising of Catholic ritual, was bound to have an effect on recusancy levels. As Eamon Duffy noted, by 'the end of the 1570s, whatever the instincts and nostalgia of their seniors, a generation was growing up which had known nothing else, which believed the pope to be Anti-Christ, the Mass a mummery, which did not look back to the Catholic past as their own, but another country, another world'.[22] The Elizabethan triumph of Protestantism sealed the fate of Catholicism in England. Mary's reputation stood little chance amongst the jingoistic myth-making of generations of historian-propagandists, who would associate Catholicism with treason.

NOTES

1 *Pope Pius V's Bull against Elizabeth*, 1570, *Regnans in Excelsis*, http://tudorhistory. org/primary/papalbull.html, accessed 12 August 2013.

2 Stanley Bertram Chrimes, however, argues that 'it is perhaps a fundamental point – the very full measure of control over the episcopate attained by Henry VII may have constituted a condition precedent without which his son might well have been confronted with a far greater degree of opposition from the Church than in fact he experienced when it came to the crisis. To many clergy and others, it must have seemed that papal power in practice was no great thing, and that its abolition was not so significant as theorists made out.' S. B. Chrimes, *Henry VII* (Berkeley and Los Angeles: University of California Press, 1972), p. 244. For a discussion of this issue see P. I. Kaufman, 'Henry VII and Sanctuary Church History', *Church History: Studies in Christianity and Culture*, 53/4 (December 1984), pp. 465–76.

3 S. Schama, *History of Britain: At the Edge of the World? 3000 BC – AD 1603* (London, BBC Worldwide Ltd, 2000), p. 308.

4 'Count Feria to the King, 1', 21 November 1558, CSPS (Simancas), vol. 1.

5 Ibid.

6 J. Knox, *The first blast of the trumpet against the monstruous regiment of women*, The English Scholar's Library 2.1558, ed. E. Arber (Cambridge, Massachusetts: Harvard University Press, 1878), p. 1. Digitised version: Project Gutenberg: http://www.gutenberg. org/files/9660/9660-h/9660-h.htm, accessed 17 August 2013.

7 T. Lanquet, T. Cooper, R. Crowley *An epitome of chronicles Conteyninge the whole discourse of the histories as well of this realme of England, as al other countreys, with the succession of their kinges, the time of their reigne, and what notable actes they did . . . gathered out of most probable auctours. Firste by Thomas Lanquet, from the beginning of the worlde to the incarnacion of Christe, secondely to the reigne of our soueraigne lord king Edward the sixt by Thomas Cooper, and thirdly to the reigne of our soueraigne Ladye Quene Elizabeth, by Robert Crowley.* (London: Printed by William Seres *in ædibus* Thomæ Marshe, 1559).

8 P. Kewes, 'The Exclusion Crisis of 1553 and the Elizabethan Succession', in S. Doran and T. S. Freeman, eds., *Mary Tudor, Old and New Perspectives* (Basingstoke: Palgrave Macmillan, 2011), p. 52.

9 For a discussion on Crowley see, J. W. Martin, *Religious Radicals in Tudor England* (London and Ronceverte: Hambledon Press, 1989), pp. 147–70.

10 S. Doran, 'A "Sharp Rod" of Chastisement: Mary I through Protestant Eyes during the Reign of Elizabeth I', in Doran and Freeman, eds., *Mary Tudor*, p. 21.

11 R. Bancroft, *Dangerous Positions and Proceedings: Published and Practised within this Island of Britain under Pretence of Reformation and for the Presbyterial Discipline* (London: A. and J. Churchill, 1712), p. 63.

12 J. Clapham, *Elizabeth of England: Certain Observations on the Life and Reign of Queen Elizabeth*, ed. E. Plummer Read and C. Read (Philadelphia: University of Philadelphia Press, 1951), p. 56.

13 R. Grafton, *A Chronicle at Large and Meere History of the Affayres of Englande and Kinges of the Same, Deduced from the Creation of the World, unto the First Habitation of*

thys Islande: And so by Contynuance unto the First Yere of the Reigne of Our Most Deere and Soureigne Lady Queen Elizabeth, vol. 2 (London: J. Johnson, 1809), pp. 538–48.

[14] W. Warner, *Albion's England, the third time corrected and augmented* (London: 1592), pp. 176–8.

[15] V. Houliston, '"Her majesty, who is now in heaven": Mary Tudor and the Elizabethan Catholics', in Doran and Freeman, eds., *Mary Tudor*, pp. 37, 42.

[16] Cited in A. Whitelock, *Mary Tudor, England's First Queen* (London, Berlin, New York, Sydney: Bloomsbury Publications, 2009), p. 305.

[17] Ibid.

[18] D. Loades, *The Reign of Mary Tudor: Politics, Government and Religion in England, 1553–1558* (London and New York: Longman, 1991), p. 390.

[19] L. Porter, *Mary Tudor, the First Queen*. London: Piakus, 2009, p. 413.

[20] For a discussion of this theme see J. Vidmar, *English Catholic Historians and the English Reformation, 1585–1954* (Brighton and Portland: Sussex Academic Press, 2005), chapter 1.

[21] D. Lewis, *The Rise and Growth of the Anglican Schism*, trans. N. Sanders (London: Burns and Oates, 1877).

[22] E. Duffy, *The Stripping of the Altars: Traditional Religion in England, 1400–1580* (New Haven and London: Yale University Press, 2nd edn 2005 [1st, 1992]), p. 593.

The Catholic Fifth Column and the Consolidation of the British Nation-State

THERE WERE MANY FACTORS that were responsible for the relative protection of Mary Tudor's reputation during Elizabeth's reign. Traditional deference to the female gender evoked hesitancy among chroniclers to associate Mary with heinous deeds. Deference also to the Crown itself dissuaded the publication of excessively critical opinion of Mary. But the most compelling reason for restraint was fear of offending Elizabeth, the queen's public disapproval of Knox, as noted, serving to deter further intemperate remarks about her sister.[1]

Such self-discipline, however, would not last much beyond Elizabeth's reign itself. Although some restraint in evaluating the Marian period continued to be present during the early Jacobean period, it would not last long. By the end of it, with Protestantism firmly entrenched as the state religion, objective opinion would be drowned out by trenchant anti-Marian voices. A trend was beginning to emerge that would become increasingly familiar in anti-Marian polemic. For instance, in the 1607 version of Thomas Webster's play *Sir Thomas Wyatt*, Mary continues to be depicted as a legitimate monarch, but her policies and actions are shown to have been misguided. Religious sterility, damaging entanglement with Spain and poor judgement generated by feminine passions was, for Webster, all that formed Mary's legacy. His picture of a heroic Elizabeth could not have been more different.[2]

Something that was altogether more sinister and dangerous for Catholics that was steadily creeping into the corpus of themes on the Marian period, was the notion that Catholicism and Englishness were incompatible. In 1605 the lawyer Edward Coke developed a theme in his *Law Reports*, first popularised by Foxe, that Catholicism was incompatible with English common law.[3] Coming in the wake of the Gunpowder Plot, whose conspirators Coke had prosecuted, the theme proved popular. Henry VIII's curt utterance in Parliament on 11 May 1532 accusing the clergy of being 'but half our subjects, yea, and scarce our subjects', had prophetic content. This theme in turn tied in well with the centrepiece of Foxe's martyrology that extolled those who had fallen victim to the Marian inquisition as martyrs for the ancient faith. It did not, however, go unchallenged. The leading recusant priest, Robert Persons, who had robustly refuted Foxe in 1603,[4] published in 1606 his *Answere to the fifth part of Reportes lately set forth by Syr Edward Cooke Knight, the Kings Attorney General*,[5] a similarly forceful repudiation of Coke's argument. Persons, who was continuing a theme first propagated by Mary's archbishop of Canterbury, Reginald Pole, and then by the recusant writers, Nicholas Harpsfield and Thomas Stapleton, during the 1560s,[6] argued that those whom Foxe called martyrs had been the purveyors of a belief system alien to England, and as such were not martyrs at all, but stubborn recalcitrants who rejected repeated attempts by their interrogators to save them from the fire.[7]

For all their protests, however, Catholic apologists were forced on the defensive at a time when suspicions about the agenda of the Stuart kings were increasing, something that the royal penchant for Catholic brides was fuelling further. Although the fortuitous avoidance by James I of assassination at the hands of the Gunpowder Plotters may have temporarily arrested these suspicions against him personally, the plot itself lent further voice to those associating Catholicism with treason. With hispanophobia reaching 'fever pitch' during the 1620s when once again a Spanish Catholic bride was being sought for James's son, Charles, 'Mary Tudor provided an obvious stick with which to beat those pushing for another Spanish match',[8] given Mary's own 'disastrous' Spanish marriage. John Reynolds's pamphlet *Vox Coeli* ('The voice of heaven'),[9] published around 1623, depicts a ghostly conference in heaven between the deceased royals Henry VIII, Edward VI, Mary, Elizabeth, Prince Henry (eldest son of James I) and Queen Anna (of Denmark, wife of James I), in which all the interlocutors, except Mary, urge James to abandon his plans for a Spanish bride for his son. The pamphlet was a sequel to Reynolds's *Votivae Angliae* ('The desires of England'),[10] in which he beseeched James to end his restraint towards Spain and go to war with it. 'Mary's supposed views', Teresa Grant noted, 'had become useful shorthand for exposing the evils of the Spanish and the Catholics.'[11]

The portrayal of Catholics as conspirators and traitors was indeed an ominous portent. Shortly before the start of the Civil War, the image of Catholicism as a threat to England's liberty was reinforced by suspicions that King Charles was harbouring crypto-Catholic views. John Pym, the leader of the parliamentary opposition to the king, delivered a scathing attack at the start of the Long Parliament on creeping Catholic influences in English politics. He warned of 'tenets of papists', 'corrupt clergy' together with the 'agents of Spain [. . .] undermining our religion [. . .], setting out difference between the king and his subjects' and seeking 'an union between us and Rome'.[12] Such portrayals reflected the perceived nature of the Catholic threat and would only subside in intensity once the threat was deemed to have been neutralised. As far as the depiction of Mary was concerned little was added over the next few decades to the well-trodden tradition which paralleled condemning Mary's reign with praising her virtues. Reverend Thomas Fuller's narrative of *Church History of Britain*, published in 1655, typified this approach. Mary was 'melancholic in mind, unhealthy in body', generally unsuccessful in politics and 'more prone to her beads than her books', yet she was 'a worthy princess' who had been manipulated by her 'bloody councilors'.[13]

Political considerations of the late seventeenth century would again, however, alter the way writers approached the Marian period. With the conversion to Catholicism of James, the duke of York, Charles I's second son, the prospect of a return of Catholicism, under royal patronage, raised considerable concerns among Protestant political circles. Stakes were raised further when it became clear that King Charles II, Charles I's eldest son, was not going to produce a legitimate heir, leaving James as his successor.

Hostility towards Catholicism was heightened following the discovery of a Catholic 'plot' to assassinate Charles and place James on the throne. The renegade clergyman, Titus Oates, together with his associate, a fanatical anti-Jesuit, Israel Tonge, concocted a money-making scheme centred on a fabricated Jesuit-led conspiracy against the king. In 1677 Oates entered the service of Roman Catholic Henry Howard, sixth duke of Norfolk, as chaplain to the Protestants of the household. Later received into the Catholic Church itself, Oates became well connected among Catholic circles. In 1678 the two schemers publicised their fictional plot and though it seemed far-fetched, especially given Oates's reputation as a perjurer, it was given credibility by its validation by a prominent justice of the peace, Sir Edmund Berry Godfrey. The tale was given even more authority after Godfrey was found with his throat cut a few weeks later.[14] Fabricated eyewitness testimony pinned the crime on Catholic priests, setting off a frenzy of anti-Catholic terror that subsequently led to the execution of thirty-five people. The public outcry was to play into the hands of the anti-Catholic Whig Party, who commenced in 1679 a campaign in Parliament to have the duke of York excluded from the succession.[15] Although passions eventually subsided and in 1685 James ascended the throne, Oates's concocted calumny would have a devastating impact on the way in which Catholicism was to be popularly depicted. Mary, as its royal standard bearer, would be subject to particular vilification. The restraint that had hitherto governed attitudes towards her rapidly evaporated amidst the Exclusion Crisis and an atmosphere of anti-Catholicism in general. Pamphleteers warned that persecution of Protestants on a par with that witnessed under Queen Mary would occur if James were to ascend the throne. 'For this reason the people seem to cry out with one voice', noted one anonymous pamphlet hysterically, 'No popish successor, no idolater, no Queen Mary in breeches, no tyrant over the conscience, no new persecutor of protestants in our land', it concluded.[16]

Playwrights eagerly joined the fray. Their vivid depictions of Marian executions made lasting impressions on the watching crowds. *The Coronation of Queen Elizabeth*, for instance, performed in London in 1680, portrayed fictionalised scenes of Mary, being rewarded with sainthood by the pope for the terror that she inflicted on Protestants.[17] As fears of a return of 'popery' were ever more widely expressed, the need to vilify Mary as cruel, brutal and tyrannical, intensified. It was during this time that the sobriquet 'Bloody Mary'[18] started to be established to represent Mary and her administration. In the wake of Edward VI's reign, noted an anonymous ballad of 1674, 'Then bloody Mary did begin; In England for to tyrannize'.[19] Offering encouragement to ever more hyperbolic accounts of the Marian period were cheap reprints of the goriest extracts from Foxe's *Book of Martyrs*.

The most significant tract of its times on the theme of the Catholic menace was the multi-volume *History of the Reformation of the Church of England*,[20] by the Scottish theologian, preacher and polemicist, Gilbert Burnet. Published between 1679 and 1713, the work surpassed even Foxe for its influence and political impact and would hold sway over anti-Catholic polemic for a generation. The first edition appeared at the height of the Oates plot as a response to a new reprint of Nicholas Sanders's *Origin and Growth of the Anglican Schism*. Political in tone, it foretold calamitous consequences were a Catholic monarch to ascend the throne. Although Mary was pious and learned, Burnet noted, she 'did not much mind any other affairs but those of the church', abiding to 'the dictates of Rome with nice scrupulosity and conscience'.[21] Burnet's omissions in his analysis here, however, are glaring. He made no reference, for instance, to the serious quarrels that emerged between Mary and the pope over issues involving both her husband and Cardinal Pole (see chapter 8). It was an inconvenient truth that would have invalidated his assessment of Mary's relationship with the papacy. Burnet's innovation lay in his claim, which was to form a key component of the legend of 'Bloody Mary', that her main motive for persecuting Protestants was not so much rooted in religion as in revenge owing to her 'great resentments of her own ill usage in her father and brother's times'.[22] He had no doubt that Mary, under 'the bloody counsels of Gardiner',[23] was the main culprit in her administration's persecution of Protestants. So hated was she that the death of this queen 'of Spain by marriage [. . .] was little lamented'.[24]

Much of Burnet's tale is set during the uncertainty over the succession after the death in 1702 of William of Orange, the Protestant nephew and son-in-law of James II. William had ascended the throne with Mary, James's eldest daughter, during the tumult of the Glorious Revolution of 1688, which saw James fleeing England after he had been abandoned by the Protestant establishment and confronted by William's army. The Bill of Rights of 1689 subsequently barred Catholics from ascending the throne. But having produced no surviving legitimate heirs, William and Mary left the Crown vulnerable to a takeover from the Catholic claimant from the Stuart line, James Francis Edward (the Old Pretender), who, upon the death in exile of his father, James II, in 1701, had declared himself king of England and Scotland. In the renewed uncertainty, the Act of Settlement was passed in 1701, to reinforce the prohibition of Catholics from the line of succession. Scotland, though reluctant to abandon its Stuart succession, was ultimately compelled, under pressure from England, to accept the Act, which paved the way for the Act of Union in 1707 between England and Scotland; this in turn formally established the Protestant British state. All this offered Burnet much to champion. In so doing, he made a considerable contribution to the process of associating tyranny with Catholicism, and freedom and Protestantism with Englishness/Britishness. His services earned him many accolades, including a commendation from both Houses of Parliament,[25] as well as an appointment in 1689 to the bishopric of Salisbury.

In 1713 the political situation prompted Burnet to revise his stance on Mary somewhat. With the Old Pretender and half-brother of the dying Queen Anne, again seeking recognition as king, potentially with the aid of a foreign army, it was politically expedient to assign a greater share of the blame for the burnings of Protestants that occurred during Mary's reign onto 'king Philip and some of his Spaniards' than to Mary herself. According to Burnet, the Spaniards at the Marian court were supposed to have suggested that 'the only sure method to extirpate heresy' was by 'the setting up of an inquisition in England'.[26] As for Mary herself, she was 'a poor harmless woman, weak though learned, guilty of nothing but what her religion infused in her, so carried to an indecencie of barbarity, that it appears that Bonner himself was not cruel enough for her'.[27] One is left under no illusion that it is Catholicism that is on trial here, not Mary. 'Here is that', Burnet warns, 'which those who look towards a popish successor must look for, when that evil day comes.'[28]

Dissent against any part of the mounting consensus on the Marian period made it difficult to make a mark. A few commentators, however, did offer a counter-argument. The theologian and non-juror[29] Anglican bishop, Jeremy Collier, for instance, in his *Ecclesiastical History of Great Britain*, published in 1714, took issue with the key aspect of Burnet's thesis. Although he concurred with Burnet that Mary's religion 'was uppermost with her, and she valued her conscience above her Crown', he argued 'her zeal was ill directed' by an 'unhappy management' of Gardiner and Bonner, who 'seemed to have pushed her upon severities beyond her temper'. Moreover, he continued, 'this Queen', whose 'private life was strict and unblemished [. . .] was not of a vindictive implacable spirit', something that 'may be inferred from her pardoning most of the great men in Northumberland's rebellion' (see chapter 7). He furthermore commended her 'resolution' and 'martial vigour' during the Wyatt insurrection, particularly 'her speech at Guildhall, when she 'declared herself ready to march in person' (see chapter 8). Her concern for her kingdom was further demonstrated, Collier continued, albeit with an unwitting contradiction of his earlier statement regarding her prioritisation of religion, by 'the stand she made upon the Pope's encroachment in obstructing a new legate' (the pope insisted that Reginald Pole should be replaced by William Peto – see chapter 8) and the deep melancholy she fell into upon the loss of Calais.[30]

Collier's picture of Mary, however, was too balanced for a time when Catholics were being increasingly socially and politically marginalised and vilified in the wake of the Act of Union. Such was the anxiety about a Catholic revival in Britain that the Succession to the Crown Act was passed in the same year as the Act of Union to reinforce further in law the exclusion of Catholics from the throne.[31] In so doing, it dramatically broke the rules of dynastic succession. As such, in 1714, following the death of Queen Anne, who left no heir, fifty-five Catholic candidates for the succession were passed over in favour of the Protestant George Louis, Elector of Hanover, who became George I.

In short, it was Protestantism, or more precisely anti-Catholicism, that made Great Britain possible. The new nation, though possessing little cultural and ethnic homogeneity, accommodated sufficient religious commonality to frame and assert an identity. Although, as Linda Colley has noted, the British peoples were at odds, 'in so much of their culture and secular history, the English, the Welsh and the Scots would be drawn together – and made to feel separate from much of the rest of Europe – by their common commitment to Protestantism'.[32] The Protestant nation-state that emerged, therefore, was a product of unintended consequences rather than of design. But once established it was too profitable to be abandoned in favour of the old ways. Wealthy and powerful men were now tied to the new national Church through financial gain. To emphasise national unity in the face of a Catholic threat, the new national culture required the celebration of new 'national' events and heroes in place of the old religious rituals of the enemy. The breaking of customs and communal ties and the huge reduction in the number of religious rituals, which had so liberally peppered the annual calendar, encouraged the growth of individualism and class distinction which had been in humbler times subsumed in the communal worship of a higher authority. Although alms-giving continued, thrift and the pursuit of wealth undermined considerably philanthropic activity and communal responsibility, a particularly harmful development in these socially calamitous times of this cultural revolution.

Certainly, from a political and materialistic perspective, Protestant confessional unity was to serve Britain well. Reflecting the anti-Stuart Whig triumphalism of the Hanoverian period, it enabled the country to confront its European foes like Catholic France and to create and expand a huge empire most of which consisted of peoples who were not Christian.[33] This was undoubtedly a messianic mission manufactured by extensive state propaganda which fostered a collective memory (in place of the old one) in a continuing drama of Protestant triumph over Catholic folly. The forlorn, though ill-fated, Armada or the hapless Guy Fawkes could hardly compete with the cult of Gloriana, or the triumph of Protestant monarchy in the early eighteenth century. That so much of the Protestant narrative of the national story was loaded with myth was immaterial to the national storytellers. Hearsay and anecdotes of Catholic atrocities embedded, for instance, in the recollections of French Huguenot refugees who came to Britain in the late seventeenth century would reinforce popular stereotypes of oppressive and cruel Catholicism and would fit in well with the image of 'Bloody Mary' that was being cultivated. The Marian reign indeed offered the most expedient material with which to attack Catholicism. With no effort at contextualisation and peppered with bias and prejudice, propaganda on Mary served to warn of the dangers of Catholicism to Britain's freedoms. The need for constant vigilance against the Catholic menace was shockingly brought home by the Jacobite invasion of England in 1745 under the command of 'The Young Pretender' Charles Edward Stuart, popularly known as Bonnie Prince Charlie, the son of 'The Old Pretender'. And when in April 1746 the Jacobite cause was decisively defeated at the battle of Culloden, self-righteous relief was all too audible among Protestant polemicists. Had the Jacobites triumphed, preached William Prior in 1750, 'soon should we have seen our rivers redden with Protestant blood and the flames of martyrdom blaze in our street. These are not mere conjectures or distant probabilities; but the almost necessary consequences of the supposed success of our enemies'.[34]

The image of 'flames of martyrdom' that Prior had conjured up, unmistaken in its intention, would find more vivid expression in the repopularised editions of Foxe's *Book of Martyrs*. These cheap reprints of reprints, full of scathing anti-Catholic commentaries, were to reach much larger audiences than the original ever did. They raised issues ranging from the Spanish Armada to contemporary continental persecutions of Protestants and would etch the legend of 'Bloody Mary' firmly on the collective memory of the nation.

Some editions painted a picture of Mary that was even farther removed from those depictions contained in the works of her most critical Elizabethan and Stuart detractors. Henry Southwell, for instance, in his *New Book of Martyrs*, published in *c.* 1780[35] had no misgivings to posit that 'The whole progress of her reign does not furnish us with a single instance of merit in her, either as a woman or a sovereign. On the Contrary', he continued, 'all her actions were of the most horrid and gloomy cast, and the barbarities she committed during her sovereignty were so great as to exceed description.'[36] The most influential edition was Paul Wright's *Fox's Original and Complete Book of Martyrs Or, an Universal History of Martyrdom*, published in 1782,[37] which would run through seven further reprints by 1810. It enjoyed immense popularity, readily appealing to the prejudices of the time. Its gruesome accounts lent themselves well to audiences all too ready and willing to draw parallels between contemporary events and Mary's policies.

Accompanying the reprints of Foxe's work, were other popular sources, notably inexpensive pamphlets such as *Old Moore's Almanac*, as well as other almanacs that passed for the tabloid press of the time, which fed ever-burgeoning anti-Catholic imaginations.[38] They recalled hackneyed themes – the pope was the anti-Christ, 'bloody Mary' was a serpent, and the Stuarts, if they ever returned, would bring ruin upon the land.[39] Reinforcing this imagery was the Protestant pulpit from where anti-Catholic bile was frequently disseminated. 'Witness what your Fathers told you in their Day', advised John Baker in his sermon, *Popery the Great Corruption of Christianity*, delivered at Salters Hall, London in 1735.[40]

But it was not only the popular press that gorged on anti-Catholic prejudice. From sophisticated journals, like the literary *Monthly Review* to celebrated academic histories, like John Oldmixon's *History of England*, published in 1739, the commentary did not deviate too much from the popular path. Oldmixon, for instance, was insistent on Mary's total lack of virtue. The people who supported her accession because they believed that 'she was the Rightful and Lawful heir', he claimed, had been 'blinded' to the fact that 'her heart be ever so much papist, that it was capable of sentiments for barbarous and bloody, that they are a disgrace not only for her sex, but to humanity and abhorrent to all religion and virtue'.[41] For him the 'accomplishments both of mind and body' of the sixteen-year-old Queen Jane 'were infinitely superior to the princess Mary's [who] without satire, had not one valuable or agreeable quality of soul, nor one beautiful and amiable feature or grace in her person, comparable to the noble and lovely endowments of Queen Jane'. In challenging those who said that she was pious and zealous, he argued that 'If there can be true piety in idolatry, hatred, revenge and cruelty she must be allowed to be pious, and if true zeal is to be met with bigotry and blind-devotion, she was zealous'. His conclusion was uncompromising – she was 'inveterate in her hatred, and merciless and bloody in her revenge'.[42] As far as her governance was concerned she did nothing that was of any value, other than for her cousin, the Holy Roman emperor, Charles, a traitor like her and her supporters. Oldmixon's picture of Catholics as traitors, persecutors and inept administrators standing in the way of progress offers the dominant theme of his work. 'It is worth observing', he asserts, 'that the papists, and their abettors have, from that time to this, had the greatest contempt, or rather, hatred, to the trade and interest of this nation and when in the administration, have been always ready to sacrifice it to foreigners: the reason is obvious; trade is a child of industry and is fed and maintained by liberty, which is the bane of persecution and without persecution papists, and their abettors, can have no joy nor comfort in life, their happiness consisting only in the misery of others.'[43] That such a view should come from Whig writers, who dominated history writing at the time, should not surprise. What is remarkable is that this image of Mary was so widely entrenched by now that it transcended political as much as class divides.

Indeed, many Tories, the sworn enemies of Whigs and traditionally associated with the legitimate Stuart claim to the throne, were of a similar mind as far as Mary was concerned. Thomas Carte, for instance, the non-juror Anglican cleric and strong sympathiser of the Stuart succession, having been forced to flee to France in 1722 in the wake of treason allegations against him, was as eager as any Whig to pass off hackneyed opinion as history. 'No nation ever had a more signal deliverance', he argued, 'than the divine providence now wrought for *England*, by taking off *Mary* in so critical a moment, on the eve of a peace; which would have enabled her and *Philip* to pursue their detestable scheme for subverting the continuation of the kingdom and enslaving a disunited people'.[44] As for Mary herself, she was

> stiff, formal, reserved, sour, haughty and arrogant [...] everything in her looks, her air, her carriage and manner, was forbidding [...] She did not care, or know how to oblige; did all things in an imperious and grating way, choosing to be feared, rather than beloved. Scarce ever was there a person so utterly void of all the agreeable qualities [... Her religion was] of a low kind; that of a bigot, and choked with superstition. Her fundamental defects were an insatiable pride, a furious impetuosity, a wilfulness to which she would have sacrificed the world and an insatiable avarice. [In these] she equalled [her father] but wanted his judgment in the exercise of them.

Without any discernment or subtlety, Carte concluded that 'Every dreary year of her inglorious reign was blackened by remarkable disaster and by such acts of injustice, rapine violence, oppression and tyranny [...] and having reduced the nation to the brink of ruin, she left it, by her seasonable decease, to be restored by her admirable successor to its ancient prosperity and glory'.[45] Even those more nuanced in their assessment of Mary, like the Tory Anglican cleric, Laurence Echard, who recognised Mary to be 'a Lady of great virtue', accused her of having poor judgement, and engaging in vengeful 'barbarous cruelties' and of pursuing unjust wars.[46]

By the end of the seventeenth century perceptions of Catholicism as a threat to peace and liberty and of Mary as a cruel, tyrannical bigot devoid of any redeemable virtues were well entrenched in Britain's collective psyche, and had become central pillars of the country's national ideology. Enlightenment philosophers would reinforce these images, albeit for different reasons. In crystallising critical thought on religion, they saw no place in society for any illegitimate authority, secular or religious or even for cultural sentimentality. Since the Enlightenment represented a triumph of militant rationalism, its exponents shared a desire to undermine dogmatic religion, believing that truth could be arrived at through a combination of reason and empirical observation. It was inevitable, therefore, that Mary would attract critical assessment from Enlightenment writers. David Hume, in his influential *History of England* published in 1775, saw no reason to deviate from the received version of events. Although he had no truck with Whiggism, he, like many other Enlightenment thinkers, harboured a fundamental aversion to all organised religion, especially Catholicism, holding it to be a source of intolerance and oppression. In Mary and her administration he saw all the hallmarks of an oppressive and irrational administration. 'Obstinacy, bigotry, violence, cruelty, malignity, revenge, tyranny' formed her personality, and as 'a weak bigoted woman, under the government of priests' she presided over 'the most furious religious persecution'.[47] Although Hume did credit Mary with 'a resolution and vigour of mind', which she used, for instance, to oppose the pope, he insisted that she governed without any great credit. The popularity of Hume's *History*, which ran to over sixty editions from its publication up to the start of the twentieth century, contributed much to uphold the legends that had built up around the Marian reign. The work made a particular effort to appeal to women with its broad sweep across a gamut of social themes over and above routine male-centred political history.

Reinforcing the written messages was pictorial imagery, which offered some of the most hard-hitting anti-Catholic polemic. Thematically some of the most uncompromising were those of the satirist William Hogarth, who pulled no punches in his assault on religion in general and Catholicism in particular. In his etching, *Credulity, Superstition and Fanaticism* of 1739, for instance, a reworked composition based on an earlier unpublished plate *Enthusiasm Delineated*, he sought to highlight what he saw were the pitfalls of fundamental religion. The main character in the composition is a

Fig. 1. *O the Roast Beef of Old England (The Gate of Calais)*, 1748,
William Hogarth (1697–1764). Courtesy of the Tate, London.

seemingly bigoted preacher who is trying his utmost with the aid of puppets
of a witch and a devil, to get across his message about the dangers of sinful
deeds. His sermon is greeted, however, with indifference by the congregation
that is engaged in various frivolous and lascivious activities. The expressions
of agony and torment that are depicted on some of the faces together
with a diseased brain at the foot of a thermometer measuring various
states of emotion metaphorically depict traditional beliefs as superstitious
folly. Hogarth's most famous work, however, *The Gate of Calais* (otherwise
known as *O the Roast Beef of Old England*), is unmistakably anti-Catholic.
It juxtaposes several leitmotifs of British anti-Catholic propaganda (Fig.
1). The parasitic Church of Rome is depicted as an obese Capuchin monk
who is presented in stark contrast to the ill-fed and down-trodden women
huddled to the side. The crucifixes around their necks suggest that, despite
their misery, the women continue to cling on to their superstitions. This
image of blind obedience is reinforced by the penitents in the background
beyond the portcullis who are kneeling before a doom-mongering priest.

The two anxious looking soldiers, though armed, are attired in bedraggled uniforms to suggest they receive scant reward for their services to the state. The imagery of oppression and poverty is contrasted by the man representing English prosperity, carrying the large sirloin of beef. While the monk licks his lips, the soldiers suspect foul play and ready themselves to make an arrest. Anti-Catholicism, xenophobia, patriotism rolled into one masterly representation of popular contemporary prejudice.[48]

No less partial in outlook was a range of texts that emerged in the early nineteenth century which sought to carry the legends on the Marian period to children. One of the most enduringly popular and influential of these tracts was Maria Collcott's *Little Arthur's History of England*, published in 1835. For all its tender and affectionate tone, its political and religious verdict on Mary was merciless. 'Though I have not the happiness to be a mother', Collcott wrote, 'my love of children has led me to think a good deal about them, their amusements and their lessons.'[49] In a perverse sense of irony, she professed that she has 'always held the history of our own country to be important in education',[50] yet proceeded to paint an image of Mary based on a grotesque tissue of lies that ventures way beyond the worst prejudices and misrepresentations of the past. 'Mary, the daughter of Henry VIII and Catherine of Aragon, his first wife, was so cruel', Collcott noted at the beginning of her chapter on Mary, 'that she is always called Bloody Mary',[51] who presided over a reign devoid of any positive achievements. All she did, apparently, was to execute opponents and rebels, repeatedly offend people, and fail to execute her sister, Elizabeth, only because Elizabeth was ill at the time she was summoned to her execution.[52] As such, 'Everybody now began to be sorry that Mary was queen', which provoked a number of people to rebel under the command of Sir Thomas Wyatt. To preserve the consistency of her argument, Collcott distorted history to an extraordinary extent, ignoring the successes that even Mary's most ardent detractors credited her with. During Wyatt's rebellion, therefore, it was not Mary who rallied her forces against the rebels but the duke of Norfolk, who by doing so saved Mary from a grim fate.[53] Philip, her husband, in turn was 'as ill-tempered and almost as cruel as the queen' and her bishops, notably Gardiner and Bonner, 'were the most cruel I ever heard of [who] went on doing the most cruel and wicked things'.[54] In short, 'Nothing did well in the cruel queen's reign'.[55] What was so remarkable was not so much that Collcott's *History* had been published well into the nineteenth century but that its publisher, John Murray, continued to keep it in print until 1975.

This 'vast superstructure of prejudice', writes Linda Colley, was 'a way of seeing (or rather mis-seeing) Catholicism and Catholic states'. It was an outlook that 'had grown up since the Reformation, if not before, which was fostered by successive wars with France and Spain, and which encouraged many Britons, irrespective of their real income, to regard themselves as particularly fortunate'.[56] The commercial prosperity of Britain in relation to that of Europe appeared to confirm this view among many Britons that was 'coloured and made more roseate by their overwhelming Protestantism. And it was on this strong substream of Protestant bias from below that the British state after 1707 was unapologetically founded'.[57] The marginalisation of Catholicism in law was a powerful source of its illegitimacy in the eyes of the public. So pervasive was societal acceptance of the anti-Catholic penal codes, under which Catholics could be disinherited, imprisoned and financially crippled by taxation, that even after the crushing of the Jacobite threat at the Battle of Culloden in April 1746 those who sought to soften the restrictions on Catholics attracted the chagrin of the Protestant polemicists.[58] When the First Catholic Relief Act of 1778 made modest legal concessions to Catholics, it provoked anti-Catholic riots, first in Scotland in 1779 and then in London in June 1780. London's so-called Gordon Riots in particular unleashed a frenzy of destruction against Catholic targets, during which 300 people died and another 200 were wounded.[59] The Catholic military threat from foreign adversaries may have subsided, and the pope may have recognised in 1766 the Hanoverian dynasty as Britain's lawful rulers following the death of the Old Pretender, Catholicism nevertheless continued to be associated with oppression, backwardness and treason. Generations of overlapping interests – confessional, Whig, Enlightenment/atheist – would embroider this image further, turning Protestantism in the process into the supporting pillar of England's (later Britain's) reinvented national identity; or at least portraying Catholicism as being alien to all that was British. This left an indelible mark on Britain's collective psyche which could not be readily erased and which was also to govern the anti-Marian narrative. 'To the majority who defended the establishment', write Duffy and Loades, 'Mary was at best the victim of Spanish manipulation, at worst a wicked tyrant who had tried to defy the "manifest destiny" of a Protestant realm.'[60]

NOTES

[1] See Doran, 'A "Sharp Rod" of Chastisement', pp. 32–3.

[2] For a discussion of the polemic on the Marian reign during the Jacobean period, see T. Grant, '"Thus like a nun, not like a princess born": Dramatic Representations of Mary Tudor in the Early Years of the Seventeenth Century', in Doran and Freeman, eds., *Mary Tudor*, pp. 62–77.

[3] V. Houliston, *Catholic Resistance in Elizabethan England: Robert Persons's Jesuit Polemic* (Aldershot and Burlington: Ashgate, 2007), p. 7.

[4] R. Persons *A Treatise of Three Conversions of England from Paganisme to Christian Religion* (St Omer, 1603).

[5] Houliston, *Catholic Resistance in Elizabethan England*, p. 7.

[6] Houliston, '"Her majesty, who is now in heaven"', pp. 42–3.

[7] Houliston, *Catholic Resistance in Elizabethan England*, pp. 93–117.

[8] Grant, "'Thus like a nun, not like a princess born", p. 63.

[9] T. Cogswell, *The Blessed Revolution: English Politics and the Coming of War, 1621–1624* (Cambridge: Cambridge University Press, 2005), p. 290. See also P. Salzman, *Literary Culture in Jacobean England: Reading 1621* (Basingstoke: Palgrave Macmillan, 2002).

[10] Both pamphlets are sometimes attributed to Reynolds' contemporary pamphleteer, the radical Protestant and anti-Spanish and anti-Catholic preacher, Thomas Scott.

[11] Grant, "'Thus like a nun, not like a princess born'", p. 63.

[12] M. Jansson, ed., *Proceedings in the Opening Session of the Long Parliament: House of Commons, 3 November to 19 December 1540*. 2 vols. (Rochester, New York, and Woodbridge: University of Rochester Press, 2000), vol. 1, pp. 35–6.

[13] T. Fuller, *The Church History of Britain, from the Birth of Jesus Christ to the Year MDCXLVIII*, new edition in 6 volumes, rev. J. S. Brewer (Oxford: University Press, 1845), vol. 6, pp. 195, 200, 247–8.

[14] The murder of Sir Edmund Berry Godfrey remains a mystery to this day.

[15] Oates, for his part, having had his allegations disproved, was flogged and imprisoned for perjury for a second time. Earlier he had been ordered to pay James substantial libel damages. He was released in 1688 and granted a pension in the wake of James's deposition.

[16] Anonymous pamphlet, *Vox populi, Vox Dei; or England's general lamentation for the dissolution of the Parliament, 1681*, in *A Collection of scarce and valuable tracts, on the most interesting and entertaining subjects; but chiefly such as relate to the history and constitution of the three kingdoms, selected from an infinite number in print and manuscript; in the royal Cotton, Sion and other public libraries, particularly that of the late Lord Somers*, 2nd edition, revised, augmented and arranged by Walter Scott. 8 vols. (London: T. Cadell, et al, 1812), vol. 8, p. 302.

[17] *The Coronation of Queen Elizabeth, with the restauration of the Protestant religion, or, The downfal of the Pope : being a most excellent play, as it was acted both at Bartholomew and Southwark fairs, this present year, 1680, with great applause and approved of and highly commended by all the Protestant nobility, gentry and commonalty of England, who came to be spectators of the same* (London: 1680).

[18] T. S Freeman, 'Inventing Bloody Mary: Perceptions of Mary Tudor', in Doran and Freeman, eds., *Mary Tudor*, p. 81.

[19] Cited ibid.

[20] G. Burnet, *History of the Reformation of the Church of England*, ed. N. Pocock (Oxford: Oxford University Press, 1865).

[21] Ibid., vol. 2, p. 591.

[22] Ibid.

[23] Ibid., p. 590.

[24] Ibid., p. 592.

[25] E. Duffy, *Saints, Sacrilege and Sedition: Religion and Conflict in the Tudor Reformations* (London, Berlin, New York and Sydney: Bloomsbury Publications, 2012), p. 37.

[26] Ibid., p. 33.

[27] Ibid., p. 31.

[28] Ibid., p. 35.

[29] Non-jurors in the Anglican Church refused to pledge allegiance to William and Mary because they felt legally bound to the oath of allegiance they took to James II.

[30] J. Collier, *Ecclesiastical History of Great Britain, Chiefly of England from the First Planting of Christianity in this Island*. 2 vols. (London: Samuel Keble and Benjamin Tooke, 1714), vol. 2, p. 406.

31 The full title of the Succession of the Crown Act of 1707: *An Act for the Security of Her Majesty's Person and Government and of the Succession to the Crown of Great Britain in the Protestant Line.*

32 L. Colley, *Britons: Forging the Nation, 1707–1837* (New Haven and London: Yale University Press, 1992), p. 18.

33 For an excellent discussion of the contiguity between Protestantism and British foreign-policy interests see A. C. Thompson *Britain, Hanover and the Protestant Interest, 1688–1756* (Woodbridge: Boydell & Brewer, 2005).

34 Cited in C. Haydon, *Anti-Catholicism in Eighteenth-Century England, c. 1714–80: A Political and Social Study* (Manchester: Manchester University Press, 1993), p. 26.

35 The full title is *The New Book of Martyrs; Or Complete Christian Martyrology Containing an Authentic and Genuine Historical Account of the Many Dreadful Persecutions* (London: c. 1780).

36 Cited in Freeman, 'Inventing Bloody Mary', pp. 85–6.

37 Its full title is *Fox's Original and Complete Book of Martyrs: Or, an Universal History of Martyrdom. Containing Accounts of the Lives, Sufferings & Deaths of the Protestant Martyrs in the Reign of Queen Mary the First . . . Originally Composed by the Rev'd. John Fox. M.A. Now Revised and Corrected by a Minister of the Gospel, Paul Wright* (London: R. Balfe 1782).

38 Colley, *Britons: Forging the Nation*, p. 20.

39 Haydon, *Anti-Catholicism in Eighteenth-Century England*, pp. 43, 46.

40 Ibid, p. 43.

41 J. Oldmixon, *The History of England: During the Reigns of Henry VIII. Edward VI. Queen Mary. Queen Elizabeth. Including the History of the Reformation of the Churches of England and Scotland . . . Also Including a History of Mary, Queen of Scots* (London: T. Cox and R. Hett, 1739), p. 213.

42 Ibid.

43 Ibid, p. 227.

44 T. Carte, *A General History of England*. 4 vols. (London: 1752), vol. 3, p. 353.

45 Ibid., p. 354.

46 L. Echard, *The History of England, from the First Entrance of Julius Caesar and the Romans to the End of the Reign of James the First*. 3 vols. (London: Jacob Tonson, 1707), vol. 1, pp. 757, 786–7.

47 D. Hume, *The History of England from the Invasion of Julius Caesar to the Revolution of 1688*. 8 vols. (Dublin: United Company of Book Sellers, 1775), vol. 4, pp. 379, 380.

48 Haydon, *Anti-Catholicism in Eighteenth-Century England*, pp. 46–7.

49 M. Collcott, *Little Arthur's History of England* (London: John Murray, 1866), p. iii.

50 Ibid., p. iv.

51 Ibid., p. 156.

52 Ibid., p. 157.

53 Ibid., p. 156.

54 Ibid., p. 157.

55 Ibid., p. 159.

56 Colley, *Britons: Forging the Nation*, p. 36.

57 Ibid., p. 43.

58 For a discussion of this see Haydon, *Anti-Catholicism in Eighteenth-Century England*, chapter 5.

59 See ibid., p. 49 and chapter 6.

60 E. Duffy and D. Loades, eds., 'Editors' Introduction', in *The Church of Mary Tudor* (Aldershot and Burlington: Ashgate, 2006), p. xi.

✛ 3 ✛

Catholic Apologia and Attempts to Buck the Anti-Catholic Trend

T HE HIGH LEVEL of anti-Catholic prejudice conspired against any Catholic attempt to set the record straight, and in this respect matters had not improved since Elizabethan times. A few writers, however, did try to buck the trend.

The Catholic clergyman Hugh Tootell, writing under the pseudonym Charles Dodd, offered a reasoned survey in his *Church History in England*, a multi volume work published between 1737 and 1742.[1] Anti-Jesuit in tone, his apologia sought to appease received Protestant opinion that considered Jesuits to be the main culprits of anti-state rebellion. It was an Appellant strategy designed to convince the British authorities that Catholics in general were not the enemies of the state. His view, however, that the Reformation had been orchestrated by a few avaricious men, was far removed from contemporary received Protestant opinion though it would be echoed by many Protestant commentators during the Victorian period. 'The rich spoils which King Henry VIII had obtained by the disgrace of Cardinal Wolsey', he noted, 'only whetted his appetite for a more plentiful feast.'[2] His view on the Marian period was similarly askance, being significantly at odds with prevailing mainstream opinion. Although he acknowledged the excesses of the Marian administration, he attempted both to justify, if not to condone, its policies within proper historical context, and to challenge erstwhile negative assessments of some of its protagonists like Bishop Edmund 'Bloody' Bonner, as well as Mary herself. 'Where John Foxe produces records, he may be credited', he noted, 'but as to other relations, he is of very slender authority' with the consequence that 'Queen Mary's memory be odious to vulgar and ignorant, who charged her personally with all those seeming hardships the reformers suffered under her reign yet her very enemies [...] have been obliged to confess that she was a princess in all respects worthy of that high status in which providence had placed her.'[3] Despite this, he continued, 'the bloody reign of queen Mary is the nurse's language to all Protestant children, and an article they are carefully instructed in from the cradle. Not only those that were active in that persecution, but the whole Catholic church is charged with these proceedings'.[4] Some two and a half centuries later John Guy echoed this point, warning of needing to be wary 'of the bias of John Foxe and other Protestants writing in Elizabeth's reign who prefer us to believe that Mary did nothing but persecute'.[5]

Dodd also raised the crucial question of whether Mary was legitimate in challenging heresy in the way that she did, highlighting the fact that both Protestants and Catholics alike during the sixteenth century deemed those who had been convicted of heresy to be deserving of suffering the ultimate penalty. If 'persecution upon account of conscience' was allowed by law, he noted, and if 'several bishops, clergy, and others became delinquents by disobeying [. . .] the communion of that church in which they were baptized and educated; and after being reconciled, relapsed again into the errors they had renounced [then] could there ever be a greater provocation, or better grounds to put such laws in execution?'[6] Although Dodd's work was limited in its impact and tainted in the eyes of contemporary Protestants because of the author's Catholic heritage, its attempt to contextualise the Marian reign was ahead of its time.

The modest enhancement of the civil liberties of Catholics during the latter half of the eighteenth century made the promotion of the Catholic cause a little easier. Many Catholic writers, in exploiting the improvement in conditions, sought to demonstrate their loyalty to the Crown by distancing themselves from temporal papal authority. Echoing the Appellant position of the Elizabethan period, the Cisalpine Movement, for instance, was more concerned with making a political statement than challenging historical fiction, hoping that in doing so it would bring forward the full emancipation of Catholics. However, in taking great liberties with historical truth writers like Father Joseph Berrington and the lay Catholic lawyer, Charles Butler, ignored 'nearly the whole of papal claims, and this was', writes John Vidmar, 'a serious theological complication'.[7] Their view that the popes were usurpers of temporal authority differed little from that of Henrician caesaropapists while their justification of Elizabethan persecution of Catholics as having been legitimate owing, in their opinion, to the extreme papal, recusant and Jesuit provocation, conformed to received state ideology on this matter.[8] Yet for all their efforts at appeasing Protestant opinion cisalpine writers failed to endear themselves to the Protestant mainstream, simultaneously drawing indignation from England's bishops (vicars apostolic). Moreover, contrary to their self-proclaimed importance their impact on the process of Catholic relief and emancipation was limited. The controversial nature of their national Catholicism, so despised among orthodox quarters, was never going to lead a great movement of Catholic historiography. But this was never their aim.

If historiographical revisionism was to occur it would have to involve a different breed of writer, a professional historian, who would start to place confessional loyalty aside in favour of a search for historical truth. As noted above, the Reformation almost immediately spurred on Catholics to chronicle events as they saw them. Generally, however, these works were no different in style from those of their Protestant counterparts. Few of the writers were trained historians. Rather, they plied their trade in other professions – philosophy, law and such like. What emerged from this rich, though not particularly scholarly tradition (with a few notable exceptions) was confessional polemic.[9] But although Catholic polemic suffered from the same flaws as that of Protestants, the latter of course had the advantage of representing the dominant tradition in the country and as such was able to form the mainstream, flaws and all. Catholic writers, conversely, had an uphill struggle to be heard in a climate of prejudice and hostility in which just being a Catholic exposed you to danger. Occasionally, apologists of the Marian reign did have something important to say that went beyond mere confessional solidarity, as noted above, but generally speaking the age of the great revision had not yet come. But come it would and it would be assisted by several factors.

Although, as we have seen, early Victorian writers would continue along the well-trodden paths of their predecessors, several factors were to bring in changes that would start the long road to the restitution of Mary and her reign. The first of these was the emancipation of Catholics in 1829. Apart from continuing to be prohibited from ascending the throne, Catholics became the political equals of Protestants. The effect of this on how history would be depicted would be considerable as now Catholics could engage Protestants in dialogue out in the open. This interaction was most ardently expressed within the Oxford Movement that emerged among 'High Anglicans' in 1833 in response to the crisis in Anglicanism in the wake of Catholic emancipation. Its exponents promoted the idea in a series of tracts, in which it was argued that the old liturgy and customs should not be the preserve of Catholics alone but should also be part of the Anglican tradition. Many of the so-called Tractarians, most notably John Henry Newman (beatified by Pope Benedict XVI in 2010), went further and converted to Catholicism. The growing legitimisation of Catholicism, therefore, emboldened Catholic writers, who became confident in exploring past controversies. With this, Marian historiography would in many respects turn full circle, containing something of the approach of writers in the years after Mary's death when the need to malign her reign for political expedience had not yet arrived. Further advancing the cause of historical revision would be the changing social norms. The Victorian preconceptions about gender sat uneasily with the idea of Mary as an irredeemable tyrant. Better she was a hysterical weak woman, which was expected of females at the time, than the ogre of old, something which was more associated with men than with women. Such gender representations also sat more comfortably with women writers of the day like Agnes and Elizabeth Strickland, who saw Mary in terms of Victorian female gentleness.

The growing professionalisation of history writing was also to have profound impact on how Mary and her times would be depicted. Hitherto, histories were compiled largely on the basis of unquestioned acceptance of previously cited sources, a practice that went a long way to explain the similarity of conclusions. However, with the foundation of the Public Records Office in London in 1838 historians were confronted, for the first time, with a comprehensive archive of material that encouraged them to engage their subject matter in a much more scholarly manner than historians of old. This new opportunity, combined with the absence of many of the political motives for demonising Catholicism, made the reassessment of received assumptions possible. The change in thinking on Mary among Protestant writers, if not on the Catholic faith itself, was clearly evident. The increasing availability of primary sources made the task of replacing prejudices with fact-based evidence easier, for those wishing to do so. By avoiding polemical styles, Catholic writers were able to render their work more ready to combat Protestant anti-Catholic prejudice.

John Lingard's groundbreaking and sober account of the *History of England*, published between 1819 and 1830, fell precisely into this category.[10] Non-polemical in style, the work drew extensively on numerous primary sources gathered from English as well as foreign archives. In his attempt to convince England's Protestants of the disastrous effects of the Reformation, Lingard did not pull any punches. Although like the cisalpines he was interested in attaining emancipation for Catholics, unlike them he was first and foremost a historian. Though at the time his work received scant recognition from the academic establishment, its influence would grow and earn extensive praise, not least from the likes of Lord Acton, no great sympathiser of Catholic scholarship, as a work that all 'educated men were obliged to use'.[11] In his assessment of so many themes of English history, Lingard was considerably ahead of his time, something that would be acknowledged in works published over a hundred years later.[12]

Lingard's appraisal of the Marian reign and Mary herself in many respects picked up where Dodd had left off, and achieved 'a balance which has only very recently been reconstructed in English historiography'.[13] Mary 'was ranked', he noted, '[even] by the more moderate of the Protestant writers, among the best, though not the greatest, of our sovereigns [who] allotted to her the praise of piety and clemency, of compassion for the poor, and liberality to the distressed'. Her character was widely regarded as 'beyond reproof' which 'exhorted respect from all, even from the most virulent of her enemies'.[14] His highlighting of her education, linguistic skills and other talents as well as what he noted were her many notable achievements such as trade expansion with Russia and realisation of various cultural projects (for Mary's programme for culture see chapter 11) painted a picture of her reign that was totally at odds with an image of sterility that had hitherto so dominated Marian historiography.[15] Like Dodd, Lingard also skilfully tackled the issue which was to tax the minds of twentieth-century revisionists, that of 'the foulest blot on the character of the queen [. . .], her long and cruel persecution of the Protestants'. Though his sense of justice led him to condemn this, he would explain, if not excuse it, by placing the persecution in historical context. Recognising that the 'suffering of the victims naturally begat an antipathy to the woman by whose authority they were inflicted', he nevertheless qualified Mary's actions against Protestants with a reminder 'that the extirpation of erroneous doctrine was inculcated as a duty by the leaders of *every* religious party. Mary only practised what *all* taught'.[16] Lingard's formula, which would be adopted by modern revisionists in their assessment of Mary, should not be seen as mere semantical sleight-of-hand but rather as an expression of his tolerance in religious matters. His denunciation of the persecution of Protestants is matched by his sympathy towards Philip's confessor, Alfonso di Castro who, in preaching at court 'to the astonishment of his hearers, condemned these proceedings in a pointed manner' as being 'contrary not only to the spirit, but to the text of the gospel'[17] (Castro's position here, however, is not wholly consistent – see chapter 12).

Favourable reporting on Mary was not confined to confessional quarters. *The Lives of the Queens of England*, by the Anglicans Elizabeth and Agnes Strickland, published during the 1840s,[18] was a similarly pioneering work which both challenged many of the erstwhile claims against Mary and acknowledged her many virtues. Like Lingard's *History*, it was based on extensive primary source material. It painted a picture of an educated woman, refined in taste, generous in her alms giving and kind hearted, who endured her mother's humiliation by her father and then her own persecution first by her father and then by her brother, only to emerge triumphant to claim her rightful inheritance. The pursuit of historical accuracy was as important for the Stricklands as it had been for Lingard but in revising some of the received version of the Marian reign, the authors were conscious of the difficulties and dangers of bucking the trend. 'It was difficult', they noted, 'because almost the whole mass of rich documents' that they used 'are in direct opposition to the popular ideas of the character of our first queen-regnant; and dangerous, because the desire of recording truth may be mistaken for a wish to extenuate cruelty in religious and civil government.'[19] This did not, however, discourage them from objectively addressing the Marian suppression of Protestants. 'Although very generous feeling is naturally roused against the horrid cruelties perpetuated in her name', they wrote, 'yet it is unjust and ungrateful to mention her maiden reign with unqualified abhorrence.'[20] Blame for the persecutions, they claimed, should lie with others, and to support their point they cited Foxe, 'the martyrologist, who calls queen Mary "a woman every way excellent while she followed her own inclination"'.[21] They also went on to credit Mary for repealing the 'tyrannical laws instituted by her father' as well as legislating many 'wholesome laws' which restored due process for charging and trying felons. In her governing, they noted, she was unbeholden to her husband, being able to make 'a proper distinction between the duty of a wife and the duties of an English queen'.[22] Moreover, somewhat daringly for the time, they noted that Mary was disposed to place 'her own sex in stations of authority of which there had been few examples before or since', having first herself 'overcome the repugnance of the English to be governed by a sovereign lady' (see chapter 8).[23] Although there was still some way to go before writing on Mary and her reign became totally free of distortion, Lingard and the Stricklands had consigned much of erstwhile Marian historiography to folklore, that is for those who wanted to take note.

But for all their professionalism both Lingard and the Stricklands were in fact guilty of introducing a new fallacy that would linger on for over a century. Both works liberally referenced source material concerning Mary's poor state of health, that had been affected further by a number of phantom pregnancies as well as by her husband's indifference towards her. While neither sought to make a political point of this, they did imply that Mary's health had affected her state of mind, something which subsequent writers used to account for what they perceived to have been her unsuccessful policies. The reader might be excused for thinking that Mary's 'frequent and obstinate maladies' as reported by the Venetian ambassador, Giovanni Micheli,[24] which 'kept her in a constant state of fear and irritation'[25] and even brought on 'self-deception like monomania'[26] could not but have impaired her judgement. Given Victorian preconceptions about gender, this was a myth that would become quickly entrenched. Even for those with good intentions it was almost as if such conclusions could not be helped.

Many writers of course had fewer objective aims and used the new source material to reinforce old stereotypes. The trend to liberate the Marian period from the myth-makers in fact remained very much on the margins of history writing. Opinion towards Catholicism itself indeed changed little. Mid-Victorian scepticism towards the motives of lay authorities that had driven the Reformation was matched only by a swaggering indignation towards the papacy and an unflinching certainty in the Protestant cause. Championing this approach was the much celebrated Whig historian

Thomas Babington Macaulay. While scathing about the worldliness and ignobility of the lay reformers, he was in no doubt that the break from Rome had been necessary for the triumph of liberty. The Church of Rome, he noted in his *The History of England from the Accession of James the Second*, published in 1849, though was 'generally favourable' to civilisation during the 'dark ages', did charge itself as its 'chief object [...] during the last three centuries [...] to stunt the growth of the human mind' so much so that under its rule the 'loveliest and most fertile provinces of Europe have [...] been sunk in poverty, in political servitude, and in intellectual torpor'. In contrast, he continued, 'Protestant countries [...] have been turned by skill and industry into gardens, and can boast of a long list of heroes and statesmen, philosophers and poets'.[27] Though Macaulay did not write specifically on the Marian period, he did note in his assessment of James I's reign that 'The cruelties of Mary's reign – cruelties which, even in the most accurate and sober narrative, excite just detestation', were responsible, together with 'the conspiracies against Elizabeth, and above all, the Gunpowder Plot, [for] the deep and bitter feeling' among people. This, he concluded, collectively provoked 'the spirit of Protestantism [to be] far fiercer and more intolerant'.[28] His limited comment on Mary did, however, offer a crumb of comfort to those seeking to exonerate her. Having eclipsed Hume's work, which harboured hostility to those aspects of history that Whigs held dear, Macaulay spared Mary's reputation further assault of the kind Hume had delivered in the eighteenth century.

Macaulay's contemporary, James Anthony Froude, conversely, had much to say on Mary and would paint a picture of her that would influence a generation of myth-makers. His great multi-volume work, *The History of England, from the Fall of Wolsey to the Death of Elizabeth*,[29] published between 1856 and 1870, though later revised, was scholarly and based on extensive primary source research, much of it hitherto untapped. But for all its pioneering nature, the work was underpinned by a clear agenda that was no less rooted in personal prejudices than the chronicles of the past had been. Deeply anti-clerical and anti-doctrinarian, Froude shared Macaulay's assessment of the Reformation as being both a free-fest of looting and gorging on Church property and a source of liberation from restrictive doctrine and clerical abuse. It was for Froude, 'the grandest achievement in English history'.[30] Suspicious of all organised religion, he was particularly anti-Catholic in sentiment. Although he was fully conscious that the Reformation had been imposed from above by 'two powerful sovereigns [...] backed by the strongest and bravest' rather than by popular will, he welcomed the progress of the Reformation. 'To the last', he noted, 'up to the defeat of the Armada, manhood suffrage in England would at any moment have brought back the Pope.'[31] Yet he also asserted that the king moved with the nation, with its backing, 'leading it though not outrunning it; checking those who went too fast, dragging forward those who lagged behind'.[32] 'In this spirit', noted Duffy, 'Froude defended the execution of More and Fisher and the excruciating death by disemboweling of the Carthusian monks of Sheen for refusing the Oath of Supremacy in 1535.'[33] It is in this context that Froude's assessment of Mary and her reign should be understood. Sandwiched between the reigns of 'two powerful sovereigns', whose faults could be excused by their contributions to what Froude considered the service of the people, was Mary's 'reign of terror'.[34]

Froude's attempt at objectivity of course was sound in many respects, which made his work all the more appealing to those who sought a more scholarly version of the past but as yet were unwilling to breach established boundaries. He acknowledged Mary's nobility and her courage in securing her rightful inheritance as well as the disagreeable task of having 'to govern with the assistance of men who were gorged with the spoils of the church, suspected of heresy, and at best indifferent to religion'[35] at a time when 'profligate profanity [...] had eaten too long into the moral life of England'.[36] But, given the huge task that confronted her, he believed that she was out of her depth. 'In happier times', he noted, 'Mary might have been a worthy queen, and Gardiner an illustrious minister; but fatal superstition which confounded religion with orthodox opinion was too strong for both of them.'[37]

Religion was not the only obstacle which Froude believed had blighted Mary's judgement. Responsible for 'shaking her mind' was a 'hysterical' nature[38] that was brought about by the succession of personal traumas that she had to suffer. Here was enough for any mischievous writer to paint a picture that contained nothing but wretchedness and despair. Where corroborating evidence was absent fantasy and hearsay filled the void. 'A lady who slept in her room', Froude noted, reportedly told France's ambassador, the duke of Noailles, that Mary 'could not speak to no one without impatience, and that she believed the whole world was in league to keep her husband from her.'[39] And so 'the unhappy queen, unloved, unlovable [...] with a broken spirit and bewildered [...] turned to Heaven for comfort, and instead of heaven, she saw only the false roof of her creed painted to imitate and shut out the sky'.[40] By dwelling on Mary's 'symptoms of hysterical derangements',[41] Froude had made explicit what Lingard and the Stricklands had implied and by doing so gave further succour to a myth that would cloud objective assessment of the Marian reign for over a hundred years. Its source was a misinterpretation of a contemporary diagnosis of symptoms Mary suffered shortly after spending some time with her mother, Katherine, in March 1531, and which would reoccur many times during her life.[42] The diagnosis of 'hysteria', a catch-all condition, attributable to a malfunction of the womb, was in fact a nineteenth-century mistranslation that was based on the Greek word for uterus, *hystera*. 'In the sixteenth century', noted Judith Richards, 'blaming the womb was a response that could be made to almost any condition that appeared in a female [. . .] Given that Mary's medical problems might have actually been almost any condition, even one shared with males, what other interpretation might be offered for her recurrent illnesses, which so frequently occurred at times of great stress?'[43]

Mary certainly experienced her fair share of stress, given the tragedies she endured throughout her life. But notwithstanding that many of her illnesses were feigned for political convenience to avoid awkward meetings with either her father or her brother, it is misplaced to attribute occasional psychological, as well as physical symptoms, to some sort of mental instability. Mary's detractors, however, did just that, pouncing on the (mis)diagnosis to imply a hysterical character that fitted in well with their assessment of her record as queen. Their view, moreover, also conformed to both the Victorian image of women as gentle creatures whose intellect was governed by emotions, and the assumption that post-Reformation Catholicism was a spent religion, and that any attempt to revive it was irrational.[44]

With Froude's assessment, what Mary had gained on the roundabouts she lost on the swings. While the 'hysterical derangement', which Froude associated with insanity, formally exonerated her for 'her cruelties', which for him too, 'stood apart from anything else in her reign', she had now become an innocent mad woman, 'entirely free [. . .] from the passions which in general tempt sovereigns into crime'. As such, he claimed, 'few men or women have lived less capable of doing knowingly a wrong thing'.[45] So if Mary was insane, who was guilty of the persecution of Protestants? For Froude her 'madness was of a kind which placed her absolutely under her spiritual directors; and the responsibility for her cruelties, if responsibility be anything but a name, rests with Gardiner, who commenced them, and, secondly, and in the higher degree, with Reginald Pole [. . . who] is not to be held innocent of atrocities which could neither have been commenced nor continued without his sanction'. Pole, in Froude's view, presided over 'the tyranny of the bishops [and] the clergy' who had been motivated by 'revenge' for 'past humiliations'.[46] Froude's conclusion was a self-fulfilling prophesy that neatly led to the assumption that her reign was useless and tyrannical. 'She had reigned little more than five years', he noted, 'and she descended into the grave amidst curses deeper than the acclamations which had welcomed her accession. In that brief time, she had swathed her name in the horrid epithet which will cling to it for ever.'[47]

Though full of factual errors on many aspects, which would in time be completely exposed, the quality of Froude's narrative and its virulent anti-Catholicism caught the imagination of the public, if not so much the academic community, which was not so easily fooled. In time, however, even academics would welcome his assessment, and would continue to peddle his errors, giving them a degree of respectability.

NOTES

¹ H. Tootell (Charles Dodd), *Church History of England from the Year 1500 to the Year 1688* (Brussels, 1737, republished Westmead, Farnborough: Gregg International Publishers, 1970). The work was originally published in Wolverhampton but for practical reasons Brussels is cited as the place of publication.

² Ibid., p. 463.

³ Ibid.

⁴ Ibid.

⁵ J. Guy, *Tudor England* (Oxford: Oxford University Press, 1998), p. 227.

⁶ Tootell (Charles Dodd), *Church History of England*, p. 92.

⁷ Vidmar, *English Catholic Historians*, p. 27.

⁸ For a discussion of the Cisalpine Movement see ibid., pp. 23–51.

⁹ Ibid, p. 9.

¹⁰ *Lingard's History of England Abridged: With a Continuation, from 1688 to 1854*, 3rd edition revised and enlarged (Baltimore: John Murphy & Co., 1875).

¹¹ Vidmar, *English Catholic Historians*, p. 53.

¹² E. Jones, *John Lingard and the Pursuit of Historical Truth* (Brighton and Portland: Sussex Academic Press), 2001, p. 79.

¹³ Ibid.

¹⁴ J. Lingard, *A History of England from the First Invasion by the Romans*, 14 vols., 4th edition (Paris: L Baudry, 1826), vol. 7 , p. 278.

¹⁵ Ibid., p. 282.

¹⁶ Ibid., pp. 277–8.

¹⁷ Ibid., p. 222.

¹⁸ A. Strickland and E. Strickland, *Lives of the Queens of England: From the Norman Conquest*. London: Colburn & Co., 1851–2.

¹⁹ Ibid., vol. 3, p. 587.

²⁰ Ibid., p. 555.

²¹ Ibid.

²² Ibid., p. 574.

²³ Ibid., p. 558.

²⁴ For Micheli's description of Queen Mary, including her state of health, see http://englishhistory.net/tudor/marydesc.html, accessed 8 April 2013.

²⁵ Lingard, *A History of England*, pp. 275–6.

²⁶ Strickland, *Lives of the Queens of England*, vol. 3, p. 575.

²⁷ T. B. Macaulay, *The History of England from the Accession of James the Second*. 5 vols. (London: Longman, Brown, Green and Longman, 1849), vol. 1 , pp. 43, 44.

²⁸ Ibid., pp. 51, 164.

²⁹ The work was revised in 12 volumes: J. A. Froude, *History of England from the Fall of Wolsey to the Defeat of the Spanish Armada* (London: Longman, Green and Co., London, 1870, new edn 1893).

³⁰ From, W. H. Dunn, 'James Anthony Froude: A Biography'. 2 vols. (Oxford:

Clarendon Press, 1961–3), vol. 1, p. 202, cited in J. A. Froude, *The Reign of Mary Tudor*, intr. E. Duffy (London and New York: Continuum, 2009), p. 8.

[31] Ibid.

[32] Froude, *History of England* , vol. 4, p. 240.

[33] Froude, *The Reign of Mary Tudor*, p. 10.

[34] Froude, *History of England*, vol. 6, p. 527.

[35] Ibid., p. 46.

[36] Ibid., p. 55.

[37] Ibid., pp. 55–6.

[38] Ibid., p. 228.

[39] Ibid.

[40] Ibid., p. 238.

[41] Ibid., p. 528.

[42] 'Augustino Scarpinello to Francesco Sforza, Duke of Milan, 664', 20 April 20 1531, CSPV, vol., 4.

[43] J. M. Richards, 'Reassessing Mary Tudor: Some Concluding Points', in Doran and Freeman, eds., *Mary Tudor*, p. 213.

[44] Freeman, 'Inventing Bloody Mary', p. 99.

[45] Froude, *History of England*, vol. 6, p. 528.

[46] Ibid, pp. 528, 326.

[47] Ibid., pp. 527–8.

✛ 4 ✛

Continuity and Revision

B Y THE TURN OF THE TWENTIETH CENTURY Mary's image had evolved
from that of a cruel tyrant to a misguided and tragic ruler, albeit kindly
and noble at heart, driven by religious bigotry, teetering on the edge of
sanity and ill-advised by wicked counsellors. Notwithstanding praise for her
achievements, the dominant strand in Marian historiography presented her
reign as a failure and primarily determined by the persecution of Protestants.
This extraordinary thesis was to survive for the best part of the century at
the end of which virtually its entire premise was to be discredited.

Key to its longevity was the work of Albert Frederick Pollard. A highly
acclaimed pioneer of modern Tudor history, Pollard too had a distinct
agenda. As a Methodist, he did not seek to defend Anglican Protestantism
as a priority, though he certainly did nothing to undermine its primacy.
Rather, it was his admiration for the British Empire and its Parliament,
both of which he considered to be the apogee of political achievement,
which framed his assessment of the Tudor age, and consequently that of
Mary and her reign. For Pollard, Henry VIII was the hero of the Tudor
saga, who was incapable of 'lust for superfluous butchery' and who 'neither
faltered nor failed' either at home or abroad.[1] And though Pollard recognised
Henry's darker 'bloodthirsty' side,[2] he downplayed it, considering his victims,
whether wives or traitors, to have been appropriately dealt with in 'a ruthless
age with a ruthless hand'[3] for the good of the realm. Astonishingly, Pollard
makes reference to Henry's debasement of the coinage only in passing[4]
while he makes no reference to inflation at all. Such a romantic image
of the founder of Britain's imperial greatness thus needed a spoiler who
came close to ruining everything. And for Pollard, Mary fitted the bill
perfectly. As a person Mary was the 'most honest of Tudor rulers [who]
never consciously did what she thought to be wrong', Pollard wrote in his
acclaimed *The history of England, from the accession of Edward VI to the death
of Elizabeth*, published in 1910. 'So far as she could', he argued, 'she kept
her court and government uncorrupt, and she tried to help the poor.' And
'In spite of her cruel treatment in youth, she was compassionate except
when her creed was concerned; and no other Tudor was so lenient to

traitors'.[5] Kindness, however, coexisted with madness of 'a mind diseased in a disordered frame'. Expecting the birth of an heir that never came, and forsaken by her husband and estranged from her people, 'Mary went on, ploughing her cheerless furrow across a stubborn land, and reaping, as the shadows fell, her harvest of hopes deferred [. . .] A pitiful woman by nature, she was rendered pitiless by the inexorable logic of her creed'.[6]

Victorian in his assessment of her character, Pollard deviated little from Victorian assessments of the nature of her reign, which he noted 'had been a palpable failure' in which 'there could only be stagnation'. In his judgement 'had Mary been content with restoring her father's system, she might have been successful. But the time for a real counter-reformation had not come in England, and there were few signs of catholic fervour in Mary's reign'. In his view, the 'reconciliation with Rome was the result not so much of popular impulse as of governmental pressure; and it stirred not a breath of spiritual fervour'.[7] It seemed to him that 'only in the pursuit of heretics did the government exhibit any vigour'.[8] Little wonder that he would conclude that 'Sterility was the conclusive note of Mary's reign',[9] a notorious though enduring *double entendre*, that mocked Mary for her many phantom pregnancies, to emphasise her failures in government.

So in tune was Pollard's thesis with the prevailing imperialist and anti-Catholic currents that it formed the essence of thinking on the Marian period both in popular and academic spheres for decades to come, Pollard's own senior academic status reinforcing its kudos. Gone may have been the Whigs from the political arena but their haughty progressiveness remained influential. 'It was widely agreed', noted Duffy, 'that the Reformation was, among other things, a vital stage along the road to modernity, the cleansing of priestcraft, ignorance, and superstition from the English psyche, a moral and intellectual leap forward.'[10]

The enduring confessional undercurrent of the anti-Marian polemic was inevitably to attract a Catholic response which varied in scholarly quality. Cardinal Aidan Gasquet, a prolific turn-of-the-century historian, offered a spirited defence of pre-Reformation Catholicism. His numerous works, notably *Henry VIII and the English Monasteries*,[11] published in 1888, and *The Eve of the Reformation*,[12] published in 1900, did much to promote the Catholic case and to address the enduring misrepresentations of Protestant polemic. Common assumptions about pre-Reformation attitudes of Englishmen, he noted, were wide of the mark. Contrary to the 'diatribes and scurrilous invectives of advanced reformers', there was an 'absence of indications of any real hostility to the Holy See of Rome [. . . and] straightforward teaching was not neglected in pre-Reformation England'. Moreover, the 'importance attached to pilgrimages by our pre-Reformation forefathers [. . .] is difficult to exaggerate'[13] while the Dissolution of the monasteries, rather than to 'serve any public purpose or to mitigate some miseries of poverty', was merely a 'sop to the greedy appetite of a vicious and avaricious monarch and his greedy favourites'.[14]

Gasquet's apologia did have its faults. The unyielding Anglican polemicist George Gordon Coulton,[15] as well as fellow Catholic priest and historian of medieval monasticism David Knowles,[16] took issue, for instance, with what they perceived to be its sloppy research as too did Geoffrey Elton in more recent times.[17] Nevertheless, for all its faults, Gasquet's work would establish a thematic framework for more meticulous historians to work within. Duffy, for instance, though critical of Gasquest's 'idealised picture of Catholic England',[18] admired the significance of his work. He went on to develop, in his scrupulously researched *Stripping of the Altars*, published in 1992, many of the themes that Gasquet investigated, offering an irrefutable case charting the vigour and popular appeal of late-medieval Catholicism.

Few reservations, however, can be expressed about the work of the Anglican convert, Monsignor Philip Hughes. Well researched and competently compiled, his works covered a range of themes on ecclesiastical history. Arguably his most notable work, the multi-volume *The Reformation in England*, published between 1950 and 1954, offered the most comprehensive and lucid narrative of the period since Lingard's *History* over a hundred years earlier. Combining wit with an assertive style, Hughes mockingly dismissed the royal supremacy as 'blasphemous rubbish', commenting sarcastically on Edward's accession, that 'The new Supreme Head of Christ's Church is a little boy of nine'.[19] Hughes shared Gasquest's view that the Dissolution was essentially motivated by plunder that made 'great business'[20] which destroyed scholarly life in England and deprived the poor of charity. So unpopular was the Reformation, he argued, which deprived the English people of their birthright that was their ancient religion that it needed to be forcibly imposed from above.[21] He also, with the authority of the competent theologian that he was, offered a convincing case against the claim, professed among others by his most ardent interlocutor, Arthur Geoffrey Dickens, that Henry's religious settlement remained Catholic. In his characteristic sardonic tone he mocked the overriding doctrine of the Henrician Church, as espoused in *A Necessary Doctrine and Erudition for Any Christian Man*, published in 1543, popularly known as 'The King's Book'. Hughes took particular issue with its claim that 'every Christian man ought to honour, give credence, and to follow, the particular church, of that region so ordered (as afore) wherein he is born or inhabiteth'.[22] 'It is, then, a man's duty in 1543', Hughes noted, 'as a thing commanded him by Christ our Lord to be what is nowadays called a roman Catholic, if he be a Spaniard or a Frenchman or a Scot – to be a Lutheran if the Elector of Saxony is his prince – or, if he is English or Irish, to be whatever at this moment Henry VIII is.'[23] The rejection of the papacy was indeed, for Hughes, a game changer as far as doctrinal authenticity of the Henrician Church was concerned.

Along with his acerbic critique of the Henrician Church, Hughes went further than anyone had gone thus far in justifying the burnings of Protestants that had occurred during Mary's reign. While arguing that the policy of burning people who had merely practised a faith that they had grown up with was misplaced, he offered intriguing contextual analysis to justify the policy. Distressing as it may be for modern sensibilities, he argued, burning was the accepted form of punishment for heresy for Catholics and Protestants alike across the whole of Europe, while the victims were for most contemporary Englishmen, contrary to subsequent Protestant propaganda, mere statistics in a violent age in which a modern humanitarian spirit was almost totally absent. 'If we were habituated to the spectacle of something like 12,000 executions yearly', he noted, '– where now there are not a dozen – for offences which varied from stealing five shillings to murder and treason, we should hardly be as impressed as we assume our ancestors to have been, by the fact of an additional number – comparatively small – now executed annually, for the crime called heresy.'[24] Such insightful observations helped Hughes's history of *The Reformation in England* to weather the test of time better than older histories of the period. Nevertheless, his highly critical depiction of the Reformation as little more than a loot fest instigated by an oppressive state for the benefit of the wealthy, as well as his apologetic assessment of the Marian period, rendered his texts suspect in the eyes of the academic establishment.

In taking such positions Hughes's great work, together with other serious Catholic histories and lesser histories such as Hilaire Belloc's very persuasive *How the Reformation Happened*, published in 1928, made little headway in drawing the nation away from the received Whiggish-Anglican version of the Reformation. Here, Froude was to triumph. His assessment of the Reformation as a popular inevitability and of Mary I as a hysterical weakling, controlled by pitiless clerics, who engaged in suppressing opponents in fits of un-English excess, eventually came to be regarded as received wisdom until very recently. From Pollard in the early part of the century to Arthur Geoffrey Dickens and Geoffrey Elton in the latter, mainstream history was to tolerate few rivals as far as the Reformation was concerned.

Even writers who were genuinely sympathetic to Mary's plight failed to challenge many of the received positions on the Marian period. Hilda Prescott, in her well-researched and highly readable biography, *Mary Tudor: The Spanish Tudor*, published in 1940, dug deep into Mary's past. What emerges is a character that is fundamentally good, though deeply affected by the tragedies of her childhood, adolescence and adulthood. Although

Prescott adhered to the view that 'All that Mary did was undone, all she intended utterly unfulfilled',[25] she made a credible attempt to explain as well as justify her policies, even those which have been cited by others as the most odious. Although a committed Protestant and the daughter of an Anglican clergyman, Prescott detached herself from confessional allegiance, which further legitimised her work. Yet for all its conventional conclusions, Prescott's work was sufficiently revisionist to render it, in many respects, an anomaly. And so long as the prevailing Protestant-political-national order held, and it still did, the traditional position, in a broad sense, would prevail. Even writers who would later make a name for themselves as exonerators of the Marian legacy were initially swept away by the contemporary currents. David Loades, for instance, wrote of Mary in his *Two Tudor Conspiracies*, published in 1965, as being an incompetent ruler 'who would have made an excellent housewife'.[26]

By the time Dickens published *The English Reformation* in 1964 one would have thought that confessional prejudice would no longer have been a determinant of history-writing on this issue, and that historians of such stature as Dickens would have known better than to allow themselves to be so greatly influenced by old assumptions. This point becomes even more salient given that his work would come to dominate Reformation studies for the next three decades, though not without increasingly being challenged. Dickens endeavoured to avoid expressing sectarian sympathies, yet notwithstanding the sophistication of his prose, his assertions and conclusions bore striking similarity to those offered by Foxe in the Elizabethan period. It would have been improbable, however, had Dickens's upbringing in a strict Methodist family not coloured his scholarly outlook.[27] For Dickens, the Reformation, even if catalysed by political rather than religious forces, was a historical inevitability, and any retreat, once it had been launched, would have been against the wishes of the vast majority of the people, such was the unpopularity and corruption of the Roman Church. Such a position in turn could conveniently depict the Marian period as a reaction that went against the grain. Although he did not deny Mary's personal qualities, he concluded, some fifty to sixty years after Pollard offered his judgement, that her reign was an utter failure, tainted by cruelty, excess and folly, and it was only its abrupt end that saved England from total oblivion.[28]

In 1977, Elton in his *Reform and Reformation* concurred, dismissing the suggestion that had Mary lived longer there is no knowing what might have happened. 'True', he noted, 'we cannot be sure, but if we may judge from what happened while she lived we must doubt very much whether she, her agents and her policies could ever really have done more than put off the consequences of the 1530s by a few years [. . .] Mary died in time [for] reconstruction to begin with confidence', he concluded.[29] Elton's motives for upholding the Whiggish-confessional version of the Reformation are less clear than those of Froude, Pollard or Dickens. Jewish in origin, having fled German-occupied Prague with his parents in February 1939, he may have perceived it wiser, as an ambitious scholar of immigrant roots, to swim with the tide rather than against it. Whatever his reasons, however, his conclusion that the Reformation was inevitable, albeit generating much more opposition than either Pollard or Dickens had realised,[30] and that the Marian reign was an utter failure,[31] was profoundly consistent with orthodox thinking.

Notwithstanding their pioneering and inspirational work in the archives, Dickens and Elton were virtually the last of their school. Both scholars would in fact repeatedly have to defend their positions against a scholarly trend that was increasingly challenging the assumptions that had underpinned history writing on the Reformation and the Marian period for so long. There were many reasons for the change in emphasis. Crucially, what was increasingly becoming clear was that the confessional and political forces that bore so heavily for so long on Britain's national story were weakening. Britain's re-engagement with mainland Europe through supra-national political and economic institutions and the diminishing significance of Protestantism in Britain's national identity opened up the possibility of redefining the national story without causing too much upset. As such, the last three decades or so of the twentieth century and beyond witnessed a burst of groundbreaking scholarship based on pioneering archival work, reinterpretation of original material and correction of blatant errors that would turn received history about both the Reformation and the Marian reign on its head. Steadily, egregious scholarly error and layers of prejudices would be peeled away to reveal a wholly different portrayal of both themes from that to which generations had become accustomed. Overseeing this huge change would be a new group of scholars – J. J. Scarisbrick, Patrick Collinson, Jennifer Loach, David Loades, Christopher Haigh, Anna Whitelock, John Edwards, Lucy Wooding, Judith Richards, Eamon Duffy and others, who would become household names in the field. Their work would also raise questions about Britain's national identity, salient questions indeed, which sooner or later will need serious attention.

*

The scholarly debate on the Marian period has focused on two aspects: the effectiveness of the reign and the personalities associated with it. The latter has drawn more attention than is usual in period studies. But because Mary's detractors, from Knox and Foxe to Pollard and Dickens, were determined to personalise the reign, often drawing spurious links between Mary's (alleged) character and physical defects and the administration's workings, it was incumbent on revisionists to approach the subject from similar perspectives. As such, revisionist biographies of Mary have woven repudiations of myths about her character with reassessments of her reign, drawing links between its nature and her character where necessary, repudiating them where appropriate. To determine why the Marian administration burned an unprecedented number of heretics it is necessary to look beyond Knox's image of Mary as 'that wicked English Jezebel' and Foxe's of 'bloody' Edmund Bonner.[32] To understand the nature of the administration, it is necessary to determine why David Hume arrived at the judgement that Mary was 'a weak bigoted woman, under the government of priests',[33] given that neither of these assertions was true. To demonstrate that the reign was not 'sterile' it is necessary to examine why Pollard chose to draw parallels between Mary's difficulties to conceive and matters of state and why he came to the conclusion at all that her rule was sterile. Although the burning of heretics remains the policy most vulnerable to criticism, it too has been subjected to extensive re-evaluation.

Face value assessment that characterised so much of old historiography has given way to detailed contextual reappraisal of both the motives of the prosecutors of the policy and the recalcitrance of the victims. It is now accepted that the policy was not governed by a desire to avenge perceived wrongs, but primarily to save the souls of the accused and that the existence of a doctrinally heterodox body of martyrs is a myth (see chapter 12). It is also no longer held that Roman Catholicism was deeply unpopular in England in 1532, or indeed some time later, but rather that it was a vibrant part of local communities (see chapter 9). It is no longer believed that the Marian restoration 'failed to discover the Counter-Reformation' as Dickens asserted or that, in essence, it was a medievalist reaction against the Henrician-Edwardian religious order (see chapter 11).[34] Neither is another Dickensian claim accepted, that Mary and Cardinal Pole, the archbishop of Canterbury and papal legate 'displayed the tragedy of the doctrinarians called to practical leadership, yet lacking the instinct toward human beings, that sense of possible in a real world' (see chapter 11).[35] Instead, it is now believed that the Marian Church not only embraced many of the Henrician novelties, that were themselves rooted in Catholic reform, but fashioned a coherent programme of reform that pre-empted many of the initiatives of the Council of Trent (1545–63), on which the Counter-Reformation would be based (see chapter 11).

We of course have no way of knowing what the precise nature of peoples' faith was on the eve of the Marian period; neither did the scholars and chroniclers of old. Twenty years had elapsed since the break from Rome during which a different interpretation of the Christian faith had been foisted on society. When Mary ascended the throne received practices and beliefs could not be overturned hastily, irrespective of the administration's intentions, particularly since the ecclesiastical infrastructure with which to do this had been so terribly depleted. One only needed to observe the persistent reluctance among sections of twenty-first-century English Catholic congregations to embrace the minor revisions to the wording of the Mass that were introduced in 2011, to appreciate the scale of the task that confronted the Marian Church in implementing the doctrinal and behavioural change that it wanted to do. We do now know, however, that five years into Mary's reign, traditional ceremonial was restored across the country to a significant extent, something that should not be dismissed as superficial or unimportant. The blandness of Protestant services, as well as the important role played by ritual of all sorts in Tudor society as a source of community coherence, rendered the restoration of traditional ceremonial a popular move (see chapter 11). Furthermore, given that religious ceremony was a pathway to faith, as Cardinal Pole so vigorously believed, the full impact of this achievement was thwarted only by the abrupt termination of the reign. The Marian Church, therefore, possessed attributes for which it had not been credited by historians of old. Religious policy apart, other policy areas have also undergone considerable reassessment. No longer is it believed that state structures, notably the Council, were a rudderless mess or that the government achieved little in restoring the country's fortunes (see chapter 8). Nor is Mary's choice of spouse in Philip of Spain now assessed with outright derision or is Marian foreign policy considered as a national disaster (see chapter 8). The reassessment of the Marian legacy has come a long way from the pernicious propaganda and factual error that dogged it for centuries.

The question needs to be asked whether this colossal reappraisal of the Reformation and the Marian period has been primarily motivated by confessional Catholic loyalties. If so then a serious charge of bias can be made against the process that could diminish the value of the new scholarship in a way similar to that which diminished traditional writing on these subjects. The charge, however, has little merit. It was inevitable that the proportion of Catholics in academia would rise in the second half of the twentieth century given the influx of Catholics into secondary education in the wake of the education reforms of 1944. And it was natural for many to be drawn to themes of medieval history, especially the Reformation, no doubt in part owing to what Duffy terms a 'sub-cultural formation, and the heightened religious preoccupations of a minority religious group'.[36] Many of these new scholars of course were lapsed Catholics, while many were not Catholic at all.

The work of those scholars with Catholic roots who engaged in the reassessment of this period does not exhibit any evidence of confessional prejudice or even 'a conscious revisionary agenda', as noted Duffy, 'but is simply the routine work of historians doing what historians always do or are supposed to do: trying to get a clearer picture of what happened in the past'.[37] In citing Geoffrey Elton's *Policy and Police*, hardly an acknowledged revisionist work, as an inspirational source, Duffy aptly stresses this point.[38] But perhaps Simon Schama emphasises the priority of modern historians in this field most convincingly. 'We all grew up', he noted, 'even a nice Jewish boy like me, with the idea that the English Reformation was a historic inevitability, the culling of an obsolete, unpopular, fundamentally un-English faith. But on the very eve of the Reformation Catholicism in England was vibrant, popular and very much alive.'[39] No confessional axe to grind here.

Yet notwithstanding the growing body of scholarly reappraisal of both Mary's character and her reign, the legend of Bloody Mary continues to enjoy much mileage. It seems that scholarly revisions do not appear to have had much influence on popular culture. 'She nodded and smiled pleasantly', recalled Matthew Shardlake, C. J. Sansom's fictional lawyer-cum-detective, of his encounter with young Lady Mary, 'though her dark eyes were coldly watchful [. . . She] turned, looked at me, and then gave a sardonic little smile.' By contrast his encounter with the thirteen-year-old Lady Elizabeth was a much more satisfying experience. 'I turned and found myself looking at the magnificently dressed figure of the Lady Elizabeth [. . .] I had met Elizabeth the year before [. . .] she had grown since then [. . .] She had acquired, too, an adult's poise, no longer displaying the gawkishness of a girl [. . .] If she was half a woman in body now, she was more than half in mind and demeanour.'[40] Film portrayals of Mary too have generally stuck to the traditional narrative of her as either the naïve though well-meaning simpleton of the 1971 television adaptation of the *Elizabeth I* or the sickly, quivering, vengeful, Mary of Shekhar Kapur's highly acclaimed film of 1998, *Elizabeth*.

Stereotypes were plentiful at an attraction in 2012 at the London Dungeon, a popular indoor theme park of medieval gore. Any visitor to the 'Killer Queen' exhibition who was unfamiliar with the recent scholarly revisions would have been left with a lasting impression of Mary as a blood-sucking, merciless woman determined to inflict the most severe pain on heretics. To draw visitors, the promotional literature featured a ghoulish image of Mary. An oversized crucifix around her neck, with a contorted face and an outstretched arm, Mary points an accusatory finger towards some wretch about to be consumed by the fire that forms the backdrop of the image. 'Bloody Mary, the deadliest daughter of Henry VIII', a flier reads:

> is ruthlessly ridding the country of heretics. In her eyes, there is only one faith and all those who believe otherwise must be punished. No

one is safe from persecution – men, women and children are all suspect in the eyes of Bloody Mary. Feel the force of her wrath, the heat of the flames and the intensity of Mary's obsession!

An animated advertisement for the same exhibition, intended to be featured on the London Underground, showing Mary morphing into a flesh-eating zombie, was so grotesque that it was banned by the Advertising Standards Authority.[41]

An even more astonishing piece of recent historical hyperbole was an episode devoted to Mary Tudor by The Discovery Channel's 2008 compendium of *The Most Evil Women in History*. Though seeking intellectual kudos by soliciting the opinions of renowned specialists like Diarmaid MacCulloch and David Loades, the programme is totally compromised by its ludicrous claims, as exemplified in its opening gambit:

> During her five-year reign she threw all of England into chaos [...
> She] beheaded traitors, murdered heretics and had pregnant women
> burnt to death in the name of her religious fanaticism. The entire
> nation lived in fear of her. The streets of English cities were polluted
> with the putrid smell of burning flesh. She created such terror that
> she's known as Bloody Mary.

The programme's credibility was further compromised by the fact that Mary is considered in the same light as the likes of concentration-camp guard and convicted war criminal Ilse Koch and the sixteenth-century torturer and serial killer, Countess Elizabeth Batory, who are some of the other candidates for the most evil women in history.

*

To say that there has been a revolution in the writing on Mary I and the Marian period would not be an exaggeration. The way that Mary, her policies and her administration in general are now viewed is hugely different compared to the way these subjects were viewed merely two or three decades ago. But while the Foxe-Dickens fantasies have been shattered for ever, the exoneration of Mary and her reign continues to encounter obstacles. And there are credible reasons why this should be so. Though considerably less of a thorny subject than it once was, the Reformation, or aspects of it, continues to govern important areas of Britain's public life. To do anything more, for instance, than to tinker with the constitutional inheritance would be to disturb a political hornets' nest for which there is little political will. Should a Catholic be allowed to ascend the throne? If so, should he be the current Stuart claimant? What impact would a Catholic succession have on the established Church of England? Should there be an established Church at all? These are just a few of the questions which the current political establishment believes should not be asked too loudly. The threat of political instability, therefore, is too great for the Reformation to be rejected totally at the political level. The Reformation story, however, also serves another constituency. The growing secularisation of society which is, in some part, rooted in a profound hostility to traditional religion in general and Catholicism in particular, still makes challenging the fundamental *raison d'être* of the Reformation impolitic in 'polite company'. For atheists and secularists the existence of 'rational' myths is preferable to the legitimisation of a religion that would make life more difficult for them than the relativist religion that Protestantism has become. As such the image of 'Bloody Mary', who attempted and failed to put a spanner into the works of religious reform, continues to enjoy much mileage in such circles. This factor alone has limited the level of initiation into historical truth about the Marian period, although one should nevertheless console oneself by the fact that the number of initiated is now considerable.

NOTES

[1] A. F. Pollard, *Henry VII* (London: Longman, Green and Co., 1919), pp. 346, 440.

[2] Ibid., p. 346.

[3] Ibid., p. 440.

[4] Ibid., pp .346, 440, 418.

[5] A. F. Pollard, *The History of England, from the Accession of Edward VI to the Death of Elizabeth* (London: Longman, Green and Co., 4th impression, 1919), p. 174.

[6] Ibid., pp. 172, 174.

[7] Ibid., pp. 172, 173.

[8] Ibid., p. 172.

[9] Ibid.

[10] Duffy, *Saints, Sacrilege and Sedition*, p. 40.

[11] A. Gasquet, *Henry VIII and the English Monasteries: An Attempt to Illustrate the History of their Suppression.* 2 vols. (London: John Hodges, 1888).

[12] A. Gasquet, *The Eve of the Reformation: Studies in the Religious Life and Thought of the English People in the Period Preceeding the Rejection of the Roman Jurisdiction by Henry VIII* (London: G Bell and Sons Ltd, 1923).

[13] Ibid, pp. 70, 245, 247, 366.

[14] Gasquet, *Henry VIII and the English Monasteries*, vol. 1, p. 322.

[15] G. G. Coulton, *The Monastic Legend: A Criticism of Abbot Gasquet's 'Henry VIII and the English Monasteries'* (London: Simpkin, Marshall, Hamilton, Kent & Co., 1905).

[16] D. Knowles, *Cardinal Gasquet as an Historian*, Creighton lecture (London, Athlone Press, 1957).

[17] G. R. Elton, *The Practice of History* (Oxford: Wiley-Blackwell, 2002), p. 96.

[18] R. de Souza, 'Confronting the Church's Past: An Interview with Eamon Duffy', *Commonweal*, 127/1, January 2000.

[19] P. Hughes, *The Reformation in England. The King's Proceedings.* 2 vols. (London: Hollis and Carter, 1956, 1961), vol. 1, p. 342; vol. 2, p. 342.

[20] Ibid., vol. 1, p. 196.

[21] Ibid., p. 144.

[22] Ninth article: the Holy Catholic Church in *A Necessary Doctrine and Erudition for Any Christian Man Set forth by the King's Majesty of England*, &c. The King's Book, 1543 Introduction by the Reverend T. A. Lacey (London: R. Browning, 1895), pp. 6–32.

[23] Hughes, *The Reformation in England*, vol. 2, p. 47.

[24] Ibid.

[25] H. F. M. Prescott, *Mary Tudor: The Spanish Tudor* (1940, rev. edn 1952 repr. London: Phoenix, 2003), p. 485.

[26] D. Loades, *Two Tudor Conspiracies* (Cambridge: Cambridge University Press, 1965), pp. 9–10.

[27] Duffy, *Saints, Sacrilege and Sedition*, p. 43.

[28] A. G. Dickens, *The English Reformation* (Glasgow: Fontana Press, 1983), pp. 355–85.

[29] G. R. Elton, *Reform and Reformation: England 1509–1558* (London: Edward Arnold, 1977), pp. 389, 396.

[30] G. R. Elton, *Policy and Police: The Enforcement of the Reformation in the Age of Thomas Cromwell* (Cambridge: Cambridge University Press, 1972).

[31] Elton, *Reform and Reformation*, pp. 377, 396.

[32] Knox, *The first blast of the trumpet*, p. 1. Digitised version: Project Gutenberg: *http://www.gutenberg.org/files/9660/9660-h/9660-h.htm*, accessed 8 August, 2013.

[33] Hume, *The History of England*, p. 379.

[34] Dickens, *English Reformation*, p. 384.

[35] Ibid., p. 385.

[36] Duffy, *Saints, Sacrilege and Sedition*, p. 8.

[37] Ibid., p. 7.

[38] Ibid.

[39] S. Schama, *History of Britain*, episode 6: *Burning Convictions*, BBC production, 2002.

[40] C. J. Sansom, *Lamentation* (Basingstoke and Oxford: Mantle, 2014), pp. 137, 140, 201, 202.

[41] The London Dungeon declined to grant permission for the reproduction of its promotional material. 'The London Dungeon, Mary Tudor promotional poster', http://www.londonnet.co.uk/competition/the-london-dungeon.php, accessed 13 May, 2013. 'Banned Bloody Mary Zombie Advert for the London Dungeon', http://www.youtube.com/watch?v=09WtEmTLp1Y, accessed 13 May, 2013.

II

Pawn and Victim

✢ 5 ✢

Mary's Earliest Years: A Childhood Blighted by Parental Discord

MARY WAS BORN IN GREENWICH on 18 February 1516. For her mother, Katherine of Aragon, Henry's first ill-fated wife, the relief was tangible, her previous six pregnancies having ended in miscarriage, still-birth or infant death. For her father, Henry, the birth was a mixed blessing. Though lavishing his new born with fatherly affection,[1] he could not help but feel disappointed by Katherine's failure yet again to produce a son (Prince Henry, his first-born, survived for barely a month before dying of an unrecorded disease in February 1511). Notwithstanding Henry's fatherly affection for his daughter, certain anxieties remained at the back of his mind, which would grow in intensity with the passing of time. With the tumultuous dynastic Wars of the Roses of the fifteenth century that tore the country apart for thirty years, still part of living memory, and with the prospect of a female ruler being a leap into the unknown, Henry's anxiety was in this respect justified. A marriage of a queen had the potential of either subjugating England to the interests of an alien power, in the event of the spouse being foreign, or of rekindling the flames of dynastic rivalry in the event of his being a home-grown noble. For now, however, Henry lived in hope that Katherine could still produce a male heir to safeguard the Tudor dynasty and consequently did not formally acknowledge Mary as his heir.

Katherine harboured no such concerns. She was the daughter of Isabella of Castile, who ruled Spain with her husband Ferdinand of Aragon as his equal for thirty-five years, having secured her throne after a five-year-long civil war against her niece, Joanna. Ferdinand and Isabella presided over Spain's reunification as well as over the *Reconquista* for Catholicism of all of the country. This saw the expulsion of Muslims from Granada, their last remaining kingdom in Spain. Together they prepared the ground for Spain's Golden Age during the sixteenth century. Isabella had been determined to give Katherine, as well as her three other daughters, a rounded education that included academic scholarship in addition to instruction in the usual

59

female arts of dance, music and needlework. This comprehensive education, together with her upbringing in such politically momentous times, was a heady combination that reinforced in Katherine the courage, fortitude, determination and political ability that she had inherited from her parents. She would demonstrate all these attributes forthrightly during her own tumultuous life. A good marriage was subsequently arranged for her with the heir to the English throne, Prince Arthur. This would form an Anglo-Spanish alliance, which for Spain was to serve to counter French power in Europe and for England as a means of consolidating the fledgling Tudor dynasty. But when Arthur died suddenly on 2 April 1501, at the age of only fifteen, merely six months after his marriage to Katherine, both dynasties were determined to maintain the valuable alliance. Thus, Katherine's betrothal to the new heir to England's throne, Arthur's brother Henry, was hastily arranged. The two were set to marry in five years' time. The marriage went ahead as planned on 11 June 1509, two months after Henry's proclamation as king of England and following a papal dispensation which allowed Henry to wed his deceased brother's widow.[2]

This arranged marriage was by all accounts based on love as much as on political expediency. Katherine, beautiful and serene, every bit a royal bride, was both a dutiful wife and a consummate companion, sharing with Henry many leisure and scholarly interests. She also stood in for him as regent during his military campaigns in Europe.[3] Their patronage of culture earned them generous praise from contemporaries, the renowned humanist Desiderius Erasmus himself likening the Henrician court more to a museum than a court.[4] And for now at least so it would remain. For Henry, however, dynastic security took precedence over any emotional attachments. As such, his marriage was no less immune to political demands than any other of his relationships, whether personal or political. In all this, his relationship with Mary would be no exception. From the moment Mary was born she became an instrument in Europe's diplomatic game.

Both France and the Holy Roman Empire, which intermittently engaged each other in warfare, were eager to establish an alliance with England which made Mary a significant lever in any negotiations. Keen to thwart the growing power of France, Henry and his chief minister, Cardinal Thomas Wolsey, saw considerable value in a potential marriage between Mary and the dauphin of France, François, as a means of cementing amicable Anglo-French relations. Reinforcing the terms of the Treaty of London, a sort of non-aggression pact among Europe's great powers, brokered by Wolsey in October 1518, was the betrothal of the two-and-a-half-year-old Mary to the six-month-old François. As a condition of the betrothal, insisted on by the French, Mary had to be recognised as the heir to England's throne. For Henry, this was not a sticking point in the negotiations as Katherine was once again pregnant, and he was hopeful for the birth of a boy who would immediately take primacy in the line of succession. But when Katherine gave birth to another stillborn daughter (the couple's first child, a daughter, had been stillborn), the betrothal, entailing the prospect of England falling into the hands of a future king of France, suddenly did not seem so appealing.

Katherine was powerless to thwart the diplomatic scheming. She was horrified that her Spanish princess daughter was set to marry the dauphin of Spain's long-standing enemy. Her father, Ferdinand, had been embroiled in an acrimonious relationship with France which now had spilled over to involve her nephew, Charles, the king of Spain and Holy Roman emperor since 1519. For Henry alliances with France were always uneasy affairs. His preference, if the opportunity would ever arise, was to conquer France, not to befriend it. It would in fact not be long before he would seek to break the newly forged Anglo-French alliance. When in 1521 Emperor Charles himself offered to step in as a suitor for Mary, arguing that France had broken the Treaty of London by invading Spanish Navarre, Henry grabbed the opportunity, with Katherine's approval, to rid himself of his entanglement with France. So at only five years of age Mary was readied to be betrothed for a second time; Charles, her cousin, was twenty-one.

Yet this betrothal had as much chance of succeeding as the previous one. Though again conditional on Mary's remaining Henry's sole heir, there was little prospect of Charles waiting for another eight years when Mary would be deemed of marriageable age. By the terms of the agreement he was in fact at liberty to marry before this time, something which he did in 1525 when he married Isabella of Portugal. In any case, the military commitment of the terms of the betrothal that had embroiled England in a disastrous campaign in France, as Charles's ally, soured the appeal for Henry of an Imperial alliance. With both Charles and Henry seeking to sever their treaty obligations, the betrothal was duly terminated in 1524. Although the end of the Spanish alliance was a major blow for Katherine, it did not undermine Charles's relationship with Mary. He would remain her ally for the rest of her life, bearing witness to her tragedies that would unfold in due course. There is no recorded evidence of what Mary thought of all of this, not that her views would have had any bearing on the diplomatic game. At the time, the infant daughter of a king was expected to obey her father's decisions.

Mary's front-line diplomatic role meant that she spent her early years in lavish luxury with a household of her own that befitted a royal princess. Visitors to the Henrician court recalled a bright, confident and vivacious child with a penchant for showmanship. By the time Mary was four she had become adept on the keyboard and was already versed in French. When she turned seven, serious attention was invested in her broader education. The nature of Mary's education, however, as with most aspects concerning her, has been subjected to much debate, being used as a political tool either to smear her as ignorant or to exalt her great intellect. The truth here, as with so much to do with Mary, has been obscured by misrepresentation. While few details about the quality of Mary's formal education are known, there exists sufficient evidence about it, as well as about her education and cultural policies during the course of her reign, to render Elton's view, that she was 'bigoted [. . .] and (not to put too fine a point upon it) rather stupid' and that 'humanism had passed her by',[5] as far removed from reality.

Although Mary was by no means a great scholar, she was a competent student, schooled in a progressive way. While Henry may have been uncertain as to Mary's status in the line of succession, Katherine was in no doubt about her daughter's rightful inheritance and eventual succession as a queen regnant akin to that of her own mother, Isabella. As such, she considered training in wifely and motherly duties as insufficient for a future queen. In ordinary circumstances, given the nature of the instruction which girls from the nobility at that time received, Mary's education would have been likely to have focused only on the furthering of piety, the preservation of chastity and the study of humane letters.[6] However, Katherine's and Henry's humanist tastes would ensure that Mary would receive an education that would go beyond what was traditionally expected for a girl to receive, heir to the throne or otherwise.

A particular influence on Mary's formation was to be the renowned Spanish humanist scholar, Juan Luis Vives. After the death in 1524 of Mary's tutor Thomas Linacre, Vives designed, at Katherine's request, a broad curriculum that spanned classical and contemporary literature, Scripture, Latin, Greek and rhetoric. It was an academic programme that he believed should be taught to boys and girls alike. Vives was by no means progressive in his views in any modern sense. For him, the pursuit of education was to foster social conformity through familiarity of appropriate behaviour and for girls specifically to preserve their chastity. Here he differed from other humanist scholars like Thomas More for instance, who viewed education more as an end in itself than as a servant of an end. However, where Vives differed from much contemporary pedagogical opinion was in his firm belief that that the social order would not be disturbed by the extension of a broad education to women. Katherine would go even further than Vives's curriculum prescribed, particularly on musical instruction. Here, Vives's view about the morally corrupting influence of music was in tune with that of many of his contemporary pedagogues.

Katherine would have none of it. Coming as she did from the Spanish court with its long-established tradition of musical patronage, she was determined that her daughter would experience extensive musical training.

Mary also acquired, at an early age, knowledge of several languages. Her competence in both areas was sufficient for contemporary commentators to notice. In 1531, the Venetian courtier, Mario Savorgnano, for instance, commented on the fifteen-year-old Mary, after he visited England, that 'She spoke Spanish, French, and Latin, besides her own mother-English tongue, is well grounded in Greek, and understands Italian, but does not venture to speak it. She sings excellently, and plays on several instruments, so that she combines every accomplishment'.[7] It is an opinion of her that seems to have endured up to her reign and beyond. 'Surely the common voice', wrote the leading theologian and historian, John Standish in 1554, 'is that her grace is not onelye moste noble, moste virtuous, moste wytte, and moste studious but also moste excellent ain learning.'[8] Unfortunately, however, apart from such commentaries from contemporaries, no written work by Mary from these years survives such as could determine her level of attainment in the subjects she studied. It should also be noted that such complimentary dedications of course contained a degree of flattery, which obscures the true level of her scholarship. Mary also studied Classics in her youth, though the extent of her knowledge in these is unknown. However, her involvement in Katherine Parr's project of translating Erasmus's *Paraphrases on the New Testament* suggests that her interest was more than cursory (see chapter 10).

Mary's formal education would continue well into her adolescence, ending in 1534 with the imprisonment of both her Latin tutor, Richard Fetherstone for refusing to take the Oath of Supremacy and her governess, Margaret Pole, the Countess of Salisbury, on a spurious charge of treason (both were eventually executed). She continued, however, to be an avid reader, though her reading by all indication was conservative, consisting mostly of devotional material by authors like Augustine, Gardiner and Erasmus, many of whose works she inherited from her mother as well as acquired as gifts from various supporters. Her piety and humanity formed the focus of subsequent dedications to her from parties grateful to her for her promotion of Catholicism. The writer John Proctor, for instance, in his translation of St Vincent Lerins's *The Waie home to Christ and Truth leadinge from Antichrist and Errour*, published 1556, praised Mary for her nobility, heavenly simplicity and virginity,[9] while her chaplain, John Angel, extolled her godliness and gifts of grace.[10] One thing that needs to be remembered, however, is that she prioritised restoring the Catholic faith over other matters and as such her work in this area was likely to have attracted the greatest praise from those promoting the faith with her.

It is true that certainty about the nature of Mary's education is lacking, and though her interests may have been more conservative than humanist, it would be incorrect to claim that humanism passed her by. The fact that she was at ease with many of her father's reforms offers further evidence for this (see chapter 10). Nevertheless, it would be equally disingenuous to assert that Mary's virtues lay more in her learning than in her humanity. It is best to err on the side of caution here; she may not have been a scholar but she was certainly no fool.

*

The diplomatic game in which Mary was so entangled failed to enhance dynastic security. In 1525 Katherine was forty and approaching the end of her child-bearing years. In June of that year, in desperation at the prospect of never having a male heir, Henry acknowledged his eldest illegitimate son,[11] Henry Fitzroy, a product of an adulterous relationship with Elizabeth Blount, a maid-of-honour in Katherine's household, and lavished him with multiple titles.[12] While there may have been little prospect of his being proclaimed Henry's heir, the option nevertheless remained, something that was to be facilitated by the 1536 Succession Act which arguably authorised the king to proclaim whomever he wanted as his successor. Katherine, at least, suspected Henry's motives and resented Fitzroy's elevation over her daughter.[13] Her concerns were allayed somewhat after Henry appointed the nine-year-old Mary in 1525 to preside over the Council of Wales and the Marches, a post traditionally reserved for the heir to the throne. But the fact that he stopped short of proclaiming her Princess of Wales, a title which would have formally designated her as his heir, indicated that he considered that all options were still available to him. Henry was also playing another, more subtle, game here. In separating Mary from Katherine, he was striking a significant blow against his wife with whom his relationship was becoming increasingly strained. This would be the first of a number of enforced separations to come between mother and daughter.

These political niceties were, however, lost on the people of England and Wales, as well as on foreign dignitaries, for whom, as far as they were concerned, Mary was the royal princess and heir to the throne. The nine-year-old Mary was certainly lauded as such. From her base at Ludlow Castle, she would engage in a number of progresses across the region, attending numerous receptions and always surrounded by royal opulence.

In 1526 Mary, a royal princess in all but name, once again was drawn into the diplomatic game. With the League of Cognac, an anti-imperial alliance formed in 1526, bearing down on Charles V, England, though not a formal member was determined to curtail the emperor's power in Europe. Consequently Henry renewed his interest in establishing closer ties with the French king, Francis, who through the League sought to avenge recent defeats by Imperial forces. He also hoped to secure the release from Hapsburg captivity of his two sons who had been taken hostage in the aftermath of Charles's victory over France at the Battle of Pavia in Italy in 1525. As such, in 1527 Mary was offered in marriage to Francis's second son, the eight-year-old Henri of Orleans only for the stakes to be raised a couple months later when Henry flirted with the idea of formally joining the League. This was an offer which he underpinned by betrothing the eleven-year-old Mary to the twenty-three-year-old French king himself. Ultimately, however, both of these schemes were destined to fall victim of the fickle nature of diplomatic alliances. In truth, Mary was as unsuitable an heir as Fitzroy was and soon, probably around mid-1527, Henry began to contemplate a dissolution of his marriage to Katherine to resolve the problem over the succession. This was set to have grave implications for Mary's status.

For a few years now he had been flirting with another maid-of-honour in Katherine's household, the young, spirited and vivacious, Anne Boleyn, having already had an adulterous relationship with her elder sister, Mary. In short, Anne was so many things that Katherine was not, opening 'the way to sexual bliss, domestic happiness and, most important of all, the possibility of a son and heir'.[14] Rejecting Henry's suggestion of being installed as his mistress, Anne insisted that she would engage in a physical relationship with him only as his wife. The ultimatum was certainly stark, not to mention daring, yet as events would show, it was something that the infatuated king was to take seriously. In fact, it became increasingly imperative for him to break, what he now came to believe, was a marriage that was divinely cursed and which had deprived him of a male heir. Did not the Book of Leviticus state 'thou shalt not uncover the nakedness of thy brother's wife: it is thy brother's nakedness' for 'if a man marries his brother's wife, it is an act of impurity; he hath uncovered his brother's nakedness. They shall be childless (Lv. 18:16, 20:21)?' The verse was enough to convince an avid reader of Scripture like Henry that his marriage to Katherine was in breach of canon law, irrespective of the fact that its application here was controversial to say the least. Notwithstanding the well-established ambiguity of the verse, was it not contradicted by the Book of Deuteronomy, which seemed to compel a brother to 'take' his deceased brother's wife as his own and have children with her (Dt. 25:5). Did the very existence of Mary also not render Henry's appeal to this Levitical verse misplaced? Seemingly not, especially as Henry's scholars reinterpreted the original Hebrew of Leviticus to mean 'without sons' rather than 'shall be childless'.[15] Whether out of scruple of conscience or personal convenience, Henry argued that his marriage to Katherine should be annulled.

There were certainly those who brazenly argued in public the latter case. In Parliament many had asserted, as the Imperial ambassador Eustace Chapuys reported to Emperor Charles, 'that the King pursued this divorce out of love for some lady, and not out of any scruple of conscience'.[16] Writing from self-imposed exile to avoid being co-opted to Henry's cause, Reginald

Pole argued powerfully against the annulment, focusing particularly on what he saw as Henry's blatant hypocrisy. 'For do you yourself not make it evident', he noted,

> that no new scruple troubled you when you dismissed your first wife, on the pretence the law prevented you from keeping her? You had her as wife for all of 20 years without any fear of the law. If the law moved you, why did it move you so late [...]? You did not make such a grave and serious mention of the divine law for some scruple of conscience. Rather you sought this precept as a false witness to assist you in covering up the shameful disposition of your mind.[17]

John Fisher, bishop of Rochester, said pretty much the same, but he did not have the luxury of exile from which to say it. Defending Katherine during the annulment hearings of the legatine court at Blackfriars in May to July 1529, Fisher stated, as reported by Campeggio, that after two years of diligent study of the matter he 'therefore, both in order not to procure the damnation of his soul, and in order not to be unfaithful to his King, or to fail in doing the duty which he owed to the truth, in a matter of such great importance, he presented himself before their reverend Lordships to declare, to affirm, and with forcible reasons to demonstrate to them that this marriage of the King and Queen can be dissolved by no power, human or divine'. He added provocatively that 'for this opinion he would even lay down his life' just like John the Baptist had after he challenged Herod 'as [it was] impossible for him to die more gloriously than in the cause of marriage'.[18] Fisher's tracts, most notably *De Causa Matrimonii ... Henrici VIII cum Catharina Aragonensi* (1530), expounded his position in greater detail.[19] His principled stand would in 1535 cost him his life. He was attainted of treason for his refusal to take the Oath of Succession to acknowledge Henry's supremacy over the Church in England.

In Henry's mind all that was required for the annulment to proceed was for the current pope, Clement VII, to declare that the dispensation from the impediment of affinity that his predecessor Julius II had issued to allow Henry and Katherine to wed, was contrary to canon law. This in turn would mean that Henry's marriage to Katherine was a so-called levirate marriage (from the Hebrew, *levir*, a brother-in-law), that is a marriage between a man and the widow of his deceased brother. It seemed, to Henry at least, that an annulment would be a mere formality. The French in fact had questioned the legitimacy of Henry's marriage to Katherine when Mary was being proposed as a future spouse to King Francis in 1527.[20] Now, however, the issue would assume a completely different emphasis.

Royal and aristocratic marriages during Henry's time were arranged and conducted usually with little regard for the feelings of the couple concerned. They were marriages of convenience, arranged either to strengthen or to preserve dynasties. And Henry's marriage to Katherine had been no exception, as noted. It was a bonus if such a marriage yielded true love between husband and wife, as apparently was the case between Henry and Katherine. Where love was not present, spouses took on mistresses and lovers to render political marriages more palatable for them, though in Henry's case any love he had for Katherine did not check his penchant for adultery. Annulments were also a potential way out of an unwanted marriage and were sought usually to procure another political alliance. They could only be granted, however, by the pope and the process of obtaining one was theoretically complex, determined by the presentation of evidence for the existence prior to any contracted union of an impediment. An impediment, in turn, could be determined by any one of a number of conditions. The existence of consanguinity based on close blood ties between the spouses, for instance, offered grounds for an annulment, as too did the coercion into the marriage of one or both spouses, the existence of affinity where one of the spouses was too closely related to the relative of a former spouse or the concealment by one spouse from the other of some grave condition, such as insanity or infertility. Yet despite what appeared to be tough conditions to meet, annulments were not that uncommon among the rich and powerful. Astute canon lawyers learned to find grounds to annul virtually any marriage, whether or not any of the determining criteria had been met.[21] It should also be noted that medieval popes were politicians as well as spiritual leaders. Frequently the boundary between the two responsibilities became so blurred as to make them indistinguishable. To achieve their political ends, popes needed to appease other rulers, particularly those who could either aid or hinder their interests. Granting annulments was one way of doing this so much so that annulments frequently became little more than political tools.

One of the seamiest annulments occurred in 1499 when Pope Alexander VI, a Borgia pope, annulled the twenty-three-year marriage between Louis XII of France and Joan, the daughter of his uncle King Louis XI.[22] The marriage had been a typical political union, the couple having had little choice in the matter. But when Louis XI's son and successor, Charles VIII died childless, Louis (XII), Charles's cousin, acceded to the throne in 1498 only to insist upon marrying Charles's widow, Anne, the duchess of Brittany, to prevent her from withdrawing the quasi-sovereign duchy from the jurisdiction of France. Having failed to show either conclusive proof of consanguinity with Joan or that he was under the age of consent when he had entered marital life, Louis, in his desperation to be rid of his wife, based his case around a preposterous claim that he had been unable to consummate the marriage owing to Joan's malformation and that he had his own performance compromised by witchcraft. Horrified by the assertion, Joan was forced to produce unsavoury eye-witness evidence that Louis had bragged that he had 'earned, and well earned a drink, for I mounted my wife three or four times during the night'.[23] Louis's case was in fact so theologically weak that it stood no chance of success had the pope not turned a blind eye to its inconsistencies in return for political favours for his family.[24] He eventually granted the annulment on the grounds that Louis had been coerced into marrying Joan by her father and his uncle, Louis XI. To annul the marriage on such grounds after twenty-three years was stretching the boundaries of canon law beyond their limits. Joan was compelled to accept the decision after which she retired to a convent where she furthered her childhood devotion to the Virgin Mary. She died there in 1505; she was canonised on 28 May 1950 by Pope Pius XII.

The 'trade in annulments'[25] provoked widespread protest against the abuse of the annulment process. In 1351, for instance, an Irish synod considered 'false and feigned reasons' and 'corrupt and suborned witnesses' to have turned annulments into farces while in 1460 the Canterbury convocation deemed annulments to be 'the scandal of the whole church'.[26] In the wake of Louis's and Joan's annulment, public opinion in France was similarly aghast. So in short, annulments were not necessarily morally justified or canonically and theologically consistent especially when the reputation of the popes who allowed them is considered. Notwithstanding Pope Alexander's record as a great patron of the arts, commissioning, for instance, Michael Angelo to redesign St Peter's Basilica, his reputation was mired in controversy. His successor, Julius II, himself certainly not beyond moral reproach, totally condemned Alexander's reign for its desecration of the Holy Church. His penchant for corruption and dissoluteness was indeed unrivalled. He did in fact have a track record of issuing scandalous annulments, not least in 1497 that of the marriage between Giovanni Sforza and his own daughter, the sexually depraved Lucrezia, on the grounds that the marriage had never been consummated. Lucrezia was declared a virgin and Giovanni impotent. The annulment was greeted with popular derision on account of Lucrezia's sexual notoriety and Giovanni's promiscuity.[27] Politics was at the heart of this seedy episode, the annulment being part of Alexander's on-going meddling in Neapolitan affairs.

In view of the history of annulments, Henry, an avid amateur theologian, may well have been justified to expect a swift conclusion to his Great Matter not least because there had been several annulments in his immediate family. In March 1527 his sister Margaret had her marriage to her abusive second husband, Archibald Douglas, earl of Angus, annulled on the grounds that Angus had been pre-contracted to another woman at the time of the marriage (Margaret's first husband had been James IV, who died in 1513 on Flodden Field fighting the English).[28] Henry's other sister, Mary, had married in 1515 his best friend Charles Brandon, the duke of Suffolk, whose first marriage to Margaret Neville had been dissolved in 1507 also for contractual reasons[29] while Emperor Maximillian, grandfather to Charles V, had his (proxy) marital contract dissolved in 1490, two years after it had been contracted. Henry's confidence of a hasty resolution to the matter was boosted further by his reliance on his 'Mr Fix-it',[30] Lord Chancellor and papal legate, Cardinal Thomas Wolsey, who assured him that little stood in the way of a successful outcome of his Great Matter. Writing to Henry from France in July 1527, Wolsey noted that 'If the pope were delivered, I doubt not he would be easily induced to do everything to your satisfaction'.[31] So from purely a procedural perspective, it is understandable why Henry became so frustrated that what should have been a routine matter turned into such a complex affair.

The actions of renegade popes, however, should not be taken as setting a precedent for future annulments. Moreover, before the political restrictions under which Pope Clement had to operate in adjudicating Henry's case are considered, it is crucial to note that from a theological perspective Henry's case was very weak, and an annulment based on it would have stretched the permissible canonical boundaries to breaking-point. For Henry and his supporters, it was a simple case of the word of God against the power of the pope, a dichotomy that found resonance in the exegesis of both reformist (Protestant) and Catholic humanist writing that stressed the centrality of original scriptural texts. But as J. J. Scarisbrick argues:

> those texts had to prove that what they forbade was forbidden *per se*, by divine or natural law, and was hence beyond the reach of papal dispensation [...] If Henry were to succeed, therefore, Deuteronomy must be explained away, or it would ruin the case which Leviticus seemed to uphold. For Leviticus, a rigorous, almost fundamentalist interpretation was required; for Deuteronomy, abolition.[32]

However, to emphasise Leviticus and dismiss Deuteronomy seemed arbitrary. Why not base an argument on the primacy of the latter over the former? Because, Henry argued, picking up erroneously on St Augustine's identification of figurative language in certain aspects of the book of Deuteronomy,[33] Leviticus was to be taken literally but Deuteronomy figuratively. Could it not be further argued that the authority of Leviticus in permitting levirate marriages had been terminated by the New Testament, just as the practice of circumcision had been? All of this combined may have seemed at the time to constitute a strong case to supporters of Henry's Great Matter, until that is, the case was examined more closely.

The main weakness of Henry's exegesis lay in its implication that Scripture contradicted itself. This position, however, was in direct conflict with fundamental Church doctrine, which insisted that scriptural contradictions were only apparent and were resolved upon deeper reflection. The resolution here was rooted in historical reality, as illustrated by a number of precedents of levirate marriages accounted for by Scripture,[34] as argued at the time by John Fisher and Robert Bellarmine, two of the foremost theologians of the time, as well as by many theologians before them, including St Augustine and St Thomas Aquinas. Fisher argued that Leviticus should be interpreted literally as prohibiting marriage between a man and his brother's wife under any circumstances, whether she be a widow or not, unless, as Deuteronomy states, 'the man dies without having a child' (Dt. 25: 5). In short, as pointed out by Cardinal Tomaso Cajetan, a contemporary of Fisher, Henry's marriage to Katherine was an example of a levirate marriage based on Deuteronomic exception to Leviticus and therefore canonically valid.[35]

With the argument dispatched to Europe's universities to resolve, Henry sought to bolster his case by contending that the original papal dispensation in 1503, allowing for his marriage to Katherine to go ahead, was canonically invalid. He argued, for instance, that the dispensation had been issued when he was only fourteen years of age and that, moreover, it had been motivated by foreign policy, involving his father and the king of Spain, both of whom were now dead. Such frivolous arguments, however, did not cut much ice. Though a minor, Henry was not below the canonical age of contracting a marriage, which at the time was seven, while any foreign policy motives could only invalidate the dispensation if deception was involved. Since improving relations between Spain and England were a motive among the parties involved for drawing up a marital contract between Katherine and Henry, the dispensation could not be declared as having been attained stealthily. The dispensation stood, which was proof of its validity.

Let us return to Henry's main case. He insisted that the impediment of affinity, that is the prohibition of marriage to one's relatives, whether blood or non-blood, was present at the point of his marrying Katherine on grounds that Katherine had been married to his brother, Arthur. Given, therefore, he argued, that the impediment of affinity was founded on divine rather than on ecclesiastical law, it was beyond the remit of papal authority to dispense with. In arguing, however, that an impediment that could not be dispensed with applied his marriage with Katherine, Henry was simply wrong. Although the impediment of affinity that had existed prior to Henry's marriage to Katherine was an impediment that could invalidate a marriage, it was within papal authority to dispense with. This was distinct from an impediment that was subject to divine as opposed to ecclesiastical authority, as in the existence, for instance, of coercion into a marriage contract of one or both parties, which would automatically invalidate a union. Henry of course was basing his argument on the presumption that the impediment of affinity derived from divine law that was rooted in Scripture. But, as illustrated above, his interpretation of Leviticus fails to bear up to scrutiny. Capping the case against Henry was a pivotal ruling by the thirteenth-century Pope Innocent III, a renowned theologian and canonist, which had validated levirate marriages among Latvian converts providing the deceased brothers died childless.[36] Retrieved by Fisher to irrefutably prove papal authority in this area of competence, the ruling was a *coup de grace* against which Henry could do little.

To reinforce his case, Henry sought to outflank Katherine on another issue. Katherine had insisted that her short marriage to Arthur had never been consummated. If true, then the marriage would have been invalid in canon law since an unconsummated marriage was not a marriage at all. This alone would have rendered any arguments over the existence of impediments of affinity prior to Katherine's marriage to Henry extraneous given that there would have been no marriage between Katherine and Arthur to dispense with. It followed from this that the only impediment that did exist was that of 'public honesty', which would have required a papal dispensation before any new marital contract could be drawn up. This in itself would generate a new controversy, which will be looked at below. Henry, however, was not going to be caught out here. He vigorously countered Katherine's claims. But to prove his case he had little more than 'a rag-bag of gossip [...] half-remembered kitchen talk and snippets of course bravado',[37] from those who had attended the young couple. One such 'snippet' was from one of Arthur's companions, Sir Anthony Willoughby, who attested to Arthur's boasting the day after his wedding night of having been 'in the midst of Spain' on the night before.[38] Such depositions were as difficult to verify as Katherine's testimony under solemn papal oath that her marriage had not been consummated[39] was to dispute. The evidence Henry assembled would, as Scarisbrick noted, 'scarcely suffice to hang a dog'.[40] It is of course possible to cast doubt on the claim she made in 1529 that Henry had confirmed her virginity on numerous occasions,[41] though it would not be untoward to expect Henry, given his pride and arrogance, to have raised objections to his marriage had Katherine indeed proved not to have been a virgin on the day of their wedding. Conversely, given Katherine's deeply held religion, it is highly unlikely that she would have lied under oath about the invalidity of her marriage to Arthur as Henry was suggesting she had for to have done so she would have been guilty of concealing mortal sins. Yet for Katherine, notwithstanding the importance of maintaining the sanctity of her marriage to Henry, as well as the legitimacy of her daughter, Mary, the Great Matter was also intrinsically tied to the defence of her personal honour. Had she been a commoner less may have been expected of her, especially in such a patriarchal age. But she was the daughter of the most renowned queen regnant in Christendom, and had more royal blood flowing through her veins than Henry. She also was in no doubt that she had been a good wife, as well as a dutiful queen, who frequently had had to endure her husband's marital infidelity.

Ironically, Katherine's insistence on her virginity could have acted against her. The original bull that dispensed with her marriage to Arthur assumed that the marriage had been 'perhaps' consummated, using the Latin term *forsan* and as such dispensed only the impediment of affinity and not of public honesty as well. What was unclear was whether the dispensation of the former also dispensed with the latter. Although some theologians, like St Thomas, claimed that it was sufficient for one dispensation to cover both impediments, most did not, so a clear position on this had not been established.[42] The ambiguity persisted because of the rarity of the situation involved. And because the circumstances that would ensue in a couple of decades were not foreseen, no-one thought of making the original bull clearer. It could be argued, therefore, that Katherine's marriage to Henry could have been invalid owing to the absence of a dispensation of the impediment of public honesty. This seemed to be a plausible, if not necessarily decisive point in Henry's favour which Wolsey had picked up on as early as 1527 after Katherine had adamantly denied to him that her marriage with Arthur had been consummated. Not exceptionally versed in canon law, Katherine had exposed herself to a potentially ruinous position. Fortunately for her, however, Henry, though fully aware of the argument, chose to ignore Wolsey's advice, either out of pig-headedness[43] or a conviction that such a technicality upon which it was based could never deliver him the coveted annulment.[44] As such he never allowed it to be tested in a court of canon law.[45] Arrogant and blinded to the flaws of his argument, Henry was convinced that Leviticus would win the day. He was in any case already mistrustful of Wolsey's motives, suspecting that his Chancellor's legatine loyalties were taking precedence over his loyalties to the Crown while Wolsey's slow progress on the matter of the annulment served to heighten Henry's suspicions of him further.

The weakness of Henry's canonical and theological case should be at the heart of any attempt to get to the bottom of the Great Matter. It is, therefore, crucial not to succumb to the temptation, as many learned works continue to do,[46] to grant foreign policy undue importance in Henry's declining chances of having his marriage annulled. Events in Italy at the time were certainly unfavourable to Henry, but whether they were decisive is doubtful. In 1527 the Imperial armies, unpaid and tired after their campaigns against the French in Italy, had mutinied and ransacked Rome. Although Emperor Charles was horrified by this, he did effectively now hold the pope prisoner. Holed up at the castle of St Angelo under house arrest, Pope Clement did reassure Charles that he would 'not grant unto any act that might be preparative or otherwise, to divorce to be made to the King and

Queen'.[47] But after his release from detention in December 1527, Clement maintained his hitherto declared position on Henry's case despite the fact that he had plenty of motives for vengeance against the emperor, which granting Henry his annulment would have amply satisfied. Five years later in August 1532, Pedro Ortiz, the Imperial ambassador to Rome, pressured the pope to reinforce Katherine's cause and excommunicate Henry in view of his adultery, claiming that the pope himself would be 'answerable before God on the day of judgement' for his inaction. However, frail and weakened by illness, Clement rejected Ortiz's demand, denying the existence of any concrete proof of sexual relations between Henry and Anne.[48] Despite Charles's shock at the actions of his ill-disciplined troops, Clement was well aware of the potential of another sack of Rome if Imperial political necessity required. And with Henry threatening schism, he was certainly not in an unenviable position.

Three years of bitter and complex wrangling involving all concerned parties followed the Imperial invasion of Rome. Henry, through his emissaries, placed an inordinate amount of pressure on the pope to relent. Yet though 'pulled hither and tither by his need for Henry, his fear of Charles and a certain residual sense of justice which could not permit him entirely to ignore Katherine's cause',[49] he refused to yield to either Charles's or Henry's demands. Eventually, however, after much delay, he conceded a commission to be held in London to investigate the facts of the case. But it was not the decretal commission empowered to grant final judgement on the case that Henry had so desperately desired. Moreover, Pope Clement instructed the Cardinal Protector of England, Lorenzo Campeggio, to oversee the commission and to delay proceedings for as long as possible in order for the case to be eventually recalled to Rome. In a desperate attempt to resolve the Great Matter before it proceeded to the London hearing, Campeggio sought to persuade Katherine to retire to monastic life, thereby releasing Henry to remarry. Theologically dubious at best, the option was adamantly rejected by Katherine, who insisted, with great steadfastness and personal integrity, on remaining loyal to the sacrament of matrimony, to which she believed God had called her. And so the commission began its hearings in Blackfriars, London on 31 May 1529. Katherine, during the first session, in what was her only appearance at the hearings, rigidly stuck to her guns, appealing to Henry not to cast her and her daughter aside. Her speech, on 21 June 1529 was a great testament to her resolve and personal virtue:

> Sir, I beseech you for all the love that hath been between us, let me have justice and right, take of me some pity and compassion, for I am a poor woman, and a stranger, born out of your dominion. I have here no friend and much less indifferent counsel. I flee to you, as to the head of justice within this realm [. . .] I take God and all the world to

witness that I have been to you a true, humble and obedient wife, ever
comfortable to your will and pleasure [. . .] being always well pleased
and contented with all things wherein you had any delight or dalliance
[. . .] I loved all those whom ye loved, only for your sake, whether I
had cause or no, and whether they were my friends or enemies. This
20 years or more I have been your true wife and by me ye have had
divers children, although it hath pleased God to call them from this
world, which hath been no default in me [. . .] And when ye had me
at first, I take God to my judge, I was a true maid, without touch of
man. And whether this be true or no, I put it to your conscience [. . .]
Therefore, I humbly require you to spare me the extremity of this new
court [. . .] And if ye will not, to God I commit my cause.

On Henry's orders further pressure was placed on Katherine by the papal
legates, but to no avail. Katherine was not to be swayed. Campeggio announced
that owing to the quantity of documentation no hasty adjudication could be
made and duly adjourned the hearings on 23 July 1529 until October amidst
acrimony and confusion. Without a resolution the case moved to Rome
and would never again return to be heard in London. Publicly humiliated
and dejected, Henry vented his anger on Wolsey, who was dismissed from
his post and subsequently arraigned on treason charges. He died on 29
November 1530 on his way to his trial. The case was looking increasingly
desperate for Henry, more so after the pope and Charles had made formal
peace at Cambrai on 5 August 1529, after which Charles was formally
crowned emperor by the pope on 24 February 1530. The Great Matter was
now to move onto a different level.

To further his cause Henry had another trick up his sleeve – anti-
clericalism. Traditionally historians have been adamant that anti-clericalism
was rife and growing. This was not the case. In truth, it never featured
significantly in English society though it was sufficiently well articulated by
a number of loud-mouths, particularly in some areas, for it to offer Henry
a means with which to attack the Church. Consequently he would invest
it with importance that it did not warrant. It was ironic that merely a few
years earlier he had been awarded by Pope Leo X the title of Defender
of the Faith for his steadfast confrontation of religious reform, which he
had not hesitated to call heresy. Now, however, Henry would embrace
religious reform, as a means with which to chip away at papal jurisdiction
in England in the hope that this would compel the pope to concede to
his demands. Unplanned and largely uncoordinated, the campaign was to
be pursued with growing urgency and vigour. Henry would draw on an
inconclusive set of documents, collectively known as the 'Collectanea satis
copiosa', which had been unearthed in various archives by his agents, chief
among whom was the reformist cleric, Thomas Cranmer. The documents

purported to prove that the kings of England historically had no superiors on earth, prince or pope, and as such they could claim supremacy over the pope on ecclesiastical matters. In this, Henry had an authoritative, if completely spurious, claim. The rights of princes, he argued, had been usurped by successive popes, rights which he would now restore to their legitimate position. His version of caesaropapism not only opened the path to a resolution of the Great Matter in his favour but also appealed to his egotistical nature. In Thomas Cromwell, the successor as Henry's main advisor to the ill-fated former Lord Chancellor, Thomas More, who was to be martyred for his refusal to acknowledge royal supremacy, Henry found an eager enforcer of his will. Under Cromwell's guidance, Parliament would approve a series of anti-papal laws, each ratcheting up the pressure on the pope to adjudicate in the favour of the king. This process would end with the king replacing the pope as supreme head of the Church in England, which led to England's separation from Rome and the creation of a wholly new Church, the Church of England. The consequences of all this for Mary were to be life-changing.

NOTES

[1] Prescott, *Mary Tudor*, p. 39.

[2] In the fickle world of international diplomacy it was a surprise that the marriage went ahead at all given that during the intervening years the value of the alliance for England waned. Isabella had died in November 1504, which restricted Katherine's authority in Spain solely to Aragon, as the union of Aragon and Castile had been based on the marriage of its two monarchs. Offending the presiding superpower of the time, however, by reneging on the marriage would have been impolitic on Henry's part, to say the least.

[3] D. Loades, *Mary Tudor* (Stroud: Amberley Publishing, 2012), p. 18.

[4] 'Erasmus to Paul Bombasius, 4340', 29 July 1518, LPFD, vol. 2.

[5] Elton, *Reform and Reformation*, p. 376.

[6] Loades, *Mary Tudor*, p. 22.

[7] 'A Tour in England, Mario Savorgnano to –, 25 August 1531, 682', CSPV, vol. 4.

[8] J. Standish, *A discourse wherein is debated whether it be expedient that the Scripture should be in English for al men to reade that wyll* (London: Robery Caly, 1554).

[9] V. Lerins (St), *Liber de Catholicæ fidei antiquitate* translated as *The waie home to Christ and truth leading from Antichrist and errour*, trans. J. Proctor (Ann Arbor, Michigan: University of Michigan, 2011).

[10] Cited in A. W. Taylor, '"Ad Omne Virtutum Genus"? Mary between Piety, Pedagogy and Praise in Early Tudor Humanism', in Doran and Freeman eds., *Mary Tudor*, p. 120.

[11] Henry is said to have had as many as six illegitimate children.

[12] Fitzroy was ennobled in 1525 at the age of six. He was given the title earl of Nottingham first and then made the duke of Richmond and Somerset. By having two dukedoms he outranked the other dukes in the land. His other titles were Knight of the Garter, Lord High Admiral of England, Warden of the Cinque Ports and Constable

of Dover Castle, Lord Lieutenant of Ireland, Lord President of the Council of the North, Warden of the Marches and Chamberlain of Chester and North Wales. He died in 1536 from consumption (tuberculosis) at the age of 16.

[13] 'Lorenzo Orio to – (a private letter), 29 June 1525, 1053', CSPV, vol. 3.

[14] Schama, *History of Britain: At the Edge of the World?* p. 299.

[15] C. Fletcher, *The Divorce of Henry VIII: The Untold Story from inside the Vatican* (Basingstoke: Palgrave Macmillan, 2012), p. 122.

[16] 'Chapuys to Charles V, 2 April 1531, 171', LPFD, vol. 5.

[17] R. Pole, *Pole's Defence of the Unity of the Church*, translated with Introduction by Joseph G Dwyer (Westminster, Maryland: The Newman Press, 1965), pp. 184, 188.

[18] 'Campeggio to Salvaiti, 29 June, 1529, 5732', LPFD, vol. 4. For details of the proceedings of the Blackfriars trial see R. Rex, *The Theology of John Fisher* (Cambridge: Cambridge University Press, revised edition, 1991), pp. 170–1; H. Ansgar Kell, *The Matrimonial Trials of Henry VIII* (Redwood City: Stanford University Press, 1976), pp. 77–87; J. J. Scarisbrick, *Henry VIII* (London: Methuen, 1991), pp. 213–28.

[19] See Rex, *Theology of John Fisher*, pp. 177–8.

[20] Loades, *Mary Tudor*, p. 28.

[21] D. L. Holmes, *A Brief History of the Episcopal Church* (London: T and T Clark, 1993), p. 182.

[22] J. R. Hale, *Renaissance Europe: The Individual and Society, 1480–1520* (Los Angeles and London University of California Press, Berkley, 1971), p. 15.

[23] Ibid., pp. 15–16.

[24] In return for the annulment Louis agreed to put pressure on Carlotta, the daughter of the king of Naples, who was at the time resident in France, to agree to marry Alexander's son, Cesare and thereby facilitate a Borgia takeover of Naples.

[25] Holmes, *A Brief History of the Episcopal Chur*ch, p. 182.

[26] Ibid., p. 183.

[27] For the history of the complex affair see R. Chamberlain, *The Bad Popes* (Oxford: Sutton Publishing, 2004), pp. 191–7.

[28] A. Weir, *Henry VIII: King and Court* (London: Random House, 2011), pp. 270–1.

[29] Brandon had been betrothed to Anne Browne, daughter of Anthony Browne, governor of Calais, with whom he sired an illegitimate daughter, Anne, in 1506. He proceeded to marry his lover's wealthy aunt, Margaret Neville, but a year later the marriage was annulled on grounds of Brandon's previous contract with Anne, whom he eventually married in 1508. She died, however, two years later.

[30] Schama, *History of Britain*, episode 6: *Burning Convictions*.

[31] 'Wolsey to Henry VIII, 29 July 1527, 3311', LPFD, vol. 4.

[32] Scarisbrick, *Henry VIII*, pp. 163–4.

[33] Reading St Augustine's *Contra Faustum* in its entirety, there can be only one conclusion and that is that Augustine does not deny the literal application of Deuteronomy but rather cites this allegory as an example of how the Old Testament continues to have relevance in the New. Moreover, he goes on to argue in his *On the Harmony of the Gospels* (Book 2, ch. 3) the case for the indisputable legitimacy of levirate marriages. He in fact cites the levirate as the reason for the discrepancies in the genealogies of Christ in the Gospels of St Luke and St Matthew.

[34] For instance, the levirate marriage between Tamar and Judah (Gen. 38).

[35] Scarisbrick, *Henry VIII*, pp. 170–3.

[36] Ibid., p. 178.

[37] Ibid., pp. 188–9.

[38] Ibid., p. 170.

39 Ibid., p. 189, n. 1.
40 Ibid., p. 189.
41 Ibid., p. 188, n. 3.
42 Ibid., pp. 189–94.
43 Ibid., p. 195.
44 J. Ridley, *Henry VIII* (London: Penguin Books, 1984), p. 163.
45 Ibid., pp. 162–3.
46 Loades, *Mary Tudor*, p. 29.
47 Whitelock, *Mary Tudor, England's First Queen*, p. 45.
48 'Dr. Ortiz to the Emperor, 21 August 1532 984', CSPS, vol. 4, part 2.
49 Scarisbrick, *Henry VIII*, p. 208.

✛ 6 ✛

Mary in Limbo

WHILE ALL THIS WAS GOING ON, Mary's life was being turned upside down. Still a child, she was forced to witness the terrible anguish that her mother was enduring. Any affection that Henry had for his daughter steadily began to ebb to be replaced by petty persecution and resentment. The stress of the situation was to place a heavy toll on Mary's health. Shortly after spending some time with Katherine in March 1531, she fell terribly ill, not for the last time, with what was diagnosed at the time as 'hysteria', a catch-all condition, attributable to a malfunction of the womb, that was to cause psychological, as well as physical symptoms. As Henry's campaign against the Church intensified his relationship with Katherine collapsed and with Mary was stretched to breaking point. The little consolation that both Katherine and Mary had in these turbulent times was each other's company, but Anne Boleyn's growing influence over Henry would see that this too would be denied them. For Anne, Katherine was the main obstacle to her plans and Mary, a competitor for Henry's affections. Perhaps, she thought, if mother and daughter were to be separated, Katherine would concede all.

For Katherine, however, to have conceded that her marriage had been unlawful would have been tantamount to her admitting both that her daughter was a bastard and that she herself had been the king's harlot for the past twenty-four years.[1] In August 1531 Henry took the radical decision to separate mother and daughter for good, partly out of his growing animosity for both, partly in a vain hope that Katherine would buckle under the strain and concede to his will. Katherine was dispatched to More Manor in Rickmansworth and Mary to Richmond Palace. Filling their place at court would be Anne Boleyn, who was to play a growing role in the unfolding saga of the Great Matter. Her impatience with the slow pace of the annulment proceedings and her growing loathing of 'the bastard' Mary would be very telling in the months ahead.

By December 1532 Anne was pregnant, having finally relented to Henry's advances a few weeks earlier. The urgency for Henry to marry her, therefore, grew ever more pressing. Here, however, there is some

confusion as to when exactly Henry and Anne married. On the one hand
Henry did not want to father another illegitimate child but on the other
hand he had to keep his marriage to Anne secret so as not to give the
pope any legal reason not to appoint the reformist Thomas Cranmer
as the new archbishop of Canterbury, whom Henry needed to annul
his marriage. The pope duly confirmed Cranmer's appointment in the
wake of the death in October 1532 of the ageing and 'disloyal' William
Warham, completely oblivious to Henry's scheming. Although Henry
and Anne were married in secret on 25 January 1533, they may well have
undergone a marriage ceremony in mid-November 1532 in order to satisfy
themselves of the legitimacy of any forthcoming pregnancy. Cranmer
did not officiate at either ceremony, having not been made aware of their
marriage until February 1533. Henry married Anne Boleyn, being still,
even by the new theology, officially married to Katherine, given that the
theological polemic that had dominated English affairs for so long was not
seen off until 23 May, when the marriage between Henry and Katherine
was formally annulled by Thomas Cranmer, merely a few weeks after the
arrival of the papal bulls confirming his appointment as archbishop of
Canterbury.[2] Prior to this, on 5 April, the convocation of English bishops
had pronounced that Pope Julius's dispensation that had allowed Henry
and Katherine to marry was invalid. In March 1533, by virtue of the Act
in Restraint of Appeals, England was declared 'an empire [...] governed
by one supreme head and king', which was confirmed by the Act of
Supremacy of 1534 that granted Henry supremacy over the Church of
England as its head. On 31 May, Anne processed to Westminster Abbey
to be crowned queen. She was greeted by silent crowds, a sure sign that
popular affection for both Katherine and Mary had not waned.

The fates of both had been sealed. Having been already told in April 1533
that she was no longer queen, Katherine was officially informed, by the Act
of Succession of 23 March, 1534 that she 'shall be from henceforth called
and reputed only dowager to Prince Arthur, and not queen of this realm'.
The Act also declared that the marriage between Katherine and Henry had
never been valid, having been 'adjudged to be against the laws of Almighty
God'.[3] Acknowledgement by anyone to the contrary was made punishable
by forfeiture of property and/or imprisonment. Though the Act did not refer
to Mary by name, it did, by implication, declare her illegitimate by passing
the succession to the heirs of Anne Boleyn. By not officially bastardising
Mary Henry left himself the option of reinstalling her into the line of
succession if the political situation demanded. Ultimately, as was argued
by Henry himself at the time, Mary was legitimate under canon law, given
that she was born of parents who at the time of her birth were unaware
of any impediments to their marriage.[4] Henry let it be known, however,

that to all intents and purposes she was a bastard and that he would treat her as such on account of her disobedience to his will. He would in fact remedy the anomalous situation in the Second Act of Succession of 1536 which did formally bastardise Mary (see below). Pope Clement offered some consolation to Katherine and Mary by finally adjudicating in favour of Katherine in the annulment case on the same day as the act was being passed. At home, however, both were now isolated.

*

Anne's child, Elizabeth, was born on 7 September 1533, though the birth of another girl dimmed Henry's excitement somewhat. Child or no child, he knew that to have his marriage universally accepted he had to break the spirits of both Katherine and Mary. Consequently, the hitherto petty inconveniences to which both had been subjected were replaced by outright persecution. To reinforce her pitiful demotion Mary had her household disbanded while she herself was dispatched to Hatfield House as a maid in waiting to the new princess of the realm, Elizabeth. Here she was given lodgings that the Imperial ambassador Eustace Chapuys observed consisted of 'the very worst room in the house'.[5] Although some have doubted that Mary's life at this point was one of unmitigated misery,[6] it is hard to imagine that it contained much joy. Chapuys's doom-laden reports on Mary's plight may have been exaggerated somewhat to provoke Charles into action against Henry, but they could not have been far removed from the truth. Forced to reside in a household that was run by two of Anne Boleyn's aunts, Lady Anne Shelton and Lady Alice Cleve, she endured the bitterness of isolation and seclusion. It was not in Henry's interest for Mary to be surrounded by friends who could raise her spirits, smuggle out letters and encourage continued resistance. He needed her to be isolated and alone, surrounded by no one but her enemies.[7]

Yet though essentially under house arrest, suffering bouts of recurrent illness, effectively bastardised, separated from her mother and estranged from her father, Mary remained defiant. She had little choice, for to have complied with England's new order, she would have effectively acknowledged her own illegitimacy as well as the invalidity of her mother's marriage. This was hardly the obstinacy of which she was accused at the time and ever since. Rather it was, as she saw it, standing up for what was right and just, a view shared by the vast majority of her countrymen as well as a great many Europeans who looked on with astonishment. For a girl of only seventeen years of age, her stance was remarkable. Not only by her defiance did she attract worsening treatment for herself from the Hatfield household. By rejecting both the Act of Succession and the Act of Supremacy, she was effectively committing treason that was placing her in growing danger. Her faith was her only source of consolation, giving her the strength to endure the numerous trials that confronted her which collectively would have broken lesser men and women.

Henry was similarly unbending, rejecting all petitions for Mary's better treatment and legitimisation, even from Emperor Charles himself. Though he would not yield to Anne's demand that he should mete out the ultimate punishment to Katherine and Mary for their treason, he made it clear that Mary would alter her situation only by totally complying with his laws. It was a position that he reinforced by forbidding her to see her terminally ill mother. Doubtless Henry's restraint in exacting the death penalty on either of them must have been governed to some extent by the emotional ties he had with both, especially Mary. Personal scruples apart, however, by executing Katherine, who was considered by anyone who mattered in Europe to be his lawful wife, and Mary, his legitimate daughter, Henry would have caused an unparalleled scandal, even by his standards, which could have brought disaster on him.

Katherine died on 7 January 1536, having been denied by Henry an opportunity to bid farewell to her daughter. From her seclusion at Kimbolton Castle in Huntingdonshire she had remained steadfast to the end. In her final letter to Henry she pardoned him for his wrongdoings against her, informing him that she prayed that God too would forgive him and begged him not to abandon their daughter. She instructed her daughter to be obedient to her father, the king, but stipulated that this should be done 'in everything save that you will not offend God and lose your own soul'.[8] Determined to be the loyal wife to the end, her own refusal to grant consent to the Act of Succession was as determined as her refusal to countenance any involvement in rebellion against Henry, which Chapuys at least was urging Charles to provoke.

Wracked with grief and still confronted by Anne's machinations against her, Mary now seriously began to entertain the prospect of escape from England. For this to happen, however, she needed the assistance of Emperor Charles. But Chapuys's efforts to engage him in Mary's plight were of limited success. The emotional attachment that Charles had felt towards Mary was not as strong as it had been towards his aunt Katherine. By the end of 1536, England had become more of a political than a personal problem for Charles. Not only did he not want to risk war with England he saw England as a potential ally in his ongoing struggle with France. His enthusiasm, therefore, to help Mary to flee the country was lukewarm at best.

If Mary hoped for an improvement in her lot she would need to rely on events at home. On 26 January 1536, the day of Katherine's funeral, Anne miscarried; the child, had it lived, would have been a boy. Impatient and frustrated, Henry began to look elsewhere for his male heir. His sights were set on a young lady at court, Jane Seymour. With this, Anne's own days were numbered, despised as she was in the country as a common harlot and with enemies among competing factions at court. A (probably) contrived plot uncovering adultery with sundry courtiers, including her brother, succeeded in removing her from the king's favours, and on 19 May 1536, Anne was executed for high treason.[9] Two days later the marriage that had scandalised Christendom and provoked England's separation from the Roman Catholic Church was declared by Cranmer to have been invalid owing to 'just and lawful impediments which, it was said, were unknown at the time of the union, but had lately been confessed to the archbishop by the lady herself'.[10] The contemporary chronicler, Charles Wriothesley, understood this to refer to a recent confession by Anne to Cranmer of the existence of a contract of betrothal between her and Henry Percy, earl of Northumberland, at the time of her marriage to Henry, something which the earl incidentally denied.[11] Eustace Chapuys, however, believed the marriage to have been annulled on grounds of consanguinity, owing to Henry's involvement with Anne's sister Mary, prior to his marriage to Anne.[12]

For Mary a window of hope had opened, or so she thought. Through a humble and contrite letter to Cromwell she hoped to engineer a reconciliation with her father. She soon realised, however, that Henry's price remained the same, total submission to his supremacy. At this point Henry could have, had his ego permitted, sought a full reconciliation with Rome given that Anne's death removed any doctrinal obstacle to this. His ego, however, not to mention his new found powers, as well the growing financial benefits of the supremacy that were coming his way owing to the appropriation of Church property, made any reconciliation with Rome unappealing. Going to the pope on bended knees admitting his guilt and pleading for forgiveness was something Henry was never going to do. Humility was not one of his virtues.

*

The political tensions that the break with Rome had provoked were becoming increasingly pronounced. 'In the spring of 1535', writes Alison Weir, 'the shadow of treason, real or imagined, and the king's wrath with those who opposed his marriage and his policies hung over England.'[13] A reign of terror was subsequently unleashed that claimed the high and low alike, including the Lord Chancellor, Thomas More, the bishop of Rochester John Fisher and numerous priests, most shockingly eighteen Carthusian monks, who were subjected to death by hanging, drawing and quartering, having been first dragged to their place of execution on their backs tied to hurdles, their heads beating against the cobbled streets. For these were times when Englishmen, not for the last time, would imperil their liberty and lives with a politically incorrect remark. Not only did it become illegal to write that the king or his new wife were schismatics or heretics, but as Simon Schama noted, 'for the very first time in English law, it was a crime to say these things'.[14] Henry now ordered that both Mary and her supporters be treated as traitors, with all that that entailed. With many of her allies having been sent to the Tower, the pressure, that she had hitherto withstood with great courage, became more than she could bear. The political executions made Chapuys fear for Mary's life for as yet she too had not acknowledged Henry's supremacy.

Mary naively entertained the thought that she could reconcile with her remaining parent on her terms. What she failed to understand was that what was solely a personal matter to her was a politically charged matter to Henry. In a series of letters she sent her father in June 1536, an imploring tone failed to mask the condition that she set for a reconciliation which was that she was prepared to submit to his will insofar as her conscience and God's laws would allow. She was to discover to her dismay that Henry was not willing to take second place to God in her loyalties and affections. He remained unmoved by the type of language that had failed both to save any of the Catholic martyrs he had had executed or to rehabilitate Katherine, so much so that he sent no reply to her first two letters. Mary's growing physical and mental anguish is clearly evident in a third letter, drafted by Cromwell himself, and sent on 14 June, in which she beseeches her father to acknowledge her pleas which she sends 'most humbly prostrate before your feet [. . .] in her great and intolerable discomfort'.[15] Although Henry did reply to this letter, he did so in uncompromising terms. On 15 June a delegation, led by the duke of Norfolk and the bishop of Chichester, Richard Sampson, arrived at Mary's home, Hunsdon. The delegates demanded that she submit to Henry's supremacy, repudiate papal authority and declare her mother's marriage null and void, with all that this entailed for her own status. To the consternation of her oppressors Mary continued to hold out. With all options exhausted, Henry finally decided to have Mary judiciously declared a traitor,[16] pending the outcome of one last chance that was offered her and it was only Cranmer, according to his secretary, Ralph Morice, who 'stayed the king's determinate mynde and sentence, in that he fullie purposed to sende the ladye Mary his daughter to the Tower, and there to suffer as a subjecte, by cause she wolde not obey unto the laws of the realme in refusing the bishop of Rome's authorite and religion'.[17] A lengthy document was drafted outlining the three aspects to which she had to submit to save herself from a grim fate. Cromwell had certainly succeeded in convincing both her and Chapuys that her life was in danger.[18]

There is no way of telling, given Henry's increasingly violent and unpredictable disposition, whether he would have carried out the ultimate sanction for treason against his daughter. It is certainly untrue though, contrary to Elton's emphatic assertion, that Mary had 'never [lived] in the shadow of death by execution'.[19] Under immense pressure and with her life in danger, Mary, on Chapuys's advice and with Emperor Charles's consent, finally relented. The tone of the submission was most galling and humiliating for her. With a stroke of a pen she signed away everything that had both sustained her and caused her so much anguish over these past years, and recognised 'the king's highness to be supreme head on earth, under Christ, of the church of England', repudiated utterly 'the bishop of Rome's pretended authority, power and jurisdiction within this realm, formerly usurped, according to the laws and statutes made on that behalf', and acknowledged the marriage between the king and her mother, the late Princess Dowager, to have been 'by God's law and man's law incestuous and unlawful'.[20]

Compounding her anguish of having signed away her birth-right, betrayed her mother's memory and renounced her faith,[21] was the taint of Nicodemism. This was a term derived from the leading Pharisee and member of the Sanhedrin, Nicodemus, who secretly sought solace from Christ, while outwardly remaining a pious Jew for fear of persecution.[22] Pope Paul III refused to countenance any public pardon for her. She may well have signed the articles of submission, as Chapuys recorded, without having read them, but her actions did little to exonerate her in the eyes of the Church. Arguments that her submission had been purely for external effect fell on deaf ears in Rome. For Pope Paul, canon law offered no room for exceptions to martyrdom, as the ultimate sacrifice for the faith, lest the memories of Catholic martyrs be compromised. One may only speculate whether the submission of leading conservatives like Bishops Stephen Gardiner and Edmund Bonner eased her conscience. She after all had much more to lose.

Henry himself suspected that Mary's submission had been insincere, knowing fully that it had been extracted under duress. Perhaps under 'extreme psychological pressure' she had been brainwashed,[23] but this seems unlikely in view of what the alternative to her submission was. To reinforce his daughter's submission to his will, Henry cruelly subjected her to sign yet more humiliating documents before she could be readmitted to court. Not only did she have to formally acknowledge Elizabeth as princess but was also compelled to officially inform both Charles and his sister, the highly influential Mary, queen of Hungary and governor of the Netherlands, of her submission.

Henry's concerns about Mary's loyalties were heightened during the social tumult that gripped northern England by the end of 1536. Growing social and economic problems had been compounded by the effects of increasingly radical religious 'reform' that had swept away many of the traditional religious rituals that had been held dear by the general population (see chapter 11). This situation, together with Cromwell's political centralisation and meddling in local affairs, generated a very combustible atmosphere in many parts of the country that would seriously threaten the Tudor order. No place was more resentful of the regime's policies than the north, especially Yorkshire, which hosted several rebellions. The largest of these, comprising some 30,000 rebels, occurred in October 1536, and came to be known as the Pilgrimage of Grace. Though its causes were multifaceted, religion formed the overarching motivation of the rebels. Marching behind a banner of the five wounds of Christ, they petitioned in the first seven of their twenty-four Pontefract articles for a restoration of traditional religious practices, including many of the monasteries that had been dissolved as well as for the repeal of the Oath of Supremacy that had effectively rendered Mary illegitimate.[24] During his interrogation after the collapse of the Pilgrimage, Robert Aske, its key leader, spoke warmly of Mary as 'marvellously beloved for her virtue in the hearts of the people', which he claimed had been 'much grudged' that she had been made illegitimate 'by the laws of this realm, seeing she on the mother side was comen of the greatest blood parage [descent] of Christendom'.[25]

There is no evidence whether or not Mary was in any way involved with the rebels or whether she expressed any sympathy either towards them or their cause, although several members of her household were implicated in the rebellion. In all likelihood, however, following her reconciliation with her father, she seemed to have reconciled herself to the reality that little more could be done to resist Henry's religious innovations. The defeat of the Pilgrimage and the brutal execution of all its leaders, 216 in total, lords and knights, half a dozen abbots, thirty-eight monks and sixteen parish priests, could not disguise the fact that the voice of the people could not be taken for granted. The fact that many nobles, as well as members of the gentry, were among the rebels was a telling sign of the times. Matters could have turned out very differently for them were it not for poor planning and a lack of support from Emperor Charles.[26] It was only after buying time with cunning deception that Henry managed to defeat them. What the rebellion also made clear to Henry was that ending foreign and domestic plots against the regime was contingent on neutralising in the minds of the people Mary's claim to the throne.

*

For Mary the material fruits of her submission were immediate (Fig. 2). Now twenty years of age, she met her father for the first time in five years. Henry began to lavish her with copious amounts of fatherly affection, doubtless satisfied by his triumph over her. He restored her to court and bestowed on her jewels and money as well as a large household and in Henry's new wife, Jane Seymour, who had always been sympathetic to her

Fig. 2. Posthumous Portrait of Henry VIII with Queen Mary
and Will Somers the Jester. Artist unknown, 16th century.
Courtesy of Sarah Campbell Blaffer Foundation, Houston

cause, she earned a trusted friend. In fact, all evidence points to Mary's
settling into a life of conformity with the new order. It was now Elizabeth's
turn to be declared by the Act of Succession of 1536 the outcast off-spring
of a marriage that never was. Yet this was only a partial rehabilitation.
Mary was neither proclaimed a princess nor restored to the succession and
interestingly she was now formally bastardised, together with Elizabeth,
by the 1536 Act of Succession, though arguably the canon-law loophole,
noted above, that determined her informal legitimacy after the 1534 Act,
still stood. Although the birth of his long-awaited son, Edward, on 12
October 1537, allayed Henry's concerns over the security of the dynasty,
he knew that there were those, both at home and abroad, who saw Mary
as a figurehead for the Catholic cause in England and who were prepared
to scheme on her behalf. Henry's anxiety was again heightened after the
Empire and Francis had struck, with the pope's mediation, a truce in the
autumn of 1537. The intense faction fighting between Edward's and Mary's
supporters that emerged at court during Henry's serious illness in 1538,

exposed the fragility of the succession, something that was reinforced further by the pope's excommunication of Henry on 17 December 1538. By his act the pope effectively gave support to any Catholic plot against him.

Reginald Pole, a cardinal of the old Church and a Plantagenet claimant to the throne himself, hoped to rally support in Europe against 'the most cruel and abominable tyrant'.[27] Given what Henry was perpetuating, Pole's words were not an exaggeration. With the threat of invasion heightening Henry's paranoia, the king began to wage war on established Catholic families like the Nevilles, Poles and Courtenays which had served Katherine and now supported Mary. Many of their leading members were either executed or imprisoned in the Tower. It was a stark reminder to Mary that her father's capacity for cruelty was unlimited and that he would stop at nothing to ensure the security of his throne. In 1539 Reginald Pole's brother, Henry Montagu, who, despite his unswerving loyalty to the Henrician regime, was imprisoned in the Tower and duly executed on spurious evidence given under duress by his younger brother, Geoffrey. Montagu's infant son, Henry, was also taken to the Tower, never to be seen again. The ageing countess of Salisbury, Margaret Pole, was also targeted. On 27 May 1541, after two years of imprisonment in the Tower, she was attainted, for which no evidence was needed, and executed. Long-serving in Mary's household, having previously given Katherine many years of loyal service, Margaret was well past child bearing age and as such was no threat to the succession. Her execution, therefore, served little purpose other than to satisfy a personal grudge. The real reason for her execution was her consanguinity with the treacherous Cardinal Pole and her unrepentant association with the old faith. It was yet another personal blow to Mary who regarded her as a second mother. For Henry, Mary's political isolation was paramount.

England had certainly entered a dark and uncertain period. So great did Henry perceive the threat from the Continent as being that he entered into another political marriage, Jane having died a few days after giving birth to Edward. In January 1540 he married Anne, the daughter of the Protestant duke of Cleves, who as a member of the Protestant Schmalkaldic League was himself engaged in a struggle with Imperial forces. Haplessly arranged by Cromwell, the marriage proved ill-fated, as Henry and Anne never really warmed to each other. Henry put this down to her unsightly looks, that he claimed were at odds with the portrait that Cromwell had commissioned the renowned court artist, Hans Holbein, to paint in order to entice Henry into the marriage. In reality, however, Anne's appearance was more conventional than propaganda of a much later period etched on popular memory. The marriage was annulled in July 1540 on grounds of non-consummation, its failure being more to do with compatibility issues than with Anne's appearance. In any case, the alliance with Cleves ultimately proved unnecessary as France and the Empire duly renewed hostilities by the end of 1540. For Cromwell, however, the marriage proved his undoing. Having saddled Henry with a woman whom the king found unappealing, he fell victim to his enemies at court, who played on Henry's fickle character to rid themselves of the much-hated figure. The leading religious conservative, the duke of Norfolk, was particularly eager to see the back of him, and in addition saw an opportunity to place his niece, Katherine Howard, in the king's eye as successor to Anne as his spouse. In June 1540 a bill of attainder was drawn up against Cromwell and he was duly executed, something which Henry almost immediately regretted. Anne, on the other hand, continued to live in England, being widely admired for her dignity and humility. During her short reign as queen, she struck up a close friendship with Mary that was to last until Anne's death in 1557.

Mary's role in the murky politics of the Tudor court continued to be peripheral. She continued to be mainly used as fodder in the diplomatic game of arranged marriages. Numerous suitors were considered, notably Don Luiz, the brother of the king of Portugal; but this was little more than posturing on Henry's part, given that his best interests were served by keeping Mary single and in England. Any foreign marriage, particularly to a Catholic prince, threatened to revive Mary's succession claims, which was the last thing that Henry wanted to do. In fact Don Luiz, not wanting to demean himself by marrying Henry's illegitimate daughter, made Mary's relegitimisation by an act of parliament a condition of any marriage contract, something that Henry flatly refused to sanction.[28] Unmarried and with her best years passing, Mary resigned herself to live a quiet life of courtly seclusion.

Yet in many ways it was a life that suited her. Though appalled by the injustices of her treatment, she remained humble at heart, her strength of will, courage and fortitude fortifying her in her ongoing physical and mental anguish. Deeply pious, she indeed resigned herself to suffer for her faith. And it was a faith that would remain marginalised even after Cromwell's execution and the triumph of religious conservatives at court. In spite of the return to England of traditional religious practices by virtue of the Six Articles of 1539, which replaced the more radical Ten Articles of 1536, England would remain firmly outside Rome's orbit.[29] As far as Henry was concerned the theology of the country had been settled, though he would continue to use religion politically through a series of heresy hunts against one faction or another in a game of divide-and-conquer that was a characteristic feature of his rule or to satisfy foreign policy alliances which vacillated from Catholic to Protestant powers.[30] Those who continued to flout Henry's order would pay with their lives, often on trumped up charges to justify their execution and satisfy the king's latest strategy.[31] In a curious, though horrific scene in July 1540, that was to characterise the fickle and confused religious situation, three Catholics, the theologians, Thomas Abel and Edward Powell, once confidants of Katherine during her divorce proceedings and Father Richard Featherstone, once chaplain to Katherine and tutor to Mary, suffered traitors' deaths for refusing to submit to Henry's supremacy. Alongside them the reformers Robert Barnes, Thomas Garret and William Jerome were burnt for heresy. Prior to this, all six were drawn through the streets on hurdles, in three pairs, a Catholic and heretic on either side of each other. The English Lutheran exile, Richard Hilles, wrote to his fellow reformer Heinrich Bullinger in the wake of these executions about the prevailing situation:

> The reason of their execution is unknown to me; but it was reported to have been for treason against the king. However, to confess the truth, people were not so active in inquiry, or in investigating matters, as they were wont to have been, because it is now no novelty among us to see men slain, hung, quartered, or beheaded; some for trifling expressions, which were explained or interpreted as having been spoken against the king; others for the pope's supremacy.[32]

*

The last years of Henry's reign were comparatively stable for Mary. The arrival in July 1543 of Henry's sixth and final wife, Katherine Parr, his penultimate one, Katherine Howard, having been executed in February 1542 for treason, was in many respects a blessing for Mary. Not only had Katherine Howard been five years Mary's junior, she had also been the cousin of Anne Boleyn. Mary's respect, therefore, for her fourth step-mother had been somewhat limited, and hence she sought to avoid the queen as much as possible. Her relationship with Katherine Parr, conversely, was on a different level. Being only five years older than she was, Katherine was more of a sister than a step-mother to her. They shared scholarly interests and became good friends, Mary seemingly unperturbed by Katherine's evangelical leanings. Their collaboration on a much-acclaimed translation into English of Erasmus's *Paraphrases upon the New Testament* attests to this (see chapter 10).

Notwithstanding taking a new wife, Henry was increasingly sickly, which limited the prospect of new heirs. As if sensing that his time was approaching he sought to consolidate the succession yet again. Henry's sole male heir, Edward, was only six years of age and prone to bouts of sickness.[33] Securing the succession became increasingly urgent. For this he turned to his illegitimate children, time having mellowed him and memories of past battles fading away. In February 1544, a new Act of Succession was passed by Parliament which overturned the Act of 1536. Though the new Act maintained Edward as heir, it declared Mary and Elizabeth, in that order, as his successors in the event of Edward's not begetting any heirs. Strangely, however, neither was formally relegitimised.

Though demoted to second place in the line of succession and still effectively declared a bastard, Mary spent the last years of Henry's reign in relative peace. The recurrent illness that had plagued her earlier years did return and there were of course the realities of her life to contend with, which she had long accepted with grace. But there was one anxiety at least, that of her continued unmarried status, which she would fret over. For a woman in her late twenties who loved children and who longed for affection this was a particularly harsh torment to bear, which no material consolation could allay. Used as she was in the diplomatic game, she lamented that 'it was certain', as reported the French diplomat, Charles de Marillac, to King Francis, that 'there was nothing to be got but fine words, and while my father lives I shall be only the Lady Mary, the most unhappy lady in Christendom'.[34] She spent her time doting over the infant Edward, to whom she was godmother, and furthering her scholarly interests. But the relative tranquillity of these years was not to last. Political turmoil and personal anguish would soon return to her life.

NOTES

[1] Prescott, *Mary Tudor*, p. 52.

[2] Henry had satisfied himself, however, that he had been free to marry again, believing that his marriage to Katherine was null. For details of this controversy see 'Appendix II, the date of Henry VIII's marriage to Anne Boleyn', in D. MacCulloch, *Thomas Cranmer: A Life* (New Haven and London: Yale University Press, 1996), pp. 637–8.

[3] The first Act of Succession, 1534, *Luminarium: Encyclopaedia Project – England under the Tudors*, http://www.luminarium.org/encyclopedia/firstactofsuccession.htm, accessed 12 July 2013.

[4] S. E. Lehmberg, *The Reformation Parliament 1529–1536* (Cambridge: Cambridge University Press, 2008), p. 198.

[5] 'Eustace Chapuys to the Emperor, 3 January 1534, 1', CSPS, vol. 5. Part 1.

[6] J. M. Richards, *Mary Tudor* (Abingdon and New York: Routledge, 2008), p. 58.

[7] Prescott, *Mary Tudor*, p. 61.

[8] 'Letter of Katharine of Aragon to her husband, King Henry VIII. 7 January 1536', http://englishhistory.net/tudor/letter5.html, accessed 12 August 2013.

[9] Though the plot is generally regarded as unfounded, it is believed by some to have some substance. See, for instance, G. W Bernard, *Anne Boleyn: Fatal Attractions* (New Haven: Yale University Press, 2011).

[10] C. Wriothesley, *A Chronicle of England during the Reign of the Tudors from 1485 to 1559*, ed. W. D. Hamilton. 2 vols. (London: Camden Society, 1777), vol. 1, p. 41.

[11] Ibid.

[12] 'Eustace Chapuys to Monseigneur de Granvelle', 18 May 1536, CSPS, vol. 5, part 2.

[13] A. Weir, *Six Wives of Henry VIII* (London: Vintage, 2007), p. 280.

[14] Schama, *History of Britain: At the Edge of the World?* p. 308.

[15] 'Mary to Henry VIII, 14 June 1536, 1133', LPFD, vol. 10.

[16] Ridley, *Henry VIII*, p. 274.

[17] R. Morice, 'Anecdotes and Character of Archbishop Cranmer', in J. G. Nichols, ed., *Narratives of the Days of the Reformation* (London: Camden Society, 1859), p. 259.

[18] Loades, *Mary Tudor*, p. 57.

[19] Elton, *Reform and Reformation*, p. 376.

[20] 'Princess Mary's Submission, 15 June 1536, 1137', LPFD, vol. 10.

[21] Whitelock, *Mary Tudor, England's First Queen*, pp. 88–9.

[22] Nicodemus is later presented in Scripture as accepting the truth and defending Christ at the time of his trial, as well as assisting Joseph of Arimathea in the embalming and burial of Jesus.

[23] Loades, *Mary Tudor*, p. 60.

[24] 'The 24 Articles of the Pilgrimage of Grace rebels', *Luminarium: Encyclopaedia Project – England under the Tudors*, http://www.luminarium.org/encyclopedia/24articles.htm, accessed 12 August, 2013.

[25] J. Edwards, *Mary I: England's Catholic Queen* (New Haven: Yale University Press, 2011), p. 55.

[26] Guy, *Tudor England*, p. 152.

[27] Ibid., p. 100.

[28] Ridley, *Henry VIII*, p. 277.

[29] 'The Ten Articles', *Luminarium: Encyclopaedia Project – England under the Tudors* http://www.luminarium.org/encyclopedia/tenarticles.htm; 'The Six articles', http://www.luminarium.org/encyclopedia/sixarticles.htm, accessed 2 December, 2012.

[30] See Ridley, *Henry VIII*, pp. 339, 343–4, 355–6, 359, 372–3, 397, 400.

[31] Ibid., p. 397.

[32] 'Richard Hilles to Henry Bullinger', in *Original Letters*, p. 211.

[33] C. Skidmore, *Edward VI: The Lost King of England* (London: Weidenfeld & Nicolson, 2007), p. 27.

[34] 'Marillac to Francis I, 3 June 1542, 371', LPFD, vol. 17.

✤ 7 ✤

From Troublesome Daughter to Troublesome Sister

Henry died on 28 January 1547. It is not known how Mary reacted to her father's death though whilst queen her attitude towards his memory was deferential rather than affectionate. Materially at least, he had provided well for her in his will. She was given a financial settlement that made her the fifth or sixth peer in the land.[1] She also took possession of vast estates among which were thirty-two principal manors and a number of smaller ones, as well as several palaces and castles, including among them her erstwhile home, Hunsdon, the impressive Newhall Palace, the former home of both Anne Boleyn and Katherine Howard, and the fortified Framlingham Castle. It is from the latter that she would launch her own claim to the throne a few years later.

Henry left the court in the hands of competing factions. Leading the council were Edward's uncle, Edward Seymour, the duke of Somerset, who had granted himself the grandiose title of Lord Protector. Initially, Mary's relationship with Somerset's Council was cordial. Continental Catholic powers may have regarded Mary as Henry's only legitimate off-spring and Henry himself as a heretic and schismatic, but Mary, however, fully endorsed Edward's succession. But a clash between her and the Council was rendered inevitable by the failure of religious conservatives during the last years of Henry's reign to dislodge the reformers from the court. Outwardly Mary may have lived a contented life surrounded by her new found opulence and wealth, though inwardly her conscience would be stretched to the point of open rebellion against the Council and increasingly against her brother too. Somerset, though not a religious radical, was inclined towards reformist views as too was the Council. The precocious Edward, on the other hand, having been schooled in the new thinking by radical tutors, would come to strain his deep affection for his strong-willed sister to the limit.

The injunctions of 1547, which outlined compulsory practices for both the clergy and lay people, the first English Prayer Book of 1549 as well as the repeal of the Six Articles offered an indication of the religious direction in which England was heading. Together they abolished numerous sacred Catholic rituals as well as clerical celibacy and the Latin liturgy, preserving the doctrine of transubstantiation only implicitly. Mary had been prepared to tolerate her father's Church settlement, but she was determined not to abide by Somerset's innovations. His use of statute to enact them made no difference to her as she challenged his entitlement to do so on matters of religion on account of Edward's minority. It was a view echoed by many members of the Council, such as Bishop Stephen Gardiner, who questioned whether a nine-year-old boy had the authority to determine religious doctrine.[2]

In her first act of public defiance against the Edwardian religious legislation, the first of many, Mary organised a Mass in the old Latin rite at one of her residences, Kenninghall, on the Pentecost of 1549 in protest at the introduction of the new prayer book across English parishes on that day. Upon hearing of Mary's action, the Council immediately ordered her to defer from any such activity in the future. At thirty-three, however, Mary was not the adolescent girl who had been bullied into submission by an overpowering king. Bloodied by years of grief and torment and materially endowed with considerable power, she was not going to be cajoled into submission again. Her confidence was doubtless reinforced by the support she received from Charles, though the extent to which this impacted on her actions is difficult to ascertain. She had after all defied her father when Charles's support for her was lukewarm and was governed primarily by the interests of his Empire. Now, though not unsympathetic to Mary's cause, he continued to be primarily motivated by political issues and supported it insofar as it gave him leverage over a Council that he felt he could unduly influence.

In January 1549 he instructed François van der Delft, who had succeeded Chapuys as Imperial ambassador in 1545, to inform the Council in the strongest possible terms that he would 'suffer no pressure to be put upon our close relative' to alter her religious views in any way. Charles issued further instructions to his ambassador in May to secure from Somerset a written guarantee allowing Mary to practise her faith unmolested by state authorities.[3] With England already at war with Scotland and France, the Council was compelled to grant Mary some religious freedom so as not to provoke the emperor into any threatening action. Although Somerset refused to give a written guarantee on grounds that it would be inconsistent with the laws of the land, he did, however, offer van der Delft verbal assurances that Mary, in view of her royal rank, could celebrate the Catholic Mass in private for as long as Edward was a minor. Irritated by Somerset's intransigence, the ambassador informed him that the emperor would not permit Mary to make any more concessions to her faith even if she wanted to, something which Somerset took to confirm that Mary was a mere pawn of Emperor Charles. Notwithstanding Somerset's accusations, Mary had little choice other than to seek protection from abroad, given her almost total isolation from England's political elite.

Mary was safe for the time being. The rebellions in Norfolk, led by the gentleman Robert Kett and in the West Country in 1549, provoked in part by the religious changes, eased the pressure on her further as Somerset's precarious position ruled out any radical move against her. However, in an age of flux Somerset's assurances were flimsy. In fact, not long after he had given them, he was dismissed from office in November 1549, his disastrous domestic and foreign policies as well as his autocratic method of governing provoking the Council to remove him from office. His successor as head of the Council, John Dudley, the earl of Warwick and latterly the duke of Northumberland, styled himself Lord President in a bid to appear more innocuous than his reviled predecessor. And for a while even adherents of the old faith looked in hope to his purported Catholic sympathies. But these hopes were dashed pretty quickly as his actions were to prove far removed from any personal religious views that he may have held. In April, the Council warned Mary about allowing servants from her household to attend her Masses, claiming that attendance would be in breach of previous verbal agreements which stipulated that such Masses were to be strictly private affairs. The warning came as a prelude to an intensification of religious reform that would occur over the next few years.

Amidst the turmoil Mary was to be placed under growing pressure to comply with the ever more radical religious laws. History appeared to be repeating itself, except for the adversaries who confronted her: a child king and a council. Ever regretful of her initial submission, she was determined 'rather [to] suffer death, than stain my conscience', as she wrote to van der Delft in May 1550, pleading with him 'to help me with your advice, so that I may not be taken unawares'.[4] Though Emperor Charles's ever-present threat to England limited the pressure that Mary was being placed under by Edward's regime, it was not going to save her indefinitely. When France and the Empire renewed hostilities in 1550 the need to appease Charles faded. With no formal permission to practise her faith, Mary would once more find herself in grave danger that was sufficient for her again to contemplate escape.

Her justification for leaving England was strengthened by the rapidly changing religious situation. Initially Charles was hesitant to agree to such a hazardous operation, given the logistical difficulties involved in smuggling her out of the country from under the noses of the tight security that had been assigned to her. He also believed that the best chance of her regaining the throne in the event of Edward's premature death was for her to stay put and risk the dangers that confronted her. Eventually, however, he was persuaded to agree to the venture, not least because of persistent lobbying from his sister and the regent of the Netherlands, Mary of Hungary.[5] Imperial ships were to anchor off the coast of the Essex town of Maldon, from where Mary was to be whisked off to the Netherlands.[6] The plan, however, was never realistic and was aborted at the last moment, having been discovered by the English authorities. With escape now closed to her, Mary resigned herself to fighting for her faith, her birthright and if necessary her life.

The immunity from persecution that Somerset had given her increasingly looked like the hollow gesture that Mary had always suspected it was. The Council now was even denying that it had ever been given at all. Conveniently for the regime van der Delft, to whom these assurances had allegedly been made, died in June 1550 and any letters regarding the issue, if they ever were written, could not be traced.[7] Faced with the prospect of having the celebration of Mass in her household prohibited, as she had been personally informed to that effect on 28 Aug 1551 by the Chancellor, Richard Rich, Mary's defiance now went into overdrive. In a series of letters between her, the Council and Edward, an extraordinary battle of wills ensued. Writing to the Council in January 1551, Mary insisted that her 'household were given entire freedom to have the Mass celebrated, and to attend other ceremonies performed in the manner used in my late father's time'. She went on to reiterate that she consented to no religious changes and desired 'that all may be left as the late king his father left it, until his Majesty has reached the age to judge for himself. It seems to me not suitable that he should be robbed of freedom by laws and statutes on spiritual matters passed during his minority. No such thing has ever been seen in any Christian kingdom; and God knows whether his Majesty may not take it amiss in time to come'. She concluded in defiant tone: 'I now request you to take this as my final answer to any letters you might write to me on matters of religion'.[8]

The following day the precocious Edward himself was to add his voice to religious matters. Strongly reformist in outlook, he would insist on his sister's compliance with the new religious order. In his reply to her defiant missive to the Council he revealed his growing irritation with what he regarded as her obstinacy. In so doing, however, he showed his own position to be as uncompromising as hers. 'It appears', he notes, 'by your letters that you have persuaded yourself that you may continue in your erring ways in virtue of a promise which you claim to have received, though we truly know that the said promise was not given with the intention you lend to it. My sister, you must learn that your courses were tolerated when our laws were first promulgated.' Now, he insisted, she must abandon her 'error', arguing, in what was clearly a prompt from the Council, that his youth, contrary to her claims, was an advantage in weighing up the arguments. He asserted:

> for perhaps the evil has endured in you so long that it is more strongly rooted than we suppose, and this but troubles us the more, fearing that our youth may not permit us to gauge the extent of the evil, if we are to judge by what we perceive at present. Truly we do not wish to presume beyond what our age concedes; that is to say, in matters yet doubtful we place no reliance in our own wisdom; but in those things which are plain we believe there is no difference (between us and older men).

His youth, he continued, was no impediment to 'acknowledging us as your sovereign lord' for 'if we were to grant you license to break our laws and set them aside, would it not be an encouragement to others to do likewise?' In his own hand, Edward concluded even more chillingly, perhaps giving some insight into the kind of England he would have presided over had he survived into adulthood:

> I could not tolerate practices that have been condemned as bad; see good statutes broken with impunity, nor connive at such deeds as if the laws were to be taken lightly, nor support some with favour whilst others are justly punished. Truly, sister, I will not say more and worse things, because my duty would compel me to use harsher and angrier words. But this I will say with certain intention, that I will see my laws strictly obeyed, and those who break them shall be watched and denounced, even as some are ready to trouble my subjects by their obstinate resistance, and by disturbing the provisions made in my ordinances and statutes by their disobedience.[9]

In her reply Mary continued to insist that she had neither broken any laws nor incited anyone else to do so. She beseeched her brother 'most humbly to believe that I have never had any other intentions or desire towards you than to wish that all prosperity and honour may fall upon your Highness' and that she acted only in accordance with the promise of exemption that she had been given. Though she acknowledged that the terms of the promise were now in dispute, she beseeched him again 'to suspend your judgement on spiritual matters until you reach riper and fuller years, and then with better knowledge and understanding your Majesty will exercise your freedom to decide according to your pleasure'.[10]

The proverbial swords had certainly been drawn. Her reception at court that March by her brother was cold, devoid of the brotherly love that had hitherto characterised their relationship. Writing in his *Chronicle* in the wake of his meeting with his sister, Edward could hardly contain his disdain for her religious views and disobedience. He told his councillors in March:

> How long had I suffered her mass in hope of her reconciliation how now, being no hope which I perceived by her letters, except I saw some short amendment I could not bear it. It was said, I constrained not her Faith, but willed her not as a King to Rule, but as a subject to obey.[11]

In August, twenty-four councillors 'at length agreed' that Mary's disobedience 'was not meet to be suffered any longer, making thereof an Instrument signed with their Hands, and sealed to be on Record'.[12]

In view of Edward's growing hostility towards his sister, it was increasingly difficult for Mary to claim that he would convert to her faith once he came of age and came to his senses. One can only speculate what would have happened to her and the country had Edward lived into adulthood. Mary, for one, certainly resigned herself to the ultimate sacrifice. She wrote to her brother in August 1551 that 'rather than to offend God and my conscience, I offer my body at your will, and death shall be most welcome than life with a troubled conscience', reiterating 'that she would lay her head on a block and suffer death', if she was compelled 'to use any other service than was used at the death of the late King, her father'.[13] Unable to break Mary's resistance, the regime turned towards her servants, whose defiance was much easier to crush. It was a tactic that Henry often used against her. In this instance several of her closest advisors, notably Edward Waldegrave, Sir Francis Englefield and Sir Robert Rochester, found themselves in the Tower in August 1551, while her chaplain was ordered not to celebrate the Catholic Mass in her house, an order that now embraced Mary as well as her servants.

At a point when matters seemed on a knife-edge, foreign policy intervened again to ease the pressure off Mary. The resumption of war between the Empire and France in 1552 threatened to damage England's cloth trade. As such, the Council was compelled to appease Mary of Hungary, who a year earlier had actually urged Charles to invade England, something which she suggested 'would not be impossible to conquer, especially now that it is a prey to discord and poverty' and which 'would enable us to protect our shipping'.[14] Although an invasion was never attempted, Charles probably thinking his sister's assessment of the chances of conquest to be over-optimistic, it remained a possibility which reinforced in the minds of the councillors that Mary posed a threat to England's Protestant order. Consequently, conciliatory gestures to her followed.

Pressure for her to abide by recent orders subsided somewhat and in March her three household officers were released from detention. Short of imprisoning Mary, there was little the Council could do to enforce the king's will and a pragmatic stalemate continued right up until the end of Edward's reign.[15] Having taken up an invitation to court in June, Mary was not subjected to any haranguing about her faith, despite the regime's determination to pursue ever more evangelical reforms, characterised by the introduction in November of the second *Book of Common Prayer*, which abrogated any ambiguities in worship that the *First Book* had generated. Clerics who would not comply with the new order were to be swiftly replaced by those who would. The bishop of London, Edmund Bonner, for instance, an erstwhile vocal advocate of Henry's supremacy, became an arch-opponent of Edwardian religious innovations, for which he was deprived of his post and subsequently imprisoned. His replacement, Nicholas Ridley, a zealous reformer, launched a frenzy of destruction in churches across the land that was to have them stripped of their altars and other representations of the old faith, reducing its rituals to what was considered the bare minimum for worship (see chapter 9).

For all the outward expressions of deference that Mary received from the regime, her position remained precarious. But, as so often in the past, fate intervened. In February 1553 Edward contracted a cold which would develop into a life-threatening condition. Northumberland, the chief architect of Mary's woes, and Edward, who at sixteen had become a principled Protestant, were determined to keep Mary off the throne, though it is unclear which of the two was more prominent in the plot. The conspiracy that they jointly hatched sought to disinherit Mary as well as Elizabeth – Mary on account of her illegitimacy, which Henry never explicitly reversed, and Elizabeth on account of her mother's disgrace – in favour of Edward's Protestant cousin, the great-granddaughter of Henry VII, Lady Jane Grey. Moreover, neither Mary nor Elizabeth was as yet married, and as such the fear was that in the event of their marrying a foreigner, the Crown could pass to an undesirable foreign power. Jane conversely, who had recently married Northumberland's son, Guildford Dudley, was a safe bet. Initially, however, Edward's so-called *Devise for the Succession to the Crown*, penned in his own hand before he was aware of his imminent death, passed the succession to 'Lady Jane's heirs male' only, that is male heirs of Jane's mother, as well as those of Jane herself and her sisters, in the event of Edward having no issue of his own or there being no male heirs to succeed him.[16] At that point Jane's mother, Frances Grey, duchess of Suffolk, would govern as a regent until the birth of a male heir.[17] Whether or not Northumberland's arrangement for his son Guildford Dudley to marry Jane was part of the plot is unclear.[18] It did, however, ultimately serve both his and Edward's interests.

By March Edward was aware of his grave illness, most probably bilateral bronchopneumonia, an untreatable disease at that time.[19] *The Devise*, initially written as a school exercise,[20] now required urgent revision. Most probably prompted by Northumberland,[21] Edward altered it to make Jane his successor, and included her sisters in the line of succession,[22] excluding both Mary and Elizabeth. The *Devise* was to be authorised by letters patent and not

Parliament, which was certainly questionable in law, given that many MPs by now considered that acts of succession required parliamentary approval. But although many at the time (and ever since) questioned the authority of letters patent over parliamentary statute in matters of succession, they had little time, with the king's death imminent, to effect any objections. As such, letters patent were drawn up and countersigned in June by over a hundred men of England's political class, though by some, notably the Lord Chief Justice, Edward Montagu, very reluctantly. For Montagu there were serious questions concerning the legality of the process.[23] For one, notwithstanding the absence of Parliament from the process, did Edward, as a minor, have the authority to settle succession merely by letters patent? It was only the prospect of a restoration of Catholicism, and all that this could potentially entail personally for the leading men of the land, which eventually swayed the doubters to approve Edward's succession *Devise*.[24] Northumberland needed to keep Mary ignorant of his plans for long enough to be able to put them into action, hoping that with French support he could stave off any attempts by Charles to intervene on her behalf. But even before Edward's death on 6 July 1554 Mary got wind of his intentions and managed to escape to her estates in Norfolk. Yet with key state figures seemingly behind Edward's scheme and with Jane and her supporters ensconced in the Tower of London and in control of its armoury, Mary's chances of becoming queen looked slim, so much so that even Charles was reluctant to assist her.

All was not lost for Mary, however. For one, her decisive actions at this point, taken when she was separated from her key advisors, including the vacillating Imperial ambassador, belie claims by historians that she lacked political acumen and was wholly dependent on Charles and his diplomats. As it happens, her distance from Imperial power contributed to her eventual success, helping to dispel claims by her enemies that she was a Habsburg stooge. Her vast wealth gave her much leverage in securing support and fighting men, whose ranks were soon to swell to some 30,000 strong. Moreover, her long 'apprenticeship' at court during which she both witnessed and endured political intrigue, fortified her for the task ahead. Notwithstanding her own defiance and determination to succeed, she enjoyed the support of the vast majority of the public, which greeted Jane Grey's proclamation as queen without any marked enthusiasm. No one present, reported the emperor's ambassadors, 'showed any sign of rejoicing, and no one cried: "Long live the queen!" except the herald who made the proclamation and a few archers who followed him', something that was indicative of 'the state of feeling in England towards the Lady Mary'.[25] The sixteen-year-old Jane was a relative unknown and her association with the unpopular Northumberland was much loathed. Northumberland was particularly despised in Norfolk, Mary's stronghold, for having brutally suppressed the Kett rebellion in the summer of 1549. Popular support for Mary was based on more than just an instinctive inclination for fair play that acknowledged Mary as the legitimate queen. Those who declared for her were fully aware of her intention to restore Catholicism to England, a fact which traditionally historians have downplayed.

The Council, on the other hand, was primarily motivated by political expediency, so much so that Northumberland could not count on the loyalty of its members. The longer Mary remained at large, the more Northumberland's assurances of her imminent arrest seemed hollow, even more so in view of the tactics that he deployed. With his personal unpopularity already counting against him, he embarked on a counter-productive campaign of vengeance against those who had declared for Mary, like Lord George Howard, whose home, Sawston Hall, was razed to the ground. Departing London on 14 July 1553 with an expedition against Mary, Northumberland left himself exposed in the Council. In fact, sensing Northumberland's defeat, the Council began to waver, especially as he was not present to cajole it. One by one the councillors began to abandon Northumberland's cause. On 18 July its resolve cracked totally as it placed a ransom on his head. The following day, London officially declared for Mary, provoking two recent converts on the Council to Mary's cause, Earl Arundel and Lord Paget, to venture to Framlingham to inform her of her triumph.

Ignorant of developments in London, Mary was readying herself for a fight, though as it turned out this was not needed. Having been already proclaimed queen, Mary rode triumphantly into London on 3 August 1553, Northumberland's cause having collapsed around him. The contemporary chronicler Charles Wriothesley reported great joy and jubilation at the new queen's arrival in London:

> Accompanied with gentlemen, squires, knights, and lords, with a great number of straungers all in velvet coates rydinge before her [...] with all the Kinges trumpetters, harrouldes, and sergeantes at armes', [Mary, lavishly dressed and bejewelled, was] 'greeted by the Lord Mayor and his brethren the aldermen [...] And all the streets by the way as her highnes rode standing so full of people shoutinge and cryinge Jesus saue her Grace, with weepinge teares for ioy, that the lyke was neuer seene before.[26]

'The joy of the people is hardly credible, Sire', confirmed the Imperial ambassadors, 'and the public demonstrations made at the entry have never had their equal in this kingdom.'[27] Without any Imperial assistance and against huge odds the people's princess secured the throne with a people's army, Mary's great dignity and humility, yet utter determination to press a just cause, being telling in the end. Her triumph by any standards was indeed impressive, but her political inheritance was certainly not enviable.

NOTES

[1] Edwards, *Mary I*, p. 67.

[2] Richards, *Mary Tudor*, p. 91.

[3] 'The Emperor to Van der Delft, 10 May 1549', CSPS, vol. *9*.

[4] 'Van der Delft to the Emperor, May 1, 1550', CSPS, vol. 10.

[5] 'The Emperor to the Queen Dowager, 25 June 1550', CSPS, vol. 10.

[6] For correspondence regarding the plot see 'Report of Jehan Duboys on the matter concerning the Lady Mary, drawn up in full and as nearly as possible in the actual words spoken, Middle of July', CSPS, vol. 10.

[7] For a detailed explanation of the circumstances of the immunity see footnote 6, CSPS, vol. 10. See also 'The Emperor to Van der Delft, 10 May 1549', CSPS, vol. 9.

[8] 'The Lady Mary to the Council of England, January 27 1551', CSPS, vol. 10.

[9] 'Edward VI to the Lady Mary, 28 January 1551', CSPS, vol. 10.

[10] 'The Lady Mary to Edward VI, End of Jan. or early Feb', CSPS, vol. 10.

[11] *Edward VI's Journal*, entry dated 18 March, 1551, in G. Burnet, *The History of the Reformation of the Church of England*. 4 vols. (New York: D Appleton and Co., 1843), vol. 4 , p. 214.

[12] Ibid., p. 216.

[13] ' Mary to Edward', APCE, vol. 3, pp. 338–40.

[14] 'The Queen Dowager to the Bishop of Arras, 5 October 1551', CSPS, vol. 10.

[15] Loades, *Mary Tudor*, p. 121.

[16] J. G Nichols, ed., *Literary Remains of Kind Edward the Sixth*. 2 vols. (London: J. B. Nichols and Sons, 1857), vol. 2, p. 561. The document can also be found in *Luminarium: Encyclopaedia Project – England under the Tudors*, http://www.luminarium.org/encyclopedia/edward6devise.htm accessed 12 August, 2013.

[17] E. Ives, *Lady Jane Grey: A Tudor Mystery* (Chichester: Wiley-Blackwell, 2009), pp. 137–9. Strict genealogical succession would have meant that Frances Grey, duchess of Suffolk, Jane's mother and Henry VIII's niece, should have been named as first in the line of succession but apparently she had waived her claim to the throne. Ibid., pp. 157, 35.

[18] What obscures clarity about Northumberland's intentions is that before finalising the marriage between his son and Jane Grey, Northumberland had been planning to marry his son off to Jane Grey's cousin, Margaret Clifford, the countess of Derby, whose maternal grandparents were Charles Brandon, first duke of Suffolk and Mary Tudor, former queen consort of France and daughter of King Henry VII. It remains uncertain whether this marriage plan was part of a conspiracy to alter the succession or simply a scheme to forge alliances with powerful families.

[19] See Edwards, *Mary I*, pp. 80–1.

[20] Loades, *Mary Tudor*, p. 125.

[21] D. Loades, *John Dudley Duke of Northumberland 1504–1553* (Oxford: Clarendon Press, 1996), p. 240.

[22] Edward stipulated, however, that Jane would be an exception to male rule. If either she or her sisters would have only daughters then the succession should pass to the next male heir.

[23] Eric Ives argues in *Lady Jane Grey: A Tudor Mystery*, that Jane was the legal heir as Henry's Act of Succession was not binding on Edward.

24 Montagu agreed to sign the letters patents on condition that they were to be ratified by Parliament, called for 18 September 1553, which, owing to Edward's death in July, never convened.

25 'M. M. de Courrières, de Thoulouse, Simon Renard and Jehan Scheyfve to the Emperor, 10 July 1553', CSPS, vol. 11.

26 Wriothesley, *A Chronicle of England*, vol. 2, p. 93.

27 'The Ambassadors in England to the Emperor, August 6, 1554', CSPS, vol. 11.

Mary the Politician

M<small>ARY WAS CROWNED</small> at Westminster Abbey on 1 October 1553. She needed a papal dispensation for the ceremony to be conducted under the old Prayer Book, which remained the only legal form of worship. The feasting of the occasion could not disguise the mammoth task that confronted the new administration which 'might have daunted the strongest heart'[1] As England's first queen regnant at a time when women were not considered to be natural political leaders, her inheritance was indeed uninviting. At home she faced an empty treasury, considerable debt, inflation and financial turmoil. She had to tackle the consequences of successive poor harvests and the ensuing famine and rural depression, as well as plague, a rapid rise in mortality, religious confusion and economic and social distress. The contemporary chronicler, John Stow, paints a very bleak picture of life at the time, writing of 'quartan agues' raging 'more vehemently than they had done the last year passed, where through died many old people and especially priests, so that a great number of parishes were unserved and no curates to be gotten and much corn was lost in the field for lack of workmen and laborers'.[2] Abroad, France was up to no good particularly in its role in stirring up Ireland's rebels. Calais, England's remaining possession in France, was poorly defended and vulnerable to a French attack and Scotland was re-emerging as a potential threat. Such uncertainty heightened the need to take the difficult decision as to which of the two great continental powers, France or Spain, should England ally itself with. It was this consideration that was central to the subsequent controversy surrounding Mary's choice of spouse.

Mary's character was complex, the product of both inherited traits and experiences as a neglected child and an imperilled and disinherited princess. She was dignified and kind hearted, yet fearless and courageous, loyal to her servants and simple and sincere in her manner though not someone to suffer fools gladly when confronted by presumption. She was not of great intellect and she could be indecisive and stubborn, but it is somewhat harsh to claim, as Hilda Prescott did, that 'for her misfortune [she] lacked all those gifts of intuition, judgment and political aptitude that Elizabeth had in such full measure'.[3] Her limitations, so Dickens argued, were reflected in her first Council, which was of such 'great numbers and notorious disunity' that 'it lacked antennae, breadth of view and authority to enjoin prudence upon the queen'.[4]

The men who served her were indeed a mixed bag, none of whom she fully trusted. And that included her able, through quarrelsome Chancellor, Bishop Stephen Gardiner. Though imprisoned by Northumberland for his conservative religious views, Gardiner was, in Mary's mind, tainted for having supported both Henry's annulment campaign against her mother and the break with Rome. But notwithstanding her inclination for mercy, her political acumen compelled her to retain many of Edward's councillors. It was easy to identify her most loyal servants, those who had been successful in placing her on the throne, but who had limited political experience. What was difficult was who to pick from the Johnny-come-latelies, those who belatedly attached themselves to her cause in the light of her certain victory. Her father doubtless would have wreaked vengeance on such traitors, overriding the political concerns of the day. Mary, conversely, defied her later reputation for harshness and political imprudence. Of those involved in the Northumberland conspiracy, for instance, only the duke himself was executed in the immediate aftermath. Jane Grey and her husband, the duke's son, Guildford Dudley, were eventually executed after several months in 'honourable imprisonment'[5] in the Tower and only after the involvement of Jane's father, the duke of Suffolk, in the Wyatt rebellion of January 1554 that sought to replace Mary with her sister Elizabeth as queen (see below). Though both Jane and Dudley were innocent of involvement with Wyatt, they were deemed too dangerous to be kept alive. Until then Mary's conscience, even against the advice of the emperor, could not allow her to execute them.[6]

It was perhaps most unfortunate for Mary that the man who bore the greatest influence on her was not an Englishman at all but the new Imperial ambassador, Simon Renard. Mary trusted Renard almost by default for no other reason than his close association with her cousin, the emperor, whom she trusted without reservation. Here, maybe Mary's judgement was left wanting. It is also unfortunate, given Renard's questionable reliability as a witness, that he is one of the main sources of information on both the intrigues and in-fighting in the Council as well as on the relationship between the Council and Mary. His excessively disparaging reports on rifts between the monarch and her Council were in no small part the result of his need to justify his own 'special relationship' with the queen and his attempts to convince her that his advice, particularly on the contentious issue of her search for a spouse, was more prudent than the Council's.[7] This anomalous relationship between Mary and her Council, which perhaps she should have resisted, is something that Renard very much encouraged.[8] Often matters were not even discussed in the Council until Mary had already made a decision. Although in some respects Renard's observations were 'probably justified', they must nevertheless be approached with great caution,[9] especially if it is considered, as Porter noted, that he 'had no direct knowledge of how its (the Privy Council's) business was actually transacted and wanted to represent it to Charles V in the worst possible light'.[10]

It cannot be denied that Mary did create a Council that was at times unwieldy, consisting as it did of forty-four men, many of whom quite frankly hated one another. If Philip's ambassador to England, Count Feria, is to be believed then a reign of confusion and disorder prevailed at the core of Mary's administration. 'I do not know who is the worst of them from the point of view of your Majesty's service', he wrote to Philip on 10 March 1558 about his perception of the situation in the Council, in the wake of Calais's fall to the French:

> but I do know that those to whom you have shown the greatest favour are doing the least for you. Pembroke, Arundel, Paget, Petre, the Chancellor, the Bishop of Ely and the Comptroller are the leading members of the Council, and I am highly dissatisfied with all of them. They do nothing but raise difficulties, whatever one proposes, and never find any remedy. The Privy Council has so many members that it seems no one has been left out, except William Howard who was formerly Admiral; and numbers cause great confusion.[11]

Feria's assessments, however, like those of Renard, need to be approached with caution, prioritising as he did in his dispatches the interests of his master, just as Renard did in his. The actual attendance of the full Council during the last year of Mary's reign averaged eleven[12] with much of the work of government being carried out in committees of the Council that emerged in early 1556 under the guidance of the new Lord Privy Seal, William Paget.[13] There was also an inner ring of select councillors which Philip encouraged to develop.[14] For Mary to have created a smaller Council for the sake of efficiency would have been politically inexpedient given that she would have needed to exclude both men like Petre and Paget who only recently had sought her demise[15] and men like Rochester and Gardiner who had backed her in turmoil. The cull of Edward's Council, however, was substantial. Of the thirty-three members serving in Edward's last Council, twenty-two, whom Mary considered too unpalatable to work with, were excluded.

Critics of Mary's councils are eager to draw attention to their unwieldiness and to the inexperience of the men who Mary chose to serve on them. 'The councillors', Loades noted, in his first study on Mary, 'were not as incompetent as Feria believed, and much of his annoyance was caused by the fact that they had no desire to comply with his wishes. They were, however, beset with uncertainty and bitterly divided, so that the impotence of the English Council was common knowledge among European diplomats.'[16] Among those whom Mary inherited, Loades claimed, there was 'no strong minister' and Mary herself 'lacked the discrimination to appoint one' so much so 'that her own limitations were ruthlessly exposed'. This situation was to make her 'permanently conscious of her inadequacy [. . .] A woman of exemplary piety and domestic instincts, who would have made an excellent housewife, she was compelled to wrestle with problems which would have baffled wiser heads'.[17] Although Loades's assessment of Mary's political abilities may have mellowed somewhat over the years, reference to 'excellent housewives' having been abandoned, his misgivings about her remained. He especially continued to reproach her for not having dropped 'most, if not all, of the Framlingham council', which he maintained lacked 'adequate experience and ability to run the country'. Such 'dithering', he notes not only sent out confused messages but also allowed the 'self-serving' Renard to establish too close a relationship with her. Inexperience and self-confidence, moreover, inhibited her from healing divisions when they appeared, Loades concludes. Philip's influence here, when he was present in England, in remedying this situation was telling.[18]

But notwithstanding the factionalism and inevitable mutual animosity that existed in the Council between Mary's hitherto supporters and opponents, the 'potential for conflict within Mary's administration', as Guy noted, 'must not be exaggerated'.[19] For one, the system of committees and sub-committees off-set, to a large extent, the Council's frequent unwieldiness. In any case, factionalism in the Council was nothing new, having been customary in recent reigns. Furthermore, the size of Mary's Council, consisting of men with a broad range of skills, should not be necessarily viewed as an impediment to efficient governance.[20] 'Discussion and debate', Porter concluded, 'however heated, did not equate to debilitation. There had been many and frequent arguments among councillors in the two preceding reigns. Perhaps the most remarkable thing about Mary's Council is how well, not how badly, it worked.'[21] In short, Mary managed to assemble her Council hastily and effectively in very trying circumstances and by the end of her reign went on to form an administrative machine that in general, as Loades argued, despite his aforementioned misgivings, 'worked with commendable efficiency'.[22]

A further feature of Mary's administration, largely neglected by historians, was the role women played in her entourage of advisors. The core of Mary's Privy Chamber, for instance, consisted largely of women, many of whom were married to leading politicians of the day, such as Anne Petre, wife of the Secretary of State, Sir William Petre. Though no women occupied a key political post, which were all reserved for males, some, like

Susan Clarencius, the Mistress of the Robes, and Jane Dormer, a personal confidant, played important informal roles. Clarencius especially came to wield significant influence in controlling access to the queen on a number of key issues.[23] To have had so many women in authoritative positions was a significant departure from prevailing trends that generally demanded submissiveness from women to the patriarchal order. Emperor Charles, for one, expressed concern about the undue influence of women in Mary's administration.[24] Although the dearth of biographical information on Mary's female confidants makes it difficult to research the role of women in Mary's administration, it alone cannot explain the neglect of the theme, particularly in recent times when the issue of women's equality has been in such vogue. Perhaps if Mary held more 'progressive' religious views, feminist writers would have paid her more attention. There is a strong suspicion, however, that anti-Catholic prejudices have stood in the way of combating erstwhile prejudices of another kind.

Undoubtedly, Mary was less adept than either her father or Elizabeth at resolving disputes in the Council, but she nevertheless attempted, with significant success, many overdue reforms. Beyond the dramatic restoration of Catholicism (see part three), reform of the financial system had a lasting effect on England's economy, where again the creativity of the Marian administration was evident. For instance, as A. G. R. Smith argued, the reform of the coinage in 1554 'established the basic pattern of financial administration for the rest of the Tudor and early Stuart period'.[25] It could have been more successful had it not been for the on-going economic problems, compounded by inherited indebtedness, foreign policy commitments, inclement weather conditions, and successive crop failures in 1555 and 1556, which doubled food prices and caused widespread famine.[26] These circumstances also compromised attempts to establish greater financial efficiency, though despite the difficulties, much here was achieved by the second half of the reign.[27] Moreover, the continued circulation of counterfeit coins that were still being produced to alleviate the effects of debased Henrician and Edwardian issue undermined the administration's attempts at genuine recoinage. Here the Marian authorities were not totally blameless. As Christopher E. Challis argues, their own debasement strategy in Ireland and their 'sheer failure of nerve' to implement a comprehensive plan for full recoinage that was ready to be implemented by the summer of 1557, probably because of fear of adding to the contemporary upheavals, certainly played a part in the continuing coinage problem.[28] Challis, however, added that

> whatever the shortcomings of Mary and her advisors may have been it seems hardly justifiable to support Pollard all the way. Just as no one could sensibly argue that Mary's death eradicated England's need for a sound and stable currency, so it is clear that Elizabeth could never have

tackled the problem of the coinage either as quickly or as effectively as she did, had it not been so thoroughly aired amongst government officials in the immediately preceding years.[29]

In short, though the Marian administration struggled throughout the reign to cope with the demands of the economy, it cannot be accused of lacking inventiveness in trying to meet them. Its achievements in turn off-set to an extent the burden of debt that it bequeathed to its successor.[30] Of course much of the debt that Mary had left indeed had a lot to do with Philip's foreign policy adventures (see below), but it was the failure of the Tudor regimes preceding her (and Elizabeth failed in this too), in addition to the failures of the Marian financial system, to create 'a proper method [. . .] of harnessing the wealth of the country to the needs of the government, which ultimately meant that the revenue system could not cope with the expensiveness of contemporary warfare'.[31]

Of similar long-lasting importance was Mary's active support for the development of what Robert Tittler called a 'national urban policy'. Under Henry VIII *ad hoc* schemes were initiated to address specific urban difficulties[32] but under Mary a consistent policy was developed to deal with a variety of issues from depopulation to unemployment. For instance, initiatives like the Retail Trade Act of 1554, the Weavers' Act of 1555 and the Woollen Cloth Act of 1557 prioritised towns over the countryside in the production of cloth in order to rejuvenate 'decayed, destroyed and depopulated' urban areas.[33] Further reinforcing the central government's 'support for the privileges of corporate towns and boroughs' was the Militia Act of 1558, which made towns and boroughs directly accountable to the Crown for the mustering of their inhabitants.[34] The Act also provided the basis for Elizabethan and early Stuart administrations to raise armies. The enduring impact of the Marian naval reforms should also be acknowledged, which not only enabled the country to confront France effectively between 1557 and 1559 but also laid the foundations for Elizabeth's naval endeavours.[35] Despite 'what one has been led to expect on the part of mid-Tudor government', Tittler concludes, 'conscious support for urban communities at Westminster became more precise in detail, more comprehensive in scope and more regular in execution than ever before',[36] which, he argued, formed 'much of the basis for the relative stability of the Elizabethan regime'.[37] Looked at closely, therefore, the Marian administration generally worked well, which belies the claims that emerged after her death that she left Elizabeth a chaotic and rudderless system.

Accusations of ineptness in her dealings with Parliament are also misplaced. Upon ascending the throne Mary declared her intention to be a parliamentary monarch in line with the precedents that her predecessors had established,[38] a commitment she reinforced by relying much less on proclamations than both of the Edwardian administrations had done and Elizabeth would do.[39] Although Mary may have been less effective than either her father or sister in dealing with Parliament directly, she nevertheless managed to arouse little more than token opposition to her policies among MPs on issues of crucial importance such as religion and her marriage.[40] Only on the issues of succession and the fate of former ecclesiastical property would Mary encounter serious opposition on which she would need to compromise.

Notwithstanding the occasional spats between Crown and Parliament, much of MPs' ire was based on personal grievances rather than on political motivations. The heated exchanges of the session of January 1555 over Mary's attempt to restore first fruits and tenths tax to the pope, which the Henrician regime had garnered for itself, for instance, were probably due more to MPs' protesting against having to remain in London over the Christmas period than to their defending any political convictions.[41] Sometimes the administration's management of Parliament was weak, particularly during its early sessions and sometimes Council faction-fighting spilled over into Parliament, which was unusual, though not unprecedented. Generally, however, Crown–Parliament relations for the period were normal, marked not only by a remarkable degree of continuity but also, contrary to traditional claims, by a considerable degree of legislative creativity, as noted. Indeed, as Loades argues, 'it is not sufficient to label the legislation of these parliaments as conservative and unimaginative'.[42] Perhaps the administration exaggerated threats of sedition, given that it did in fact confront far less social unrest than its recent predecessors did and perhaps it was not very innovative in dealing with social problems it did, however, emphasise 'thorough and systematic restoration', and not just in religious affairs. It was genuinely determined to improve the efficiency of legal practice, and was committed to supporting established economic interest.[43] As such, Guy's claim that 'Mary I will never appear creative'[44] fails to convince.

For all the accusations of weakness and indecision that have been levelled against Mary, she was at the heart of the political decision-making process. Hardened by life, she never baulked at confronting her male advisors when she deemed it necessary, and that went as far as excluding her husband Philip of Spain from matters of state (see below). She may have been 'a submissive wife', but she was also a 'shrewd politician'.[45] The 'picture of Mary', as Porter argued, 'as a woman who had little grasp of what was going on, who could not work with her politicians and was essentially run by her cousin, Charles V, is entirely false'. In short, 'she was no pushover'.[46]

Many within England's political class, however, suspected that Philip commanded undue influence over English affairs which in turn aroused in

Parliament suspicions of his agenda, something that was aggravated by his inability to communicate his intentions in English. Moreover, his frequent absence from England served to reinforce the view that he was merely using England as a pawn for his own foreign policy adventurism. While most of England's leading men accepted the *fait accompli* of Mary's intention to marry Philip, some, particularly from the lesser ranks, remained unconvinced about the assurances included in the marriage agreement that had been drawn up by Parliament that Philip would be little more than a consort. Fears of foreign policy folly and of a full restoration of Catholicism as well as of an imminent invasion of England's court by Spanish gentlemen, were tangible enough to send a rebel army into the field in January 1554 under the command of Sir Thomas Wyatt. Encouraged by French intrigue, the plot to unseat Mary was planned to consist of several coordinated risings which would see Mary replaced by Elizabeth. The new queen would then be married off to Mary's erstwhile suitor, Edward Courtenay (see below), who himself was to lead a revolt in Devon.

Wyatt was poised to take London by the end of January, Mary's meagre forces not being expected to present much of an obstacle. But while her Council was vacillating and Gardiner advised compromise, Mary stayed resolute, even offering to fight herself. Abandoned by most of her councillors and courtiers, she rallied her available forces with a stirring speech at Guildhall on 1 February 1554 that in both content and delivery was every bit as rousing as Elizabeth's famous address to her troops at Tilbury on 9 August 1558 in the face of the approaching Armada. This was not the inept politician of anti-Marian fantasy. The speech is worth recalling:

> Nowe louing subiectes, what I am ye right well knowe, I am your Queene, to whome at my Coronation when I was wedded to the Realme, and lawes of the same (the spousall Ring wherof I haue on my finger, which neuer hetherto was, nor heereafter shall be left off) you promised your allegeaunce and obedience vnto me [. . .] And this I say to you in the woorde of a Prince, I can not tel how naturally the mother loueth the childe, for I was neuer the mother of anye, but certainely, If a Prince and gouernour maye as naturally and earnestly loue her subiectes, as the Mother doeth the Childe, then assure your selues, that I being your Ladie and Maistres, doe as earnestly and as tenderly loue & fauour you. And I thus louing you, cannot but thinke that yee as heartely and faithfully loue me, and then I doubt not, but we shall geue these rebelles a short & speedy ouerthrow.[47]

The impact of the speech proved decisive in galvanising support against Wyatt's forces, a fact that even John Foxe was compelled to admit. Yet it was recorded by generations of historians as a mere footnote, overshadowed by her sister's address to her army at Tilbury. After some delay, Wyatt was driven back, and eventually surrendered without much of a fight, but Mary was not to know the ease with which he would be defeated. Her determination to fight against seemingly bleak odds was illustrative of both her courage and political foresight.

The clemency and leniency that she extended to the rebels is another example that defies the image of a bloodthirsty ruler of anti-Marian fantasy. Although becoming disillusioned with the consequences of her hitherto merciful approach towards her opponents, she continued to display a level of leniency that was out of keeping with the times and against the advice of Emperor Charles who urged greater severity.[48] Of the 480 convicted of treason only 90 were executed including Wyatt and the duke of Suffolk, as well as the other leaders of the rebellion. Another 285 were pardoned before they were convicted. Lady Jane Grey and her husband, Guildford Dudley, as already noted, were the unfortunate victims of the plot. The gruesome sight in several parts of London of executed traitors was moderated by further displays of clemency. Royal pardons, for instance, were extended to the Kentish rebels after they had been paraded through the streets on their way to their executions. Others still, like Sir Nicholas Throckmorton, to Mary's chagrin, escaped execution owing to acquittals by sympathetic juries.[49] The mercy that Mary extended to the Wyatt rebels offers a stark contrast to that of her father's vengeful treatment of the leaders of the Pilgrimage of Grace, which unlike the Wyatt rebellion was not even a protest against the Crown.[50]

The most sensitive issue in the aftermath of the rebellion, however, was what to do with Elizabeth, who had undeniably been compromised by it. The lack of conclusive evidence to implicate her directly in the uprising did not allay suspicions against her, which called her loyalty to Mary into question. Her own admission, when questioned in the Tower after the rebellion, that she had received a message from Wyatt, served to confirm in the minds of her enemies that she was a liability to Mary's throne. Her failure to report the incident further raised suspicions against her. Renard for one urged Elizabeth's execution, frustrated with what he saw were legalistic niceties that had convinced Mary to do otherwise.[51] Irrespective of what Mary's conscience dictated, it was Philip who ultimately saved Elizabeth from the axe. The last thing he would have wanted was for Mary, Queen of Scots, who was betrothed to the heir to the throne of France, to have succeeded Elizabeth as Mary's heir. What would have removed the threat of Protestant succession, which Mary had not managed to do in Parliament, would also have given Francis an advantage that Philip could not tolerate. Temporal concerns here took precedence over confessional affiliations. Concerns over Elizabeth's involvement were the likely reason Courtenay was saved from the block too. Exiling the man who knew about the extent of Elizabeth's involvement in the plot was preferable to having him expose her under intense interrogation.[52] The circumstantial evidence against Elizabeth, which at the very least pointed to her foreknowledge of the plot, would have sufficed to have had her condemned for treason at other times. Instead, she was subsequently to live in relative comfort in Woodstock Palace, Oxfordshire, albeit under close supervision. This was certainly not the severe incarceration that Foxe referred to in his accounts.[53] Although murmurs and rumblings continued against the Spanish marriage, as well as against Mary's religious and foreign policies, they would never again provoke open rebellion.

*

Mary's foreign policy was complex. She has been often attacked for reducing England to little more than a pawn of Habsburg interests. However, this is a view that at the time was based more on fears of Spanish intrusions than of actual realities, and ever since more on anti-Marian sentiment than on measured opinion and which does not bear up to serious scrutiny any more. For one, the first eighteen months of Mary's reign were incident free abroad as well as one of triumph and relative tranquillity at home, the trouble with Wyatt notwithstanding. It was not until early 1555 that matters began to turn in foreign affairs, though many of these, such as the machinations against her by the new pope, Paul IV, either were beyond her control or, as the loss of Calais in January 1558, were not the disasters that they subsequently were purported to have been.

Much of the criticism of her foreign policy was provoked (and has been ever since) by her choice of spouse. It was naturally assumed that Mary would marry not only to produce an heir but also to be directed in the manly arts of politics. Given the prevailing trend that wives should be subordinate to their husbands, Mary's choice of husband carried with it enormous significance for the fate of England. And with Mary now thirty-seven years of age, and rapidly approaching the end of her child-bearing years, haste was of paramount importance. Mary herself sought to marry quickly to secure her Catholic inheritance, and deny the throne to her sister Elizabeth. But she was determined to marry someone of her own choosing, something which unsurprisingly provoked considerable concern among her leading subjects, who were keen on her marrying someone whom they perceived would not compromise either England's or their own interests. And this meant her marrying an Englishman.

Mary's choice of husband, Prince Philip of Spain, the son of Charles V, has been attacked by generations of historians as being one of her greatest errors, which it was claimed subordinated England to the interests of the Spanish Habsburgs and brought disasters to the country. High levels of anti-Spanish feeling in England's society, which emerged following the Reformation, ensured that her decision would not be well received. Hostility towards Spain among the common folk was generally rooted in coarse xenophobia and in some quarters in anti-Catholicism, while among the rich and powerful there was a fear that a Spanish marriage would bring with it a huge entourage of unwelcome Spanish officials who would undermine their ambitions and aspirations. Mary's own determination of strictly separating personal and public spheres as her grandmother, Isabella, had done so successfully after marrying Ferdinand of Aragon was lost on most Englishmen, who naturally assumed that her husband would dominate her in public as well as in private affairs in line with contemporary trends. What certainly was not lost on the English was the potential benefit to the Habsburgs of an alliance with England in strengthening their position *vis-à-vis* France. And this would mean embroiling England in Habsburg foreign policy adventures. So great were these anxieties that even Emperor Charles initially advised Mary to marry an Englishman. It was only after Renard has assured him of the stability of Mary's administration that he began to suggest his son as a potential suitor. It would seem, therefore, that her choice of husband was not a prudent one, that is once the English alternative is assessed.

Already a veteran of the diplomatic marriage game, Mary had never had an English suitor proposed to her. The fear that many had about a home-grown marriage was that an English spouse could potentially upset the balance of political forces among the aristocratic classes in the realm, undermining the very interests cherished by those who opposed a foreign marriage. In any case, there was a distinct shortage of suitable candidates. The most widely touted was Edward Courtenay, who, though of royal blood, had little else going for him. He was ten years Mary's junior and only recently had been released by her from a fifteen-year period of imprisonment in the Tower. He had been arrested as a young boy in 1538, together with his father, the earl of Exeter, who had been executed by Henry VIII for treason.

Mary's determination to override the concerns of her subjects was not based on some obstinate desire to show her strength. Rather, it was based on her principled belief that royal prerogative should determine her choice of spouse. Her final decision was hers and hers alone, albeit taken after extensive consultation with Emperor Charles and other close confidants as well as after much personal torment and prayer. Crucially, however, she did subject her decision to parliamentary approval. The resulting marriage agreement placed significant restrictions on Philip's role as 'king of England' which enabled Mary to skilfully juxtapose her marital duties with those of a monarch. She was adamant that her dutiful obedience to Philip as his wife would not impinge on her running of the country. Having played no part in the negotiations, Philip, as used as he was to a very patriarchal world, found his role as consort not merely odd but very offensive. Though harbouring significant reservations about the marriage, he was duty bound to his father and accepted its terms that in short reduced him to little more than an advisor. For her part, in marrying Philip of Spain and heir both to the New World, as well as to vast swathes of land in Europe, Mary married someone who was probably one of the most eligible bachelors in Europe.

The marriage ceremony finally took place at Winchester Cathedral on 25 July 1554, the feast of St James, the patron saint of Spain, merely a day after Mary and Philip had met and only four days after Philip arrived in England. The ceremony, while lavish, was replete with symbolism to denote Philip's subordinate status to appease those who remained sceptical about him and his intentions. Once the ceremony was over, both emerged clutching swords to represent their kingly status. Significantly, Philip was positioned to the left of Mary to be reminded that he was king of England only by virtue of his marriage and not through any inheritance. This order of precedence was maintained during the banquet. Philip was, for instance, served from silver plates while Mary from gold. But so intricate were these rituals that to the uninitiated their meaning would have been lost. Even their limited value threatened to be undone by the practice adopted on Imperial insistence that Philip's name should always feature first in all proclamations and acts of Parliament, lest, as Renard put it, human and divine law should be transgressed.[54] Carrying with it no political significance, the practice was nevertheless symbolically loaded to confirm in many people's eyes where the real power in England lay. Charles, to reassure the people of England that Philip had no interest in furthering his ambitions as its king, as well as to enhance Philip's dignity, transferred the crown of Naples from himself to his son. But if anything, Philip's new title further raised the suspicions of sceptics, not without some justification, who feared that he would draw England into the murky world of Italian politics (see below).

It was difficult for many, even those who understood the complex technicalities of the marriage treaty, which these rituals sought to convey, to believe that Mary's marital arrangements could depart so radically from the established norms of the sixteenth century. The issue in September 1554 of the so-called 'double coin', bearing the image of both monarchs with a crown hovering above each, provoked further controversy. What was nothing more than a polite gesture towards Philip fuelled suspicions against him further among those ready to exploit any symbolic ambiguity. Although the practice of including both monarch and consort on a coin is common today to mark royal occasions, it departed radically from contemporary tradition that excluded consorts from such imagery to denote their lack of political power. There seemed to be nothing that Mary could do to allay the fears and suspicions that many continued to hold towards Philip. In fact, it is hard to see, noted Richards, 'what else she could have done to protect herself from the charge that she had rendered herself simply her husband's instrument'.[55]

For much of the population, however, the Spanish marriage was not a problem. Wriothesley wrote of an enthusiastic reception for the king and queen of 'great provision and pageants' as they progressed through London on their way from Winchester following their wedding.[56] Personal prejudice, nevertheless, especially when it served a political purpose was not easy to combat. Reading Foxe's account, for instance, of tensions between the large Spanish entourage of several thousand that accompanied Philip to England and local populations leaves the impression that there was much ongoing Protestant resentment to the Spanish marriage.[57]

Many commentators ever since have been inclined to accept such accounts at face value. There was certainly tension between the English and the Spanish at both court and in those parts of the country where large concentrations of newly arrived Spaniards could be found. Some of these tensions were based on long-standing mutual prejudices and ignorance of one another's culture and language, some on personal rivalry and sporadic incidents. Philip did all he could to minimise the opportunities for squabbling, ordering his personnel to be on their best behavior whilst in England. But it was a difficult situation to control. Many in his entourage, having travelled reluctantly to England, a country widely considered to be a European outpost, quickly came to view its people and culture, not to mention its climate, with disdain. Awareness of the widely publicised persecution of Catholic martyrs like More and Fisher during the Henrician Reformation remained strong and had already contributed much to the negative predisposition that Spaniards had formed towards their English hosts. Quarrelsome, exceedingly prone to drinking and possessing a tendency to street violence was a common opinion about the English among the Spanish visitors,[58] who in turn fed local prejudices by their arrogance and disrespectful behaviour towards their English hosts.[59] The contemporary diarist, Henry Machyn, wrote of sporadic mutual violence and even murder, which was duly punished.[60]

All this was to be expected given the circumstances. But amidst the tensions there was also a considerable degree of mutual respect and goodwill, especially towards Philip. The entrenched resentment towards Philip in the City of London was understandable. His constant favouring of Flemish tradesmen over English and his refusal to allow the latter access to Spanish colonies in South America and Africa made him few friends in England's financial centre.[61] But generally there exists no strong evidence that Philip was as unpopular among the English as he has been frequently portrayed to have been. Most of the virulent anti-Spanish sentiment that had been provoked by the announcement of the Spanish marriage subsided considerably after Philip's arrival as most of his entourage soon left England to fight continental wars. Philip himself quickly earned considerable respect from English courtiers for his eager participation in chivalric contests and festivities that were laid on for him as well as for his dignified behaviour and constructive contributions to the administration of the country.[62]

In truth, however, Philip was too preoccupied with his own territories to be interested in England's internal affairs, especially as he received so little from them through the restrictions of his marriage treaty. He was never crowned, on the insistence of the Council, and did not even receive any lands with which to pay for his household in England. But whatever his position was, and it was by no means clear as to what it was, he was not, noted Porter, 'the grim Spanish Catholic bogeyman and foe of fearless Elizabethan England that he was so often represented. The burden of ruling creased and changed him later in life, but the Philip of the 1550s was a different man'.[63] If anything, as has already been noted, his contribution to England's administration was positive, his vigorous personality acting as a source of stability in an often divided Council, whose members he used to meet regularly.[64] But even in matters where he did have some influence, Mary ultimately had the final say. Philip, in short, 'found himself the unwilling pioneer of the role of consort to an English sovereign queen, which would only much later be developed by Victoria's Albert and Elizabeth II's own Philip'.[65] In fact, so humiliating and circumscribed was his role as consort that it is extraordinary that he agreed to it at all. It would be naïve, however, to claim that Philip did not seek to use his marriage to Mary for his own foreign policy purposes. By resurrecting the Anglo-Spanish alliance, terminated by Henry VIII's divorce from Katherine of Aragon, he hoped to reinforce his position in Italy. If this policy were to clash with Mary's or England's immediate interests, so be it, even at the expense of the Catholic faith, as Philip's protection of Elizabeth after the Wyatt rebellion demonstrated.

But Mary was certainly no dilettante in foreign affairs. She had been embroiled in the diplomatic cut and thrust almost from birth, having been betrothed at the age of two to the infant French dauphin, who was to be the first in a long line of suitors. In itself the alliance with Spain was nothing new, with both Mary's grandfather, Henry VII, and her father having made it a central pillar of their foreign policies. Mary's strategy was not merely borne out of loyalty and gratitude to Emperor Charles but out of pragmatic considerations similar to those that had motivated her predecessors and as such represented not regression but continuity.[66] Not only did the marriage gain for England an alliance with the superpower of the time but also it strengthened England's trade links with the Netherlands and Germany, though as noted above, access for England's traders to Spain's colonial possessions was not guaranteed. What trade advantages England did acquire of course came at a price. Charles gained considerable leverage to reinforce his north-eastern possessions while Philip expected and received assistance in his struggles against France. It was England's embroilment in Philip's French adventures that has attracted particular criticism from Mary's detractors. How deserved has this been?

The French king, Henry II, had been provoking Mary from the very start of her reign. France's machinations had been at the heart of Northumberland's promotion of Jane Grey as they had been during Wyatt's failed coup in 1554. France also gave Sir Henry Dudley tacit support in his attempt to unseat Mary in 1556, as well as considerable backing to Thomas Stafford who led a hundred or so Protestant exiles on an ill-fated and bizarre 'invasion' of Scarborough in April 1557. If France's constant threat to Calais, England's last possession in France, is factored into Mary's approach to the French problem, then her grounds for declaring war on France were very compelling, irrespective of any interests that Spain may have had in stopping Calais from becoming a French springboard to attack Habsburg lands. Although Philip certainly urged England to make necessary preparations to defend Calais, informing the English Council in a letter he sent from Brussels on 2 January 1558 that Calais was about to be invaded by the French,[67] he played no direct part in the final decision to declare war. Indeed, Mary had proclaimed war on 7 June 1557, using her own prerogative, thus breaking from the practice of jointly declaring on issues with her husband (see below).[68] This certainly riled Henry, who felt humiliated for having had war declared on him by a woman. Judging from the widespread hostility among Englishmen towards French nationals living in England that her proclamation of war provoked, her act was not unduly unpopular.[69]

The deputy of Calais, Lord Thomas Wentworth, had raised the alarm about the massing of French troops on the outskirts of the town on the same day that Philip sent his letter. His warning, however, came too late. On the 7 January Calais fell. Amidst the recriminations that followed, which went as far as conveniently to accuse Calais's Protestant exiles of treason, Wentworth included, Mary's and Philip's reputations were undoubtedly damaged.[70] At the time the loss of Calais was a humiliation and a psychological blow to an increasingly ailing Mary and to a country already disheartened by climatic turmoil and economic burdens. For Mary's detractors ever since, the fall of Calais was confirmation of the incompetence of her administration. In reality, however, Calais's defences had been neglected and mismanaged for some time. The Imperial ambassador, Jehan Scheyfve, van der Delft's successor, had reported in January 1551 that as far as he 'could ascertain, the English are not keeping the best of guard over there (in the English possessions round Calais), providing neither sufficient victuals nor anything else'.[71] And though it is true that the government did act incompetently to relieve the Calais garrison, England's defeat turned out in the long-term to be a financial blessing given the high cost of maintaining control of the outpost. In fact, Philip, the least to blame for the loss, came to the correct conclusion that England had no interest in regaining it. Mary may well have regretted the loss of Calais, although Foxe's account of her deathbed confession to her trusted servant, Susan Clarencius, that Calais lay in her heart,[72] probably owes more to poetic licence than reality. Parliament was certainly not willing to fund an expensive expedition to regain the town. In his report on French military activity to the Doge and the Venetian Senate, Michiel Surian, Venetian ambassador to Spain, noted that when Parliament debated whether or not 'to provide for the recovery of Calais, many members said that the times were so bad, that before undertaking a war which might be the ruin of the kingdom, the matter should be well considered; and that if the French have taken Calais, they thus took nothing from the English, but recovered what was their own; so should this opinion be that of the majority, but little assistance can be hoped for from those people'.[73]

If speculation that Northumberland had been planning to cede Calais to the French in return for military assistance against Mary[74] is considered then, as Richards noted, 'the loss of Calais – certainly deeply regretted by Mary – was not necessarily viewed as a disaster by all Englishmen until it became another part of the Protestant black legends of her reign'.[75]

Ironically where Mary experienced particular difficulties as a result of her entanglements with the Habsburgs was in her relationship with the Papacy. At the time when she was restoring Catholicism to England the new pope, Paul IV, Giovanni Pietro Carafa, was compounding her domestic problems with intrigue against her in Rome. Here, Dickens has a point when he noted that Mary's and Cardinal Pole's devotion to Rome offered some strange rewards.[76] The reasons for this were complex, having both contemporary and long-standing origins. For several decades now, the rivalry between the Habsburgs and France had dominated continental affairs, which the lesser powers, among which was England, could at best hope to influence from the sidelines. Key to European domination, in turn, was control of Italy. Philip, having been granted the kingdom of Naples by his father Charles, and who would become king of Spain in January 1556, following Charles's abdication from the throne of Spain as well as the Empire, was determined to step out of his father's shadow. His quest, however, would inevitably draw Mary into the cauldron of Italian politics.

A conflict would not be long in coming. The French, having invaded Italy in 1551, wanted now to confront in battle the un-bloodied prince and allied themselves with the pope, a Neapolitan, for whom Philip's investiture in Naples, which was a papal fiefdom, was an affront. The attempt to expel the Habsburgs offered rich pickings for both the Papacy and France. Under a Franco-Papal treaty in October 1555, Sicily was to be divided between the two, Naples and most of Milan was to go to France while Sienna and parts of Milan were to be absorbed into the Papal States. Florence, on the other hand, a ducal Habsburg protectorate, was to become an independent though pro-French and pro-papal republic. Taken outside this broader context, Pope Paul's attitude towards England cannot be fully understood.

The prospect of war with the Papacy for Mary was dreadful, especially at a time when she was restoring Catholicism to England. Together with the archbishop of Canterbury, Cardinal Pole, she tried to mediate in the dispute and counselled Philip to exercise caution. For Philip, though not yet directly involved, to threaten the pope in his own backyard was politically hazardous and religiously objectionable, not to mention insulting. The next few months saw attempts at peace negotiations between the parties. The truce at Vaucelles in February 1556 with England's mediation, between the French king Henry II and Charles, who would formally remain emperor until August, did little to resolve Habsburg-Valois tensions. The pope, though seeking a peaceful solution to the crisis, at least publicly, was of a temperamental character and all too frequently allowed his fury at the Habsburg presence in Italy to overwhelm him. Amidst the mutual recriminations, Philip finally launched a pre-emptive strike against Rome itself, which triggered French intervention in defence of the pope. Mary, caught between her loyalty to the pope and obligations to her husband, was eventually left with no choice but to declare war on France in June 1557, though, as noted above, not without good reason in defence of English interests. The muddle that the subsequent conflict in Italy became gave the warring parties few benefits. With no genuine unity of purpose between the Papacy and the French and with the Habsburgs stronger than either had anticipated, the conflict soon turned into a messy stalemate.

Philip's campaigns in France were considerably more profitable for him than his Italian adventures, giving him the laurels that he had so craved. England's military efforts in France, while not extensive, were the best among the combatants assailing Saint Quentin.[77] But as so often in the past when England rallied in support of Habsburg interests, its own interests suffered. When unexpectedly Philip and the pope settled peace terms on 14 September 1557, the English army was left stranded in France. Moreover, the victory at Saint Quentin served only to antagonise the French further, compelling the English to maintain a high state of military alert back at home. At a time of deteriorating economic conditions and political tensions in England, and of an ever increasing threat to Calais, such foreign policy adventures seemed frivolous to many of Mary's critics.

England's involvement in Philip's Italian adventure indeed was to have a devastating impact on its domestic affairs, especially on its restoration programme. Despite doing all she could to avoid conflict with the pope, to the point of denying Philip direct military assistance in Italy, Mary would inevitably attract Paul's chagrin over her steadfast support for Cardinal Pole in the growing conflict between Rome and the Cardinal. Even the cessation of hostilities between the Papacy and Philip was to have no bearing on this matter. Here, however, Paul's antagonism towards Pole is even more difficult to fathom than his hostility towards Mary. Pole himself had done much to reduce Habsburg-Valois tensions, so he was shocked when in April 1557 he was informed by Paul that he, together with the other legates from Philip's lands, was to have his legatine authority revoked. Pole actually had been referred to by name and had been recalled to Rome to face investigations for heresy. Although Paul also withdrew all his legates from Spain, his reason to strike out at Pole requires an examination of the state of the relationship between Pole and Paul some twenty years earlier.

Ever since Pole had been made Cardinal in 1536, his theology has been suspected by the then Cardinal Giovanni Pietro Carafa (the future Pope Paul IV), owing to his association with the humanist reform group, the Spirituali. Paul suspected him of being at the centre of a heretical conspiracy involving a number of other prominent cardinals, notably Giovani Morone, who was arraigned to appear in front of the Roman Inquisition on suspicion of habouring Lutheran sympathies.[78] The reigniting of Habsburg–Valois conflict reinforced Paul's antagonism towards Pole. Paul's anger was further provoked by Mary's refusal to allow Paul's replacement as legate, William Peto, to enter England. Peace between the Papacy and Philip changed matters little for Pole. The tragic fact was that Pole had long ago totally reconciled himself to papal authority after the spiritual crisis he had endured. The double irony here is indeed curious. Pole's eventual theological reconciliation with the Papacy and Mary's need for papal support for her restoration programme did little to assuage Rome's hostile attitude to both Pole and England. It was in fact Pole's personal belief in obedience to the Church which had not only allowed him to overcome any doctrinal error he may have flirted with in the past but also had explained his emphasis on discipline, obedience and ritual in the progamme for the restoration of the Church.

Despite Pope Paul's order, Pole continued to act as legate in England. 'In this respect, at least', noted John Edwards, 'the Church in England seemed, with Mary's tacit approval, to have reverted to operating as a "national" Catholic Church, as it had done in her father's time',[79] with Mary acting *de facto* under royal supremacy. In a strongly worded letter to the pope of 26 July 1557, she appealed to him 'to restore the legation in the person of Cardinal Pole', questioning why 'a legate, after confirmation by him, and after performance of so many good works that it may be said with truth that through him alone England resumed her obedience to the Church, should be recalled without cause'.[80] If there had been any hope of reconciliation between Rome and England it was dashed with the intensification of the Habsburg–Valois tensions in March 1558 over the formal succession to the Imperial Crown of Charles's brother, Ferdinand, which the pope deemed had negated proper procedure. Paul showed further disdain for England's Church by neglecting its internal affairs, causing it lasting damage. His delay, for instance, in replacing several deceased bishops by the end of Mary's reign severely reduced the capacity of the episcopal bench to challenge Elizabeth's religious settlement of 1559. Paul's inaction is placed into perspective when one considers that Elizabeth's uniformity bill passed the House of Lords by only one vote.

A further irony in all this was that Pole himself had been favourite to become pope on three occasions, first after the death of Paul III in November 1549, then in March 1555 after the death of Julius III and again after the three-week pontificate of Marcellus II, who died in May 1555. But on each occasion he had been defeated by a combination of French lobbying and Carafa's intrigue against him. Though supported by Habsburg allies, Pole was further disadvantaged by his absence from the latter two conclaves, being at the time immersed in England's restoration programme.

Although England, on balance, gained little from its association with the Habsburgs, it gained no less than it had gained from Spanish alliances of the recent past. And it was not as if its embroilment in Habsburg foreign policy had been particularly extensive or driven primarily by Spanish interests. When the need arose in June 1558, for instance, for English naval assistance to be sent to the Flemish coast following French assaults to the south, Mary dispatched her fleet to protect her possessions in the Channel Islands instead. The reluctance of her government to offer greater commitment to foreign affairs was ultimately seen by Philip and his advisors as disloyal and even treacherous.[81]

Reassessment of the Marian administration reveals a picture that is at odds with the image of Mary as politically inept. The government's reforms revealed a degree of creativity for which it has rarely been credited, while Mary's general pragmatism belies depictions of her as an uncompromising fanatic. But perhaps the greatest surprise to those accustomed to view Mary in the light of her 'bloody' reputation, is the way she approached her opponents. The picture here is far removed from the traditional portrayal of her as a merciless and unforgiving woman, bent on exacting vengeance on those who had affronted her. In both religious and secular affairs she demonstrated a degree of moderation that her father, at least, would have baulked at.

NOTES

[1] Prescott, *Mary Tudor*, p. 232.
[2] E. Howes, *Annales or a General Chronicle of England Begun by John Stow, Continued and Augmented by Matters Foraign and Domestique, Modern, unto the End of the Present Year, 1631* (London: Richardi Meighen, 1631), p. 634.
[3] Prescott, *Mary Tudor*, pp. 228–9.
[4] Dickens, *English Reformation*, pp. 355–6.
[5] Whitelock, *Mary Tudor, England's First Queen*, p. 185.
[6] 'The Ambassadors in England to the Emperor, 16 August 1553', CSPS, vol. 11.
[7] D. Loades, *The Reign of Mary Tudor: Politics, Government and Religion in England, 1553–8* (London and New York: Longman, 1991), p. 25.
[8] Ibid.
[9] Ibid., p. 28.
[10] Porter, *Mary Tudor, the First Queen*, p. 234.
[11] 'Count Feria to Philip, 10 March 1558', CSPS, vol. 13.
[12] Loades, *Mary Tudor*, p. 225.
[13] Ibid., p. 225, p. 264.
[14] Ibid., p. 264.
[15] Both men had signed the king's letters patent which conferred the succession onto Lady Jane Grey on 21 June 1553, having been cajoled by the duke of Northumberland to do so. However, after Northumberland's departure from London to confront Mary they switched sides and started campaigning in Mary's favour.
[16] Loades, *Two Tudor Conspiracies*, p. 9.
[17] Ibid., p. 10.
[18] Loades, *Mary Tudor*, p. 264.
[19] Guy, *Tudor England*, p. 230.
[20] Edwards, *Mary I*, p. 109.
[21] Porter, *Mary Tudor, the First Queen*, p. 234.
[22] Loades, *Mary Tudor*, p. 238.
[23] Edwards, *Mary I*, p. 112.
[24] 'The Emperor to his Ambassadors in England, 23 August 1553', CSPS, vol. 11.
[25] A. G. R. Smith, *The Emergence of a Nation-State: The Commonwealth of England 1529–1660*. London: Longman, 1997, p. 83.
[26] C. S. L. Davies, 'England and the French Wars', in J. Loach and R. Tittler, *The Mid-Tudor Polity, 1540–60* (London: Palgrave Macmillan, 1980), p. 161.
[27] Loades, *The Reign of Mary Tudor*, p. 254.
[28] E. Challis, *The Tudor Coinage* (Manchester: Manchester University Press, 1978), pp. 117–18.
[29] Ibid., p. 118.
[30] For detailed discussion of the Marian financial system see Loades, *The Reign of Mary Tudor*, chapters 7, 9, 10.
[31] Loades, *The Reign of Mary Tudor*, p. 361.
[32] Lehmberg, *The Reformation Parliament*, pp. 97, 212.
[33] The Woollen Cloth Act, 1554, cited in R. Tittler, 'The Emergence of Urban Policy, 1536–58', in J. Loach and R. Tittler, eds., *The Mid-Tudor Polity, 1540–60*. Problems in Focus (London and Basingstoke: Palgrave Macmillan, 1980), p. 74.
[34] Ibid., p. 87.
[35] Ibid., pp. 83–4.

36 Ibid., p. 75.

37 Ibid., p. 74.

38 Whitelock, *Mary Tudor, England's First Queen*, p. 228.

39 Loades, *The Reign of Mary Tudor*, pp. 222–4.

40 Ibid., 1991, p. 214.

41 J. Loach, *Parliament under the Tudors* (Oxford: Clarendon Press, 1991), p. 96.

42 Loades, *The Reign of Mary Tudor*, p. 221.

43 Ibid., pp. 221–2.

44 Guy, *Tudor England*, p. 226.

45 Whitelock, *Mary Tudor, England's First Queen*, p. 285.

46 Porter, *Mary Tudor, the First Queen*, p. 231.

47 'The Oration of Queene Marie in the Guild Hall', *Acts*, book 10, 1583, p. 1442.

48 The Emperor to his Ambassadors in England, 23 August 1553', CSPS, vol. 11.

49 'Simon Renard to the Emperor, 22 April 1554', CSPS, vol. 12.

50 Proportionally, however, the execution toll in the wake of the Wyatt rebellion was far higher than that in the wake of the Pilgrimage: around 90 out of 3000 rebels, 216 out of around 35,000.

51 'Simon Renard to the Emperor, 22 April 1554', CSPS, vol. 12.

52 Richards, *Mary Tudor*, p. 153.

53 'Queene Mary. Gods prouidence in preseruing Lady Elizabeth in Queene Maries tyme. Anno 1558. The myraculous preseruation of Lady Elizabeth, nowe Queene of England, from extreme calamitie and danger of life, in the time of Q. Marie her sister', *Acts*, book 12, 1583 p. 2115.

54 'Simon Renard to the Emperor, 7 June 1554', CSPS, vol. 12.

55 Richards, *Mary Tudor*, p. 161.

56 Wriothesley, A *Chronicle of England*, p. 122.

57 See for instance, 'Q. Mary. The Martyrdome of Iohn Ardeley, and Iohn Symson. Iohn Tooly', *Acts*, book 11, 1576, p. 1526; 'Q. Mary. A broyle betwene the spaniards and English men Order taken in the Parliament for Q Maryes childe', *Acts*, book 10, 1583, p. 1504.

58 According to the Spanish eye-witness chronicler, Andrēs Muñoz, see Edwards *Mary I*, 2011, p. 213.

59 Edwards, *Mary I*, p. 213.

60 *The Diary of Henry Machyn: Citizen and Merchant-Taylor of London (1550–1563)*, ed. J. G. Nichols (London: Camden Society, 1848), pp. 66–79.

61 Loades, *Mary Tudor*, p. 202.

62 Edwards *Mary I*, pp. 210–11.

63 Porter, *Mary Tudor, the First Queen*, p. 271.

64 Edwards, *Mary I*, p. 208, 270–2.

65 Ibid., p. 206.

66 Porter, *Mary Tudor, the First Queen*, p. 243.

67 Edwards, *Mary I*, p. 310.

68 APCE, vol. 5, p. 53.

69 Richards, *Mary Tudor*, p. 215.

70 Edwards, *Mary I*, p. 310.

71 'Advices from Jehan Scheyfve', January 1551, CSPS, vol. 10.

72 'Quene Mary. The vnprosperous succeße of thinges vnder Queene Mary'. *Acts*, book 12, 1583, p. 2122.

73 'Michiel Surian, Venetian ambassador with King Philip, to the Doge and Senate, 12 February 1558, 1164', CSPV, vol. 6.

[74] See E. H. Harbison, *Rival Ambassadors at the Court of Queen Mary* (Princeton: Princeton University Press, 1940), pp. 50–3; Richards, *Mary Tudor*, p. 204.

[75] Richards, *Mary Tudor*, p. 222.

[76] Dickens, *English Reformation*, p. 384.

[77] 'Juan de Piñedo to Francisco de Vargas (Extract), 27 August, 1554, 339', CSPS, vol. 13.

[78] Cardinal Morone was cleared of any suspicions by Paul's successor, Pius V.

[79] Edwards, *Mary I*, p. 325.

[80] 'Bernardo Navagero, Venetian ambassador at Rome, to the Doge and Senate, 5 August 1557, 981', CSPV, vol. 6.

[81] Edwards, *Mary I*, p. 318.

III

Creative Reconstruction
rather than Blind Reaction

✠ 9 ✠

The Challenges of the Restoration and the Nature of Later-Medieval and Early Tudor Religion

O F ALL MARY'S GREAT CHALLENGES it was her programme of restoring the old faith, from which most people had not spiritually departed, that has been in the spotlight ever since her death. The methods used to implement the programme have overshadowed her achievements in other policy areas, which were many, and arguably even more challenging. By and large it has been negatively assessed and overwhelmingly declared a failure.

Traditional Reformation scholarly argument went something like this: the Reformation happened because there was a popular demand for it. The coercive legislation that successive regimes enacted may have created a climate for reform, but conversion was a voluntary process among the people which in turn ushered in a Protestant England. Consequently, the Marian restoration was doomed to failure amidst a tide of popular resistance and anti-clerical and anti-papal sentiment. Mary's Church was trapped in a 'medieval past',[1] unable to withstand the robustness of Protestant theology or even to assimilate the Counter-Reformation that was sweeping across Europe. Mary's efforts were hampered further by the incompetence and sterility of her administration[2] that ensured that English Catholicism remained in a 'parlous situation'.[3]

This corpus of viewpoints that convinced generations of the folly and cruelty of Marian religious policy no longer commands much authority. A word of caution is needed here, however. As selective and as skewed as the work of historians of the past was, a revision of this viewpoint should not offer a mere reaction that is just as flawed. Fortunately, the passing in England of the political and ideological order that reinforced erstwhile history together with the availability of new archival sources has enabled scholarly revision to render obsolete the old received history about the nature of both the English Reformation and the Marian restoration.

'The fact that there *was* a Reformation', noted Christopher Haigh, 'does not mean that it was wanted: it does not imply that there was a deep-seated popular demand for religious change.'[4] The immediate root of the English Reformation was Lollardy, initiated in the mid-fourteenth century by John Wycliffe, a theologian and philosopher from Oxford University. In challenging key doctrines of the late-medieval Church, Wycliffe was to pre-empt Martin Luther and other continental reformers as well as shape the thought of early Protestant reformers in England. Yet in reality it is difficult to characterise Lollardy as a movement at all. Rather, it was 'a highly amorphous phenomenon',[5] whose social impact was both temporary and limited. Undoubtedly there existed reformist opinion among certain social groups, notably the emerging urban elites, but to suggest that Lollardy made significant inroads into doctrinal orthodoxy[6] is not convincing.[7] Similar conclusions can be made about anti-clericalism, which traditionally historians claimed had been widespread. Again, while there are recorded instances of anti-clerical protests there is no evidence of widespread tension between the laity and the clergy during the late-medieval to early Tudor period (see below). Criticism of the clergy was restricted to certain areas and cities and to certain vested interests. Common lawyers, notably in London, for instance, were eager to play on the marginalisation of the Church's juridical authority and as such were well represented among the contemporary critics of the Church.[8] There is little in fact to suggest that the late-medieval Church was not a thriving and popular institution whose subversion was the work of a small minority that eventually triumphed under Elizabeth largely for political reasons. 'The establishment of Protestantism as a mass religion', as Haigh put it, 'was thus a consequence, not a cause, of the political Reformation. The Reformation brought Protestantism, not Protestantism the Reformation.'[9]

This claim, however, raises the question: if the Reformation was indeed imposed from above, why did it ultimately succeed if the target audience was generally hostile? To answer this question it is important to appreciate the nature of religious practice both on the eve of the Reformation and during it.

For 'the Reformation from below' thesis to have any credibility it needs to demonstrate that Protestantism managed to establish itself rapidly among the population, both in rural and urban areas. Here the thesis immediately runs into trouble. Given that Protestantism was a faith based on the Word rather than on 'superstitious' ritual, it was never going to rapidly capture the imagination of the illiterate, who made up most of rural society in England at the time. Unsurprisingly, urban areas where most literacy was to be found, was where reformist sympathies were strongest, though even here considerable regional variations were evident. Moreover, a ritualistic religion that reflected the ebb and flow of communal rural life was likely to be more appealing than a bibliocentric religion that encouraged personal reflection over Scripture.

Attempting to rescue the 'Reformation from below' thesis by arguing that Protestantism emerged slowly though decisively as reformist doctrines became better known is no more convincing when it becomes clear that this argument too relies as much on selective evidence as the 'rapid Reformation from below' thesis does. Neither interpretation is in fact adequate to account for the complexity of the Reformation. The Reformation was certainly not inevitable and at any number of points, as Haigh noted, 'in 1529, 1532, 1536, 1538, 1539, 1540, 1543, 1546–7, 1549–50 and 1553, events could have developed in dramatically different ways if the balance of power had shifted only slightly'.[10] The Reformation was most epitomised by a struggle within successive regimes between courtly factions as well as by popular resistance against government religious initiatives, the latter manifesting itself well into the Elizabethan period to the irritation of government officials.

So what kind of religion was late-medieval Catholicism? The pre-Reformation Church, it was long claimed, had been dominated by the clergy, and offered the laity little scope to participate in either its administration or public worship. Mass was largely a mystery, hidden behind screens, and celebrated in Latin, which was incomprehensible to most people. Communion was taken rarely and good preaching was a hit-and-miss affair.[11] It appears, however, that this image was little more than a caricature. There is little doubt that both Catholic piety and the Catholic Church as an institution, especially in terms of recruitment of clergy, were flourishing. And little credibility can be afforded the oft-made claim that medieval popular religion was rooted in superstition, with orthodoxy being the preserve of the well-educated and wealthy.[12] True, medieval religious practice was very diverse, which in itself was a sign of its vigour and vibrancy, but as Duffy noted, 'within the diversity [. . .] there was a remarkable degree of religious and imaginative homogeneity across the social spectrum, a shared repertoire of symbols, prayers, and beliefs which crossed and bridged even the gulf between the literate and the illiterate'.[13]

There was in fact no sign before the Reformation that England was moving away from religious ritualism. Visual imagery and rituals were a way to both deepen faith and express devotion. From carols at Christmastide to processions at Candlemas and Corpus Christi, from devotional fasting to the elaborate ceremonies of Holy Week, the Church year offered ample scope for the laity to participate in religious activity.[14] In fact, a very developed sense of ritualism and liturgical knowledge, as well as a deep awareness of the complexities of the liturgical calendar, emerged among the laity, affecting every aspect of life. So entrenched were religious rituals that, despite being under continual attack from Protestant reformers, many of them survived well into the Elizabethan era.

However, it was attendance at Mass that was the most common religious experience and daily attendance was not unusual. Eucharistic piety, rooted in the belief in the real presence of Christ in the sacrament of Communion, was regarded as a communal practice and though the receiving of Communion was for most an annual occurrence, usually at Easter, seeing the elevated host was considered a huge privilege that brought with it abundant blessings. The communal nature of Mass in turn challenges the claim that the laity was alienated from the liturgy by rood screens and Lenten veils that separated the congregation from the high altar.[15] Proper understanding of the liturgy confirms the intricate integration of every part of it into the whole with rood screens and veils, as Duffy explains, being 'manifestations of a complex and dynamic understanding of the role of both distance and proximity, concealment and exposure [...] marking boundaries between the people's part of the church and the holy of holies [...], the sacred space within which the miracle of transubstantiation was effected or, in the case of the veil, between different types of time, festive and penitential'.[16] The high altar, in front of which was the rood screen, was in any case one altar among many in churches. At these, which were not concealed behind screens and veils, 'low' masses were celebrated. Moreover, these altars, their construction and maintenance, were frequently financed by the laity, who instructed the clergy to celebrate Masses and recite special prayers for personal reasons.

The laity, from the poorest to the wealthiest, were at the centre of parish life, contrary to the claim that the people were alienated from religious activity and that religiosity was waning on the eve of the Reformation. During the century and a half before the Reformation perhaps as many as two-thirds of English parish churches underwent significant rebuilding, alteration and refurbishment, most of which was funded by guilds and bequests of wealthy benefactors.[17] Undoubtedly some of the motives were holier than others, association with a prestigious institution or seeking self-preservation in the after-life featuring strongly among them. But generally a communal spirit rooted in a sense of piety was the overarching motive of benefactors.

It does of course have to be noted that the level of sophistication of devotion was commensurate in part with the kind of religious instruction received. While undoubtedly there was much ignorance of doctrine among both the laity and clergy, it was nowhere near as widespread as Protestant reformers claimed. Whereas preaching, for instance, was in many cases substandard, pastoral care was not. Religious instruction took many forms, from various literary sources to pictorial and carved sources as well as a wealth of religious plays. The volume of material, notably elaborately decorated primers, increased considerably with the coming of printing, which undermines the common perception that printing was primarily the tool of Protestants (see below). What is intriguing and which further challenges allegations of institutional decay and waning religiosity is that religious decorative art proliferated in many parts of the country particularly during the three decades preceding the Reformation and was particularly vividly expressed in elaborately decorated side-chapels dedicated to specific saints. Pictorial sources in both primers and among church furnishings and in side-chapels did not proliferate, as is commonly perceived, to compensate for people's ignorance of Latin. It is true that fluency in Latin was rare among the laity as well as much of the clergy. Nevertheless, as Duffy noted, the Mass, particularly the consecration, 'gave legitimacy to the sacred character of Latin itself, as higher and holier than the vernacular'.

Moreover, Latin commanded universal respect as a language that communicated the faith, its mystery evoking a sense of sacredness even to those who did not fully comprehend it.[18]

Although some devotions to saints enjoyed more popularity than others, devotions generally tended to be grass-roots initiatives rather than impositions from above. The veneration of saints not only was associated with supernatural assistance and protection on earth to ease the perilous road to eternal life but also was acclaimed as a means of worshipping God owing to the closeness of saints to Him. Moreover, veneration was more often than not a communal activity manifesting itself, for instance, in communal prayers in search of healing for the sick. Doubtless some cults of saints offered much scope for fraud and abuse of the gullible, which in turn encouraged historians and Protestant reformers to depict late-medieval piety as ignorant and superstitious. Yet devotions to saints would not have flourished and proliferated had there not been a belief in genuine cases of supernatural assistance and healing. Furthermore such devotions perhaps indicate that the medieval mind was much more attune to what constituted both the sacred and evil than the modern mind is, as immersed in relativist morality as it is. And while the scope of devotional practice was broad and diverse, it involved the full spectrum of society.

The avoidance of sin indeed was an intrinsic feature of late-medieval piety. What highlighted a sense of urgency of one's failings was the deep awareness of personal mortality. Images of death and cadaver tombs were common features in churches. To a modern mind such manifestations may seem morbid and doom-laden. But in actuality they were reflections of piety given that musing on one's mortality was accompanied by a commitment to virtuous living. Awareness of imminent death heightened a sense of urgency to make recompense for wrong-doing to one's neighbours either through altruistic deeds or intercessory prayers to ease the passage of souls through Purgatory on to eternal joy in heaven.

Belief in Purgatory was widespread, and people in fact went to great lengths to save souls, both their own and those of others. Gruesome depictions of Purgatory were always accompanied by instructions on repentance and the avoidance of sin and were designed to frighten people into virtuous living and to avoid presumptuous death-bed repentance. Far from being a place of hopelessness, as Protestant reformers dismissively caricatured it, Purgatory represented a place of hope from which the purified soul, having avoided the eternal fires of hell, could progress towards eternal joy in heaven. Participation in intercessory prayers not only served to relieve the distress of individuals but also allowed for humble worship before God. In the second volume of his *The Supplication of Souls*, published in 1529,[19] Thomas More eruditely commented on this and other issues, in reply to Simon Fish's crude and hyperbolic satire, *A Supplication for the Beggars*,[20] published a few months earlier.

It would seem, therefore, that faith in late-medieval England both among the learned and simple was complex and pious, overwhelmingly orthodox and seldom superstitious, while the Church in England itself exhibited few signs of decay.

*

Myths about the state of religiosity in England are underpinned by claims of widespread anti-clericalism, which have been cited by Protestant propagandists and historians alike as explanations for the Reformation but which have never been convincingly substantiated. Specific events like the Hunne affair of 1514[21] or references to the salaciousness of Cardinal Wolsey are cited as being representative of the Church and in turn as causes of anti-clericalism which generated 'flashpoints' among the laity[22] that moved the authorities to enact anti-clerical legislation. The Imperial ambassador, Eustace Chapuys, ironically has been an oft-cited source for claims of widespread anti-clericalism.[23] In his report to Emperor Charles in December 1529 Chapuys relates that 'nearly all the people here hate the priests'.[24] Because Chapuys would appear not to have had a vested interest in exaggerating the situation, his comments have been taken at face value. Closer inspection of the context of Chapuys's dispatches, however, suggests that something altogether different is at play here. For one, his comments were overwhelmingly motivated by anxiety over the fate of Katherine of Aragon. Such concerns, therefore, as Haigh argued, were likely to have 'made him hyper-sensitive to any challenge to the Pope or Church courts'.[25] Chapuys claimed that the people were being manipulated by the authorities to reject papal authority to 'persuade them to consent to this

[Boleyn] marriage' so that 'they will get large sums of money by the sale of Church property, and a judicious investment of the same'.[26] For all his concerns, however, he could well have been referring only to the situation in London, where he was based, one of the country's Protestant hot-spots. Or perhaps events in London led him to generalise about the situation across the country. Whatever the case may be, interpretations of his reports are certainly not straightforward.

Chronicle accounts of anti-clericalism also have to be treated with caution as many emanate from those who had vested interests to promote or axes to grind. Fish's *A Supplication for the Beggars*, for instance, adds grotesque spice to a socio-theological critique of the Church, accusing the clergy not only of reducing people to misery and wretchedness but also engaging in ubiquitous sexual promiscuity. There was plenty here to feed John Foxe's fertile imagination several decades later. Much less crude but nevertheless similarly robust in its attack on the clergy was Christopher St Germain's work, especially his *Treaties concerning the division between spirituality and temporality*, published in 1534, in which he defended the notion of royal supremacy.[27] Both Fish and St Germain were common lawyers, a group that stood to gain much from the weakening of the Church's juridical authority, St Germain, in Dickens's words, being 'the embodiment of the old hatred felt by common lawyers for ecclesiastical jurisdiction'.[28] Such works, despite their exaggeration and partiality, influenced the drafting of the anti-clerical legislation between 1529 and 1534 that restricted the Church's financial and juridical practices,[29] which in turn pre-empted the declaration of the royal supremacy itself in 1534. Even more scholarly work such as John Skelton's satirical poetry purporting to highlight Cardinal Wolsey's corruption and avarice or the hostile assessment of the Cardinal by contemporary court historian Polydore Virgil should arouse suspicion as both men harboured grievances against Wolsey for having them arrested.

Many more examples of literary tracts could be cited to labour the point. But though such works were used widely as propaganda, they cannot be deemed to be fair representations of the situation in the Church, nor a reflection of widespread opinion among the laity towards it. A minority of priests did engage in sexual practices forbidden in canon law, but the majority did not.[30] Pluralism did exist in a minority of parishes, but neglect of duty was rare as non-resident priests were almost always replaced by competent curates.[31] In fact, it was not until after the break with Rome that major problems with pluralism and neglect of parishes began to appear owing to a decline in the number of clergy.[32] The financial corruption and moral laxity of a few Church officials like Thomas Wolsey may have provided 'a lurid theme for anti-clerical demagogues' and 'a heavy bludgeon to beat churchmen',[33] but such character traits were hardly representative of the entire clergy. In fact the clergy in terms of wealth, competence, morality and education, as Dickens himself admitted, was 'as a body so heterogeneous as to defy generalisation'.[34] Neither were atypical legal cases like the Hunne affair, cited above, representative of the workings of Church courts. The case may have provoked some people of London to 'rage against the clergy' in its aftermath, as Polydore Virgil suggested, but its long-term effects were minimal.[35] Suspects were rarely treated harshly by Church courts and those who were charged usually admitted guilt. Where possible, judges urged parties to arrive at a quick agreement to save cost, belying claims that Church courts were money making bodies.[36]

The workings of ecclesiastical courts were generally fair and efficient, attracting few suits from those subjected to their rulings. Their records reveal very little evidence of widespread anti-clericalism, before the Reformation at least.[37] It is also crucial to note that the prestige associated with the sacraments, especially the Eucharist, implied an 'enormously high doctrine of priesthood',[38] whose authority to perform the miracle of the Mass was external to any temporal authority and over and above any abuses of it that may have been perpetrated.

It is most likely, therefore, that anti-clerical legislation had little to do with reform of the Church or that it was a reflection of popular discontent with the clergy but much with the pursuit of specific vested interests. The anti-clerical laws passed in 1529, for instance, were highly influenced both by merchants, especially the Mercers' Company, whose trade had been severely disrupted by Wolsey's foreign policy, and lawyers, who sensed an opportunity to enhance their client base once the authority of Church courts was undermined. Unsurprisingly, both groups were heavily represented in the House of Commons.[39] The hatred of Wolsey was such in some quarters that his enemies took the occasion of his arraignment, the proceedings for which had opened the first session of the 1529 Reformation Parliament, to attack the Church that he had served. The Wolsey factor indeed was to be a significant motive behind the passing of the first series of anti-clerical laws over and above any reformist motives that their advocates may have harboured. In fact there was to be little connection between this legislation and subsequent anti-clerical laws, given that during the intermediate years any anti-clerical zeal that had prevailed in the Commons had abated. The later legislative attacks on the Church were overwhelmingly political in nature instigated by the rising star of the Council, Thomas Cromwell. They sought to bully the pope into granting the king the annulment of his marriage as well as to enhance the prestige of the Crown-in-Parliament idea that Cromwell was championing. Opponents of the bills, and there were many, in both houses of Parliament, but especially in the Lords, were brow-beaten into compliance by threats and intimidation, not least by Cromwell himself.

Complaints against priests for not performing specific duties were inevitable as it is inevitable that all institutions staffed by mere mortals will experience dissatisfaction with their performance. The descent of the Holy Spirit upon the Apostles, which has come to be known as Pentecost, represented Christ's own reservations about leaving the Church solely in the hands of quarrelsome men. But the 'chasm' between the clergy and the laity, which Dickens claims had been steadily growing, simply did not exist.[40] In fact it is somewhat inconsistent of Dickens to claim that 'the secular clergy tended to encounter resentment as an unduly privileged caste within the national body',[41] having a few pages earlier, as noted above, stated that the clergy was a heterogeneous body that defied generalisation. As Guy noted, despite errant priests having undoubtedly abused their authority, which did irritate the laity, 'the pre-Reformation church was free from major scandals'.[42] And even Dickens concedes that 'it is possible to exaggerate the importance of particular tensions and personal feelings' as causes of the Reformation.[43] It would indeed be inconceivable that a few individual cases would have incited a popular movement. Haigh reiterates the point that anti-clericalsim did not become prevalent until the Elizabethan period when a combination of cheerless services, ritual-free worship, a dearth of priests and a haughty clerical mentality brought about by a professional cohesion that was much more pronounced than in the pre-Reformation Church, acted to alienate the laity from the clergy.[44] Anti-clericalism was therefore more a result of the Reformation than a cause of it.[45]

*

The English Reformation was a disparate affair. For one, there were several reformations or mini-reformations – the Henrician, two Edwardian and the Elizabethan – each with specific characteristics and with varying degrees of intensity. It is also crucial to distinguish between the 'official' reformation of statutes and enforcement and the much vaguer 'popular' reformation of alehouse debates, acquiescence and low and high-level defiance.[46] Indeed, notwithstanding the parliamentary resistance that was referred to above, extra parliamentary opposition to the state religious legislation was considerable, if never on the scale of continental Europe where wars of religion raged for decades. However, as noted above, a number of armed rebellions, motivated in varying degrees by animosity towards the new religious order, did flair up and some, especially the so-called Pilgrimage of Grace of 1536, presented a genuine challenge to the regime.

The relative restraint of protest has been attributed to a variety of factors, notably, as Dickens argues, to its disparateness and lack of coordinated leadership.[47] There is indeed some merit in this claim. Some protested against the marriage, others against the end of papal supremacy while others still against the Dissolution of the monasteries. The trickery, for instance, used by the king and his arch-lieutenant, the duke of Norfolk, to suppress the Pilgrimage certainly blunted its impact. But that should not take away from its potential to disrupt the Tudor order. If the manner in which the Pilgrimage was suppressed is anything to go by then Henry's coercive structures doubtlessly can be credited for being the main reason for limiting opposition to his religious reforms. Dickens himself acknowledged that the 'King was far from compassionate by temperament and he bears the moral guilt for not a few avoidable executions'.[48] In addition to the printing presses, which the state controlled and through which Cromwell disseminated a barrage of propaganda in praise of the new order, there was a widespread network of informers 'to discover all who speak or preach' against the Henrician religious changes.[49] Where organised rebellions were absent, resistance emanated from individuals such as More and Fisher. All in all, in spite of the harsh penalties at least two hundred Catholics willingly met their deaths for their faith under the Tudor monarchs while many more were killed in rebellions and post-rebellion executions (see chapter 12). The suppression of the Pilgrimage of Grace did not extinguish resistance. Cromwell's agents reported much iconoclasm and frequent flouting of religious legislation.

The cause of reform suffered a major setback with the execution of Anne Boleyn for treason in 1536. Henry, a religious conservative by nature, had never been a great enthusiast of radical religious reform and though he brutally suppressed the Pilgrimage for political reasons, he was already having second thoughts about the extent to which reform had ventured. Although in October 1538 Cromwell managed to implement yet more injunctions that further attacked the old faith, in November Henry proclaimed a halt to radical reform, starting a process that was to reverse many of the most Protestant aspects of the Reformation to date. To stop radical preaching, which he blamed for the growing disorder in the land, he ordered in 1539 for the Ten Articles of 1536, by which many Protestant principles were enforced, to be replaced by the Six Articles, which reaffirmed much of the abandoned doctrine and ceremonial.[50] Confirming the conservative reaction was *A Necessary Doctrine and Erudition for any Christian Man*, published in 1543 and commonly known as 'The King's Book', which sought to settle on-going theological battles with an emphasis on traditional belief. The same year the Act for the Advancement of True Religion restricted the reading of Scripture to certain educated quarters of society after Henry discovered that universal access to the Word of God provoked, as the Act declared, 'malicious minds [...] to subvert the true exposition of Scripture [...] by printed ballads, rhymes, etc., subtly and craftily to instruct His Highness' people, and specially the youth of this his realm, untruly'.[51] Officially, England of course remained a Protestant country, espousing much that separated it spiritually as well as institutionally from Rome, but in appearances at least, it seemed to have settled on a course of 'national Catholicism'.

However, notwithstanding the many trappings of Catholicism that the Church exhibited, political obstacles made it very difficult to turn the clock back. With Henry's death in 1547, the conservative faction led by Bishop Stephen Gardiner, which had enjoyed the king's favour, once more had to do battle with Protestant reformers. Thomas Cranmer, who had been cowed by the conservative atmosphere of recent years, was now determined to acquire the upper hand under the Protestant regent, Lord Protector Edward Seymour, the duke of Somerset. For the time being a half-way house between Protestantism and Catholicism was reached, as demonstrated by the 1549 *Book of Common Prayer* which abolished key Catholic ceremonials, as well as images, processions, clerical celibacy and chantries while retaining fundamental Roman doctrines, notably transubstantiation. It was a compromise, however, which satisfied neither reformers nor Catholics, producing regional variations of compliance. Opposition to the religious changes was a contributing motive for the rebellions that broke out in the western counties, as well as Oxfordshire and Yorkshire. Religious worship was to be further radicalised under Seymour's successor, the duke of Northumberland. The eradication of the remnants of Catholic ceremonial and doctrine was accompanied by a frenzy of destruction and looting of churches that stripped them of altars, side chapels, images, rood screens and shrines. What ensued can only be described as authorised destruction and theft on an unprecedented scale. Churches were emptied of all but what was deemed by the new religious order as the bare essentials for worship as defined in the second *Book of Common Prayer* of 1552, their plate and other valuables being appropriated by the Crown. There was to be no doctrinal compromise here. The Eucharist was declared as nothing more than a memorial, which necessitated the replacement of altars by moveable wooden tables. Traditional vestments that tracked the progress of the now defunct Church calendar were replaced by plain white surplices, and the remaining chantries were dissolved, their abolition having commenced in the last years of Henry VIII's reign. The intercessory prayers that they offered were prohibited. In fact, Northumberland was determined 'to leave nothing in the official worship of the Church of England which could provide a toehold for traditional ways of thinking about the sacred'.[52]

The wanton destruction and grand theft of Church property and the desacralising of religious ceremonial sanctioned something unsavoury, breeding a sense of detachment from Christian virtue. The English Reformation ran parallel to and complemented the rise of a new economic system that normalised the husbandry of wealth for the sake of it. Before, the possession of land and cattle was for personal consumption and excessive covetousness, and materialism was restrained by condemnation from the pulpit. Now, wealth was being utilised in a consumerist way and for the acquisition of power. As such, England was rapidly emerging as a commercial European power-house. Count d'Egmont, an Imperial ambassador to the Netherlands, wrote to Philip in January 1554 about his impending visit to England, 'that the Emperor has given us no money to make presents when called for, though more is to be done with money here than in any other country in the world'.[53] 'Needless to say', noted Prescott, 'there had been successful men, saving men, greedy and unscrupulous men in the past, but by the teaching of the church, by laws, by regulations of the Guilds, they had been hampered, and certainly their ambitions had never been sanctioned by public opinion. Now, although from the pulpit such ambitions were still denounced, a new theory of commerce was growing up.'[54] The huge land and property grab by the upper classes, especially the expanding gentry, did nothing to alleviate the condition of the poor. Neither did it further the spread of the new faith. In play here was not godly virtue but unbridled self-interest.

What indeed is striking – and this is a crucial reason for Mary's swift restoration of Catholicism – is how little progress had been made to entrench the new faith in society. In 1547, the Swiss reformer Martin Bucer observed that the English Reformation was too negative, imposed 'by means of ordinances which the majority obey very grudgingly, and by the removal of the instruments of the ancient superstition'.[55] Outside London, Essex, Bristol, Cambridge and East Anglia, Protestantism was confined to small pockets, though in rural areas it was virtually non-existent. There are many explanations for this, though beyond generalisations the picture is not straightforward. London and the eastern ports, for instance, by virtue of their geographical position, were more in contact with continental reform influences through trade with Protestant areas, than were the western coastal ports which in turn traded more with Catholic countries like Spain, Portugal and Ireland.[56] This did not, however, prevent Bristol and landlocked Coventry from developing into Protestant centres, nor northern towns like Hull, Leeds and Beverley in a region otherwise noted for the greatest resistance to religious reform. In anomalous situations like these the influence of local secular and religious elites in moulding the religious beliefs was important.

Indicators of trends in belief that have been subjected to quite a lot of analysis are personal wills, which have been used both to prove and disprove the growth of reformist sympathies. Dickens, one of the first to research this area, placed great emphasis on the increasing replacement of traditional forms of reference such as to the Virgin Mary or to saints with references exclusively to God, taking this as testament to the waning of certain beliefs.[57] Duffy, however, does not regard such omissions as a significant indicator of changing beliefs. For one, he noted, there was nothing exclusively Protestant about making reference only to God in wills. It was common before 1530 for orthodox Catholics to commit their souls exclusively to God in their wills and as such there was no theological reason why they should not continue this practice especially when it became expedient to do so to avoid legislative sanctions.[58] Moreover, in many cases wills before the Reformation that made reference only to God in their preamble included in their main bodies demonstrably Catholic traits such as bequests for Masses and requests for both intercessory prayers and works of charity.[59] So, rather than offering evidence of abandonment of traditional beliefs, the omission of traditional forms of reference during the 1540s and 1550s could just as well point to testators preferring not to be provocative in these uncertain times or it could mean nothing at all. The revival of traditional forms of wills immediately after Mary's accession, when no legislative pressure to dispense with Catholic practice was deployed, may well bear this out. It is unclear whether the revival of traditional forms of reference, noted Duffy, represents Protestants returning to Catholicism, or Catholics reasserting their beliefs with greater confidence.[60] It is simply difficult to tell. Ultimately, without a greater degree of certainty either way, the claim that the changing forms of reference in wills during this time represented waning commitments to traditional beliefs is unreliable.

Information garnered from state visitations to parishes during these years about levels of compliance with the new diktats is similarly inconclusive. Although conformity seemed to have been widespread, this in itself, Duffy argued, 'implies nothing about the beliefs of clergy, wardens, or laity in the parishes, and we are certainly not dealing here with mass evidence of spreading Protestant conviction'.[61] The mass sale of Church plate and religious objects similarly offers scant evidence for growing Protestant sympathies. Frequently, such action was taken not only to comply with legal requirements but also to prevent their confiscation by the state. Yet in spite of the harsh penalties for non-compliance with the new laws, there was much concealment of religious objects, so much so that many parishes were able to resume Catholic worship following the accession of Mary with many or most of the required objects for services.[62] That is not to deny, however, that many parishes did rid themselves of their religious objects either out of indifference to the old faith or out of genuine conviction towards the new one. The continued resistance of these parishes to the Marian restoration did in turn contribute to the failure of the Marian administration to reinstall Catholicism in many places.

*

The fate of Protestantism, like that of any new belief system, inevitably became entangled with existing religious culture and ultimately depended on complex social situations dominated by rivalries between individuals, families, social groups and entire communities.[63] It is also crucial to remember that the law was only as potent as was the determination of the unpaid local officials, such as the justices of the peace, to enforce it, given that there was neither a standing army nor a regular police force that could be utilised for such purposes.[64] Yet notwithstanding the pitfalls of generalisations about the geographical spread of religious belief and of the possible exaggeration of the levels of Catholic resistance, the unpleasant manner in which reform was being implemented certainly drew people away from its message. As Guy noted, 'Decatholicisation and looting were no valid substitutes for missionary work'.[65] Moreover, having destroyed familiar ritualism, reformers had the disadvantage of having to spread their faith by literary means to a largely illiterate population. Dickens himself conceded that the progress of proselytisation was slow and that by 1553, 'the greater part of the nation was neither ardently Protestant nor ardently Catholic'.[66]

NOTES

[1] Dickens, *English Reformation*, p. 383.

[2] Elton, 1977, pp. 376–96.

[3] Dickens, *English Reformation*, p 383.

[4] C. Haigh, 'Introduction', in C. Haigh, ed., *The English Reformation Revised* (Cambridge: Cambridge University Press, 1992), p. 4.

[5] Ibid.

[6] Dickens, *English Reformation*, pp. 41–62.

[7] Duffy, *The Stripping of the Altars*, pp. xxii–xxiii; Haigh, 'Introduction', p. 5.

[8] Haigh, 'Introduction', p. 6.

[9] Ibid., p. 8.

[10] C. Haigh, 'The Recent Historiography of the English Reformation', in Haigh, ed., *The English Reformation Revised*, p. 31.

[11] Guy, *Tudor England*, p. 22.

[12] Duffy, *The Stripping of the Altars*, p. 2.

[13] Ibid., p. 3.

[14] Ibid., p. 15.

[15] Ibid., p. 111, n. 63.

[16] Ibid., p. 111.

[17] Ibid., pp. 132–4.

[18] Ibid., p. 218.

[19] T. More, 'The Supplycatyon of Soulys 1529', in Gerald L. Carroll and Joseph B. Murray, The Yale Edition of *The Complete Works of St. Thomas More*, 15 vols. (New Haven: Yale University Press, 1990), vol. 7.

[20] S. Fish, 'A Supplycacion for the Beggars', 1559, in Carroll and Murray, The Yale Edition of *The Complete Works of St. Thomas More*, vol. 7.

21 After refusing to pay the standard mortuary fee in March 1511 to the rector of St Mary Matfelon in Whitechapel following the funeral of his dead five-week-old son Stephen, Richard Hunne was found hanged in his cell on 4 December 1514. Ever since, the Hunne affair has evoked great passions, being used by Protestants as an example of Church corruption. Hunne's accusers claimed that he had committed suicide, but the coroner's jury subsequently concluded that he had been murdered by William Horsey, the chancellor to the bishop of London, and two other Church officials. All were eventually acquitted owing to a lack of evidence, which provoked a public outcry. The case was complex. Hunne's original transgression was not initially pursued by the Church. Not until Hunne with a friend challenged the rector of St Michael Cornhill in November 1511 over the title of a tenement was he sued by the rector of St Mary Matfelon for the mortuary fee. He subsequently appeared in the ecclesiastical court of audience in April 1512, which found in the rector's favour. The case would have ended there and then. On 27 December 1512, however, Hunne attended vespers at St Mary's, only to be confronted by the priest, who refused to proceed until Hunne left, shouting at him, according to John Foxe, that he had been excommunicated. Hunne subsequently sued the priest for slander as well as counteracting a charge against the Church court in which he had been arraigned, claiming that the court had acted on authority of a foreign power and therefore had no jurisdiction in England. It was then that the Church acted, by charging Hunne with heresy. A swoop on his house found an English Bible with a prologue that was sympathetic to the Lollard, John Wycliff.

22 Guy, *Tudor England*, p. 24.

23 For instance, P. Marshall, *The Catholic Priesthood and the English Reformation* (New York and Oxford: Oxford University Press, 1994), p. 211; Dickens, *English Reformation*, p. 138.

24 'Eustace Chapueys to the Emperor, 13 December 1529, 232', CSPS, vol. 4.

25 C. Haigh, 'Anti-clericalism and the English Reformation', in Haigh, ed., *The English Reformation Revised*, pp. 59–60.

26 'Eustace Chapueys to the Emperor, 13 December 1529, 232', CSPS, vol. 4.

27 T. F. T. Plucknett and J. L. Barton, eds., *St. German's Doctor and Student* (London: Selden, Society, 1974).

28 Dickens, *English Reformation*, p. 140.

29 For a list of the laws. Guy, *Tudor England*, p. 123.

30 Guy, *Tudor England*, p. 24.

31 Haigh, 'Anti-clericalism and the English Reformation', p. 61.

32 Ibid.

33 Dickens, *English Reformation*, p. 64.

34 Ibid., p. 72.

35 Dickens, *English Reformation*, pp. 137–8; Haigh, 'Anti-clericalism and the English Reformation', p. 61.

36 Haigh, ibid.

37 Ibid., p. 68.

38 Duffy, *The Stripping of the Altars*, p. 110.

39 Lehmberg, *The Reformation Parliament*, pp. 8, 24–6, 81–2. See chapter 5 for details of anti-clerical legislation.

40 Dickens, *English Reformation*, p. 89.

41 Ibid.

42 Guy, *Tudor England*, p. 24.

43 Dickens, *English Reformation*, p. 89.

44 Haigh, 'Anti-clericalism and the English Reformation', p. 74.

45 Ibid.

46 D. M. Palliser, 'Popular Reactions to the Reformation during the Years of Uncertainty, 1530–1570', in Haigh, ed., *The English Reformation Revised*, p. 94.

47 Dickens, *English Reformation*, p. 176.

48 Ibid.

49 Duffy, *The Stripping of the Altars*, p. 385.

50 See chapter 6, n. 24.

51 *The Act for the Advancement of True Religion*, 12 May 1543, restricted the reading of the Bible in English to clerics, noblemen, the gentry and richer merchants. 'Women, artificers, apprentices, journeymen, serving-men of the rank of yeoman and under, husbandmen and labourers' were prohibited from reading the Bible. Women of the gentry and nobility were only allowed to read the Bible in private.

52 Duffy, *The Stripping of the Altars*, p. 473.

53 'Count d'Egmont to Prince Philip, 7 January 1554', CSPS, vol. 12.

54 Prescott, *Mary Tudor*, p. 145.

55 Cited in Guy, *Tudor England*, p. 223.

56 Palliser, 'Popular Reactions to the Reformation', p. 104.

57 Dickens, *English Reformation*, p. 206.

58 Duffy, *The Stripping of the Altars*, p. 508.

59 Ibid.

60 Ibid., p. 522.

61 Ibid., p. 481.

62 Ibid., pp. 491–2.

63 Palliser, 'Popular Reactions to the Reformation', p. 107.

64 Ibid., p. 109.

65 Guy, *Tudor England*, p. 223.

66 Dickens, *English Reformation*, p. 251.

The Nature of Mary's Personal Faith

ENGLAND UP UNTIL ITS BREAK FROM ROME was a staunchly Catholic country, governed, as we have seen, by a king who had been awarded the title Defender of the Faith in 1521 by Pope Leo X for his steadfast defence of the seven sacraments against Lutheran heresy. Mary made it a personal mission to restore Catholicism to England. But what kind of Catholicism was this to be? To understand this it is crucial first to examine Mary's own faith.

Mary was born in a climate of religious uncertainty when many of the key pillars of Church doctrine were being challenged by radicals like Martin Luther as well as by more conservative figures like the respected Dutch scholar, Desiderius Erasmus, who questioned the spiritual relevance of certain long-entrenched practices such as pilgrimages. The education that Mary received meant that she was well versed in contemporary religious thought as well as the ideas of Erasmus and More which her humanist Spanish tutor, Juan Luis Vives had instilled in her. Although she had sided with her mother in the annulment crisis and passionately continued to believe in the integrity of her position, she was at ease with some, though certainly not all, of the Henrician reforms. Her interest in humanism would continue into her adulthood and was most vividly demonstrated by her collaboration with the evangelical Katherine Parr, the last of Henry's six queens, on the translation into English of Erasmus's *Paraphrases on the New Testament*, which under Edward was to be placed alongside the English Bible in every parish church (see below).

Mary's faith belies the simplistic accounts that have plagued scholarly as well as popular opinion for generations of her being an unreconstructed religious bigot. Those who come to this conclusion are not only factually incorrect but are guilty of committing the ultimate historian's fallacy by totally ignoring the context of the period. Though firmly rooted in tradition, her faith was willing to embrace innovation, pretty much in line with the reformist Catholicism of her time. It needs to be remembered that the religious crisis that shook England and Europe had a profound impact on Mary. Having been punitively separated from her mother, effectively declared a bastard by her father and then, under severe pressure, having to submit to royal supremacy, Mary was subjected to an inordinate amount of emotional and physical stress which only her faith could alleviate. Prayer would offer her a sanctuary for the rest of her life when she was confronted by trials. It was in prayer, for instance, that after several weeks of doubt and personal trauma, she decided to marry Philip, a man many years her junior, whom she had never seen and who had a less than chaste reputation. So David Loades's claim that her reliance on faith 'probably tells us more about her emotional state than her piety'[1] is difficult to justify.

Loades is also sceptical about the extent to which Mary's faith was orthodox and goes as far as to claim that at this point Mary, despite her enthusiasm for the Mass, 'was not ostensibly a Catholic at all, but what her father had made her – a conservative humanist with an extremely insular point of view', whose faith was based more on personal convictions than on doctrinal orthodoxy.[2] Loades casts further doubt on her religious orthodoxy by suggesting that her submission to royal supremacy in the face of personal danger stands in sharp contrast to her protestations against Edwardian religious policy in the face of similar dangers, which he claims was indicative of a level of acceptance of the Henrician settlement which she could not extend to Edwardian deviations.[3] Her proclamation of 18 August 1553 on 'freedom of conscience', her first proclamation, in which she included her father among 'all progenitor kings of the realm' who had maintained 'their subjects in Christ's true religion'[4] certainly seemed to suggest that she did indeed accept her father's settlement as consistent with her own faith. However, given the context of the proclamation, her reference to her father is open to an altogether different interpretation. For one, the proclamation does not differentiate between the period prior to the break from Rome and that which followed it, in which case Mary could be said to have had the former in mind when issuing the proclamation. A political explanation could also be elicited. Throughout Edward's reign Mary had disputed the legality of her brother's religious reforms on account of his age. As such, her reference here to her father may well have been intended to contrast the legitimacy of his reforms, if not agreement with them, with the illegitimacy of those of her brother.[5] There is nothing conclusive, therefore, in the proclamation or in her acceptance of the Henrician settlement and her rejection of Edward's that could cast doubt on Mary's religious orthodoxy. The sister to Edward VI was not the daughter to Henry VIII, having grown further in courage and stature to oppose what she fervently believed was intolerable error. Submission to Henry, therefore, was more motivated by fear than endorsement of his religious policy.

It is also true to say that Mary had no coordinated plan of action and reacted when she felt she could take no more. This is precisely what had governed her submission to her father. Her improvised strategy could likewise be seen in her rejection of Edwardian religious legislation because she believed that neither Edward nor the Council had the authority to legislate on religious matters so long as Edward was a minor. At no point did Mary defend the Henrician settlement. In theory, of course, by arguing as she did, Mary was undermining the very faith she so vigorously upheld. What would she have done once Edward came of age? Here, however, little can be read into her religious views. Given that Edward would not have come of age for several years, hers was the strongest position she could assume without actually incriminating herself as a traitor. In the meantime she could always think of a plan B, though we have no evidence that she ever came up with one; improvisation to the end, then.

Doubts about the orthodoxy of Mary's faith have been matched by doubts about her commitment to the papacy, the claim being that her humanist opinions sat uneasily with traditional demands of obedience to Rome.[6] Those who argue this case see the years of separation from Rome as inevitably having had an impact on Mary's own religious outlook. The papacy for Mary, it is claimed, may have become an unavoidable reality after she became queen, but it did not become a central feature of her faith, which was, as that of many reformers and Protestants of the day, primarily rooted in Scripture, the decrees of the early Councils and the teaching of the Church Fathers. The First Statute of Repeal of 1553 may in this instance offer clues about Mary's position on papal supremacy. Careful to stress the continuity between the Marian and Henrician reigns, the statute insisted that 'divine service and administration of sacraments as were most commonly used in the realm of England in the last year of the reign of our late sovereign lord, King Henry VIII, shall be [...] used and frequented through the whole realm of England and all other the queen's majesty's dominions'. The context here, however, is again all important. Two things are apparent. By associating Mary with Henry, the statute emphasises Mary's legitimacy, yet at the same time implying the irregularity of Edward's religious reforms by omitting to refer to them. Nothing here, therefore, explicitly indicates Mary's endorsement of her father's religious settlement. The statute was drafted in all likelihood with domestic political interests rather than religious interests in mind at a sensitive time just after Mary's accession. Mary was already clear as to what her religious policies would be. But in order to be able to implement them she first had to ensure she had a firm political base from which to launch them. By tapping into popular attachment to traditional religious practice and ritual, which did not automatically include papal obedience, sympathy for which had waned somewhat among the people since the break from Rome, Mary was showing a level of political skill not usually accredited to her.

There is also little in Mary's humanism to suggest indifference towards the papacy. In fact her humanist beliefs were wholly consistent with contemporary reformed Catholicism, many of which would find resonance in the declarations of the Council of Trent (1545–63). To suggest that her humanist sympathies somehow conflicted with the idea of papal supremacy fails to understand the nature of both contemporary Catholicism and Mary's own faith. Henry's later reformation may have reaffirmed core Catholic doctrine, but its reiteration of the break with Rome made the Church in England distinctly Protestant. It is worth recalling Philip Hughes's witty dismissal of the supremacy as 'blasphemous rubbish', which insisted, in view of Edward's supremacy, that 'The new Supreme Head of Christ's Church is a little boy of nine'.

Mary, conversely, *was* Catholic. There was nothing obstinate about her faith. Catholicism is not *à la carte* in the same way Protestantism was becoming, depending on the whims of the ruling monarch, and as such Mary was being consistent with the faith that she so passionately believed to be true. The fact that she made no explicit commitment towards the papacy before her enthronement says nothing about her view on the restoration of papal authority. As a Catholic she would have taken this for granted. As such, Richards's claim that Mary's view 'that the papacy was crucial to the maintenance of orthodox religion [. . .] was almost certainly a fresh decision, newly arrived at, not one stubbornly adhered to since the 1530s', is not convincing.[7] No sooner had she repudiated papal authority during her father's reign than she made a request to the pope for absolution for her submission to her father's royal supremacy. This surely offers firm confirmation that she believed that Catholicism was contingent on papal authority and not merely in the 'formal sense' as Loades contends.[8] The ensuing doctrinal heterodoxy and disputes during her father's and brother's reigns, rather than persuading Mary to embrace papal authority, as Richards suggests,[9] reinforced her long held view of the need for the pope as the ultimate custodian of doctrine. This she confirmed by her insistence on as hasty a reversal as possible of the schism with Rome, suggesting that her loyalty to the papacy was more than a nostalgic craving for things past. It was domestic political considerations that delayed the union with Rome rather than any doubts about the legitimacy of Rome's authority over the Church in England. There was in fact no conflict between Christian humanism and papal authority. Her disputes with Pope Paul IV, as noted above, when she sided against Paul, first with her Cardinal, Reginald Pole and then with her husband Philip, should be seen more in terms of a clash with a particularly obstinate and irrational individual than in terms of a challenge to papal supremacy. In this she was not setting any precedents. Here, her actions were those of a politician, who understood that politics sometimes had to take temporary precedence over loyalty to the papacy. It is therefore mistaken to claim that Mary's commitment to papal supremacy was less than absolute.

Mary's restoration of papal authority in England has got her into trouble with some historians over something else. Loades, for instance, regards this commitment to Rome as a fatal mistake. Had she 'confined herself to restoring her father's settlement, her Church would have remained impeccably English, and its distinctive theology would have served such a settlement well'.[10] By not doing so and by linking her Church 'to an unpopular Papacy' she forced Elizabeth's hand 'to turn to the Protestant alternative'. Loades concludes on this point, albeit with some reservation, that without Elizabeth's Protestantism, 'John Foxe would possibly have remained in Strasburg, and much subsequent English history would have been different. However ...'.[11] This argument is indeed problematic, as Loades's hanging doubt suggests, for not only does it underestimate the orthodoxy of Mary's Catholicism but also exaggerates the popularity of the Henrician settlement. If both the successes of the Marian restoration and the level of opposition to the Elizabethan settlement are anything to go by then Protestantism in England and the rejection of papal authority were far less popular than has been suggested. English history would indeed have been demonstrably different had Mary accepted her father's settlement, but Mary was not planning to reign for five years only for her programme to be pilloried by her enemies after that. Hers was a long-haul programme that if fully implemented would not only have ensured that Foxe would occupy a mere detail on the fringes of English history but also without doubt have prevented the Elizabethan settlement, that is of course if Elizabeth had succeeded Mary at all. Catholicism would have been so well entrenched that any reversal of it would have been impossible. Mary's reputation suffered only because her premature death allowed her enemies to sully it. The reversal of Catholicism duly followed.

Mary's faith was not eclectic, given her traditional Catholic outlook. Yet it was a faith that in some parts would have been at odds with that of a pious medieval worshipper. She had several private devotions, top of which was to the Mother of God, but her efforts to restore the broken shrines, Marian or otherwise or to reclaim lost relics were limited. The one shrine that was restored during her reign, that of Edward the Confessor, was done so on the initiative of neither Mary nor Cardinal Pole but on that of local monks, though with Mary's full support. Mary's diffidence here could have been due to a realistic resignation to the fact that the focal points of the other two great shrines, that of Thomas Becket and the statue of our Lady of Walsingham, had been destroyed; the relics of St Edward had not. Moreover, religious devotion apart, there was also a political advantage that a restored shrine to the Confessor could offer which the other two shrines could not, serving as it did as a point of continuity between the saintly king and herself. This factor in turn overrode both her gender and her status of illegitimacy that she endured since her father's reign.[12] That aside, however, Mary's acknowledgement of the spiritual importance of devotions to saints again showed that her faith was very much in tune with the spirituality advocated by the Council of Trent. Though she never attempted a pilgrimage, that other fundamental feature of medieval worship, other than to the shrine of Edward the Confessor, she did personally finance a modest monastic revival from which something grander could have developed had her reign lasted longer (see chapter 11). And though she never took a formal position on any of the great contemporary theological debates concerning, for instance, Purgatory, she was, as we can assume from her own practice, a traditionalist. We may only speculate, however, that her insistence on clerical celibacy was perhaps influenced as much by her personal chastity as by sacramental prescription.

At the centre of her faith was the miracle of the Mass, whose rejection by radical Protestants, in her mind, warranted condemnation and punishment. Elton's flippant remark that 'she depended on the mass because it gave her emotional satisfaction'[13] merely revealed his unfamiliarity with Catholic doctrine and worship. Having been the cornerstone of medieval worship as well as a test of Catholic allegiance during the Henrician schism, including her own and that of her household, the Mass would now form the 'centrepiece' of England's restored Catholicism.[14] The importance attached to the Mass was not for religious reasons alone; its abandonment was regarded by Marian authorities as symbolic of the social turmoil of the time and there was no shortage of Marian polemic that associated devilish Protestantism with social decay (see chapter 11).

However, here too restoration was not mere medieval nostalgia. Of course the Marian Mass was totally Roman based on the doctrine of the true presence, adherence to which determined loyalty to the new order. But certain medieval perceptions of the Mass were challenged by Marian commentators. For instance, Thomas Watson, the Catholic bishop of Lincoln, in his highly popular collection of some thirty model sermons, *Holsome and Catholyke Doctryne Concernyge the Seven Saraments of Chrystes Church* published in 1558, drew on many humanist themes. For one, it played down the idea of Communion as the miracle panacea, and stressed instead the primacy of its spiritual role rooted in faith. Its innovative approach to the Mass was accompanied by a strong emphasis on Augustinian theology that saw salvation dependent as much on faith, grace and Christ's sacrifice as on good works. Others challenged the oft-held medieval view of the priest as a supernatural being. Bishop Edmund Bonner, for instance, in his *Profitable* and *Necessarye Doctryne*, published in 1555, wrote 'it is not the visible priest that nowe worketh thys hyghe mysterye by his own power or strengthe but it is Christ hym selfe, the invisible priest, that dothe worke it by the mysterye of the visible priest'. Marian writers used humanist methodology to prove the authenticity of the true presence, appealing to patristic sources for evidence. John Angel, for instance, in *The Agreement of the Holy Fathers*, published in 1555, cited thirty-six different Greek and Latin authorities on this matter. It would seem, therefore, as Lucy Wooding noted, that Mary's restored Mass, as the rest of her programme, was not, 'a medieval replica'. In fact the Mass that emerged, 'despite its self-conscious nostalgia for the late-medieval Church, is a much more intricate and multifaceted construct than its pre-Reformation precursor. Even with regard to this most central element of traditional Catholicism time could not stand still'.[15] With the Council of Trent suspended, 'what was happening in England', noted Edwards, 'may have seemed the best current hope, anywhere in Europe, for the implementation of the agenda of Catholic reform'.[16]

*

Mary's involvement in the translation of Erasmus's *Paraphrases on the new Testament* sheds more light on the nature of her faith. Those writers like Loades who have claimed that Mary's Catholicism was not totally unreformed have suggested that her involvement provides further evidence 'that Mary fitted quite comfortably into the circle of her father's last queen, and that there was nothing in either her intellectual tastes or devotional practice that set her apart as a rebel or a misfit',[17] and it was only her ill-health that compelled her to withdraw from the project. For other commentators, like Susan James, Mary's alleged peripheral involvement in the project was due to her conservative Catholicism which ultimately deterred her from more active association with it. James sees her abrupt termination of her work as evidence that she had never been Katherine Parr's willing collaborator. Rather it was the queen who had pressured her into collaborating in an attempt to convert her to the evangelical cause.[18] Mary consequently feigned illness, so the claim goes, to get herself out of a tricky situation. She after all had done this in the past and would do so in the future. Yet to understand Mary's involvement in the translation it is in fact as unnecessary to doubt the orthodoxy of Mary's Catholicism as it is erroneous to claim that she expediently feigned illness to avoid collaboration in a project with which she was ill at ease.

Crucial to the understanding of Mary's involvement in the translation is to determine the context in which the *Paraphrases* were seen during Henry's and Edward's reigns. It is most likely that her involvement in the project was central rather than peripheral, Mary being regarded by Katherine, 'as an academic mentor'.[19] A vital point to consider, however, is the date on which Mary's involvement started. The work may have been printed by the evangelical playwright, Nicholas Udall, in late January 1548, a year into Edward's reign, but Mary's participation in its translation commenced in 1545 on the invitation of the queen during the religiously conservative period of Henry's reign. This point is indeed crucial given that the *Paraphrases* were viewed differently by each administration. It is true that since the break from Rome, reformers regarded the *Paraphrases* as a significant source of the New Learning. But this was in large part due to wishful interpretations. Despite criticism from certain conservative quarters, neither Erasmus himself, nor other humanists like Vives or the conservative humanist, Henry Parker, The Lord Morley,[20] considered the *Paraphrases* to deviate from orthodoxy on key issues such as that of the eucharistic sacrifice. As such, as Aysha Pollnitz noted that in the late Henrician period, 'neither Erasmus nor the *Paraphrases* were inevitably linked to Lutheranism in England'[21] as they would be during Edward's reign. In fact, Udall's revisions in a second volume, published in 1552, which sought to bend the meaning of the original text, failed to disguise the difficulty that Erasmian theology had with reformed religion. 'Had Edward's government been less chaotic and more unified and disciplined', noted Gregory Dodds, 'the Paraphrases would never have ended up as required reading.'[22] In this context there is no reason, given what we know about Mary's faith, why she could not have engaged, with a clear conscience, in translating Erasmus's work.

In a letter to Mary of 20 September 1547 Katherine acknowledged Mary's health issues, though she urged her to pass her work to the chaplain whom they shared, Francis Mallet, for 'correcting' and 'repair', which may or may not suggest that the work was in need of major revision.[23] In his letter to Katherine of 1548, Udall noted that Mary took to the project with 'Great studie, peine and travaill', in order 'to promote Goddes worde, and the free grace of his gospel', but was forced to halt her work because the 'over peynfull studie' had made her ill.[24] However, in his dedication in the *Paraphrase of Acts* Udall is eager to quash any doubts over Mary's centrality in the project, stressing that he had done nothing more than 'placed the texte, and divided the paraphrase' since, as he noted, it would have been a 'cryme of great arroganceie and presumpcion [...] to entremedle' with Mary's and Mallet's work.[25] Without a manuscript written in Mary's hand it is ultimately difficult to ascertain the extent of her involvement in the project, but it is unlikely to have been peripheral or coerced in view of the close and cordial relationship that Mary and Katherine enjoyed.[26] It also needs to be noted that although Katherine's reformist leanings provoked conspiracies against her at court from religious conservatives, she was not an evangelical in the strictest sense. She and Mary, in fact, had points in common, Erasmus being one. Moreover, as Pollnitz noted, 'we should remember that Parr's own beliefs were evolving between 1543 and 1547' and sat somewhere between those of Cranmer, by whom she was increasingly influenced and her almoner, the relatively conservative Bishop George Day. As long as both Katherine and Mary both believed in the real presence, and there was nothing to suggest in Katherine's faith that she adhered to a radical Protestant position on this issue, not least because it was illegal to do so, there was no reason why both could not share scholarly interests.[27] It was probably in this spirit that Mary and Katherine collaborated in the project. And if we are to accept the aforementioned evidence from Udall and Katherine regarding the centrality of Mary's work on the translation then Mary's involvement offers an important insight into her intellect and level of education. Notwithstanding Mary's frequent, albeit minor errors, her effort was competent and 'reveals that the princess was a careful Bible reader, an enthusiastic if inexperienced grammarian, and in possession of greater rhetorical sophistication and a more nuanced and consistent religious ideology than some scholars have supposed'.[28] The fact that when she became queen she did not include the *Paraphrases* on any list of proscribed texts is further evidence not only of her enthusiastic collaboration with Katherine in their translation but also of her willingness to embrace theological revisions, albeit modest ones that did not encroach on any core doctrines. 'The picture of Mary as the vengeful Catholic traditionalist', writes Wooding, 'is obviously incompatible with this impression of the learned princess who contributed to what ironically became one of the key texts of the Edwardian Reformation.'[29]

NOTES

[1] D. Loades, 'Introduction: The Personal Religion of Mary I', in Duffy and Loades, eds., *The Church of Mary Tudor*, p. 20.

[2] Ibid., 2006, p. 18.

[3] Ibid.

[4] P. L. Hughes and J. F. Larkin, *Tudor Royal Proclamations: The Later Tudors (1553–1587)*. 3 vols. (New Haven and London: Yale University Press, 1969), vol. 2 , pp. 5–6.

[5] W. Wizeman, 'The Religious Policy of Mary I', in Doran and Freeman, eds., *Mary Tudor, Old and New Perspectives*, p. 154.

[6] L. Wooding, 'The Restoration and Language of Catholic Reform', in J. Edwards and R. Truman, eds., *Reforming Catholicism in the England of Mary Tudor: The Achievements of Friar Bartolomē Carranza* (Aldershot and Burlington: Ashgate, 2005), p. 58.

[7] Richards, 'Reassessing Mary Tudor: Some Concluding Points', p. 210.

[8] D. Loades, 'The English Church during the Reign of Mary I', in Edwards and Truman, eds., *Reforming Catholicism in the England of Mary Tudor*, p. 48.

[9] Richards, 'Reassessing Mary Tudor: Some Concluding Points', p. 210.

[10] Loades, 'The English Church during the Reign of Mary I', p. 48.

[11] Ibid.

[12] W. Wizeman, 'Martyrs and Anti-martyrs and Mary Tudor's Church', in T. S. Freeman and T. F. Mayer, eds., *Martyrs and Martyrdom in England c. 1400–1700* (Woodbridge: The Boydell Press, Woodbridge, 2007), p. 167.

[13] Elton, *Reform and Reformation*: England, p. 377.

[14] L. Wooding, 'The Marian Restoration and the Mass', in Duffy and Loades, eds., *The Church of Mary Tudor*, p. 229.

[15] Ibid., p. 257.

[16] Edwards, *Mary I*, p. 241.

[17] Loades, 'Introduction: The Personal Religion of Mary I', pp. 13–14.

[18] S. James, *Kateryn Parr: The Making of a Queen* (Aldershot and Burlington: Ashgate, 1999), p. 106.

[19] Edwards, *Mary I: England's Catholic Queen*, p. 230.

[20] Loades, 'Introduction: The Personal Religion of Mary I', p. 13.

[21] Cited in A. Pollnitz, 'Religion and Translation at the Court of Henry VIII', in Doran and T. S. Freeman, eds., *Mary Tudor, Old and New Perspectives*, p. 128.

[22] G. D. Dodds, *Exploiting Erasmus: The Erasmian Legacy and Religious Change in Early Modern England* (Toronto, Buffalo and London: University of Toronto Press, 2009), p. 25.

[23] Pollnitz, 'Religion and Translation at the Court of Henry VIII', p. 124.

[24] Ibid.

[25] Cited ibid.

[26] Weir, *The Six Wives of Henry VIII*, p. 500.

[27] Pollnitz, 'Religion and Translation at the Court of Henry VIII', p. 132.

[28] Ibid., p. 136.

[29] L. Wooding, 'The Marian Restoration and the Language of Catholic Reform', in Edwards and Truman, eds., *Reforming Catholicism in the England of Mary Tudor*, p. 52.

Cardinal Pole
and the Programme of Restoration

W HEN REGINALD POLE finally arrived in England on 24 November
1554, merely two days after the Act of Attainder on him had been
lifted by Parliament, much had already changed since Mary's accession.
By the end of the first parliament on 5 December 1553, England's religion
had been restored to what it had been during the final years of Henry
VIII, Henry's and Edward's illiberal treason laws that implicated anyone
in treason who denied royal supremacy had been repealed, the marriage
between Henry and Katherine of Aragon that had been declared invalid by
Henry had been validated, which quashed any ambiguity over Mary's own
legitimacy, clerical marriage had been prohibited, all rituals and ceremonies
were ordered to be conducted in Latin and the Mass had been restored to
its pre-Edwardian form.

Overseeing the observance of doctrinal discipline was Archbishop
Edmund Bonner. Having been an arch-defender of the break from Rome,
Bonner had abandoned his support for royal supremacy when he saw how
it had been manipulated by the Protestant councils of Edward's minority.
An opponent of doctrinal innovations, for which he had been imprisoned
by both Somerset and Northumberland, he had now been given the
responsibility for tracing and restoring to churches the property that had
been looted during the Edwardian visitations, inasmuch as this was possible;
in many cases, however, it was not. Most churches had been stripped bare
of their contents, whereas the property that had been acquired through the
monastic land-grab during the Dissolution was all but lost to the Church.
Those who had profited from the Dissolution, especially incumbent MPs,
were to prove to be a considerable stumbling block to Bonner's efforts. These
MPs, whose consent was required on all religious legislation, were not about
to become the turkeys that were going to vote for Christmas. Reporting to
the emperor on 19 August 1553, Renard wrote of an impending 'conspiracy' in
Parliament by those 'who held that property either by the liberality of the late
kings, Henry and Edward, or by purchase, who would rather get themselves

massacred than let go'.[1] Knowing that the stakes were high, Parliament was threatening to refuse to consent to Mary's ultimate demand of restoring papal jurisdiction over the Church without first securing assurances from the government on the new ownership rights over former monastic land. 'Concessions', as Pole called it, therefore, had to be made.[2] However, not only were these 'concessions' a bitter pill to swallow for Pole, as well as Pope Julius, who had initially made absolution for England conditional on the restoration to the Church of its former land, they also proved to have a significant impact on the implementation of the restoration programme, given that it denied the Church huge funds. Pole did, however, in his address to both houses of Parliament on 28 November 1554 severely admonish the owners of former Church lands, whom he referred to as temporary occupiers ('possessors') of God's property, whose faith could not be genuine as a consequence of their venial actions.[3] Damning Henry's schism as the cause of ruin in England, similar to the consequences of other schisms, he praised Mary as the courageous queen who would correct past wrongs. Two days later Parliament, barring two MPs, formally voted to reunite England with Rome after which Pole, using his legatine powers, absolved the country from its sins. With the formalities over, the practical task of restoring Catholicism would take on a new momentum.

*

The task that Pole faced in fully restoring Catholicism to England was by no means going to be easy. According to critics of Pole, it was made more testing by the fact that he himself was its chief overseer. He has been accused of shortsightedness, applying outdated methods and being out of touch with the situation in England that had arisen during his twenty-year absence. It was these reasons the argument goes, rather than a shortage of time, which ensured the failure of the restoration to take root in England. Pole is also charged by those who view Mary as an arch-conservative of reinforcing her position with his exotic and archaic approach. In truth, Pole's reputation has been sullied largely, though not exclusively, as shall be seen, for the same reasons as that of Mary. He was, as much of Protestant polemic saw him, 'Bloody' Mary's hatchetman who led a botched attempt to roll back the English Reformation, or in the words of his successor as archbishop of Canterbury, the 'butcher and scourge of the English Church'.[4] Pole's reputation suffered a further set-back by the attacks on him by Catholic sources, not least by the pope himself, who confoundedly accused him of being doctrinally suspect. Deliberate misrepresentation of his work has led to a skewed interpretation that is grossly at odds with reality and which fails to assess properly both the momentousness of what confronted him and his achievements.

His mission was certainly immense, but one which he approached with considerable enthusiasm. He drafted an ambitious programme for the restoration of the old faith, which he presented at a synod of bishops convened in Westminster on 11 November 1555, which according to José Ignacio Tellechea Idígoras was 'the most positive factor in the great attempt to restore Roman Catholicism'.[5] Pole was under no illusion that imparting doctrinal orthodoxy on a laity that had been confused by twenty years of religious turmoil would be anything other than a huge undertaking. Twenty years in the great scheme of things is not a long time. But in the personal sphere it represents fading memories and abandoned practices. And that is only for someone who has had any experience at all of what came before. For someone who has not, knowledge of things past is either non-existent or is based on second-hand information. In Mary's time, such knowledge would have been based overwhelmingly on verbal recollections from people with varying degrees of appreciation of the old ways. What made matters worse was the perilous financial situation that the Church was in, having been stripped of most of its assets during the previous two regimes. Monastic land and most of the looted property had to be written off, while tracking down the remainder was going to be a painstaking undertaking that was only going to draw attention and resources away from religious campaigning. Easing the financial pressure on the Church was the abolition by Parliament in 1555 of payments by the Church to the Crown of the 'first fruit'. This was money that used to go to the pope, but had been redirected to the Crown in 1534 by the Act in Absolute Restraint of Annates as part of Henry's campaign of bullying the pope to annul his marriage to Katherine of Aragon. The Crown continued to receive payment of 'the tenths' from lay patrons of Church benefices, though those benefices whose patron was the queen, except for those exempted for being too poor, paid their 'tenths' to Pole, which subsequently helped to finance monastic pensions. Interestingly, Rome was to receive nothing of this levy.[6]

Getting the appropriate clergy in place to implement the restoration programme was in itself a huge task. Notwithstanding England's absolution, the clergy still needed to be vetted for its suitability in accordance with canon law. The vetting process was to be determined by a complex code that was drawn up for what was an unprecedented situation which sought to distinguish heretical clerics from doctrinally acceptable ones. Frequently there existed a fine line between the two. Bishops who had adopted a heretical position and refused to recant or had married, irrespective of having been consecrated under the Roman rite before the schism, could no longer continue in their posts together with bishops who had been consecrated under the Edwardian ordinal. Bishops who conversely repudiated heresy and who had been consecrated under the Roman rite and had not married could be absolved. That was not the end of the matter, however. All of the twenty-three eligible bishops, one of whom, John Hooper, possessed two sees, had submitted to the Edwardian settlement, willingly or unwillingly.[7] Ultimately, there were very few clerics who had not been compromised in some way by the Reformation and who were available for promotion, other than those who had been exiled, like Richard Pate. He was subsequently consecrated as bishop of Worcester.[8]

In all, thirty-five bishops were to serve in the restored Church. They had been appointed partly for their conservative opinions, partly for their learning. Very few of them were actual Catholics in the full sense. In spite of their varied backgrounds, they collectively served the Church well, and with considerable commitment, though there is some scholarly disagreement as to the level of their intellectual calibre and personal zeal. For some the Marian episcopate, while possessing respectable credentials, lacked, with a few exceptions, men who could affect a lasting impact[9] while for others most of the office holders 'were distinguished by learning, many by zeal and a surprising number by both'.[10] The fact that only one Marian bishop, Anthony Kitchin of Llandaff, conformed to the Elizabethan religious settlement appears to bear this position out. Having retained his position under all the monarchs since the start of the Reformation, Kitchin secured a reputation as an incorrigible timeserver, 'who would doubtless have become a Hindu if required, provided he was allowed to hold on to the see of Llandaff'.[11] As such the Marian episcopate was a potentially formidable spearhead for genuine Catholic revival. Its collective opposition to Elizabeth's Protestant settlement sets it in stark contrast to the collective submission of its Henrician counterpart, barring John Fisher, to Henry's royal supremacy.

The fortitude of the Marian episcopate alone strongly challenges the claim that there developed both 'organic' and spiritual discontinuity between the Marian 'medieval' Church and modern post-Marian 'Counter-Reformation' Catholicism.[12] The personal cost to the Marian bishops of non-conformity with the Elizabethan order further demonstrates its dedication to the cause that they served. Duffy robustly defends the achievements of the Marian episcopate. It had more credentials, in his opinion, to assume the challenges of the post-Council of Trent Church than any other in Europe. While in France and Spain, for instance, the bench of bishops remained dominated by lawyers, in England the Marian bench overwhelmingly consisted of theologians. 'In that perspective', noted Duffy, 'Marian England was the hare to the rest of Europe's tortoise.'[13]

The situation concerning ordinary clergy was even more complex than that of the episcopate. Priests who had been consecrated under the Roman rite and had repudiated heresy could remain in their posts. Those, on the other hand, who had renounced the Catholic Church, irrespective of having been consecrated under the Roman rite, were deprived as too were any clergy ordained under the Edwardian ordinal. The issue of married clergy, of whom there were many, was particularly problematic. In short, married priests were absolved on the condition that they abandoned their wives, something which must have caused much anguish for many and tested their faith to the limit. Once vetted, the clergy needed to be instructed in appropriate conduct so that they could be purged of any recently acquired vices. Needed also were seminaries to train a new generation of priests in line with Council of Trent rulings. Aside from the administrative challenges that all this would present, implementing this programme as well as addressing the widespread problem of impoverished bishops and clergy would require colossal funds, which were simply not there. Yet without a fully trained clergy the programme of restoration would falter at the first hurdle. There was no alternative to finding the requisite funds.

For many of Pole's critics, his preoccupation with the augmentation of the Church's finances seemed like a throwback to old priorities,[14] for Pole it was an essential element of implementing his restoration programme. Even if, as Rex Pogson argues, 'Pole had placed emphasis on, say, an evangelical campaign, he would still have been forced to work for the financial recovery of the Church in England if Rome was to regain anything resembling its former influences'.[15] Despite financial and time constraints much was done.[16] The strengthening of clerical education to aid the restoration again pre-empted a key recommendation of the Council of Trent. By 1558, for instance, seminaries had been established in York, Durham, Lincoln, Chichester, and Bath and Wells, which compares favourably to the slow pace of the reform of seminaries on the Continent.[17] The idea of a comprehensive programme of seminarian education was then forwarded by Niccolo Ormanetto, the papal datary in charge of Cardinal Pole's legatine judicial machinery, to Cardinal Borromeo in Milan, who proceeded to introduce it to the Council of Trent where it was turned into a major decree.[18] A system of wealth redistribution from richer to poorer diocese was also being effectively implemented which went a long way to plug the holes that monasteries had once filled in their support for poorer parishes.

A recatholicised clergy could not fulfil its task without reconsecrated churches. This was an issue that was irking the Spanish priests who had come to England and who felt uneasy in having to celebrate Masses in what were effectively Protestant churches surrounded by unconsecrated graveyards. Once churches had been reconsecrated, the logistically problematic and financially prohibitive task of re-equipping them with the imaginary, ornaments, roods and bibles could begin in order to facilitate Catholic worship. All this had to happen at the same time as the recatechisation of large portions of the population. This in itself was fraught with problems. Although most people were amenable to Roman worship, most had never known anything other than the Protestant service, while many who remembered the old Mass undoubtedly were rusty as to its meaning and practice. And given the high mortality rate and short life expectancy there could not have been too many people who did remember it. Even the schismatic service of Henry VIII had been stripped of much more than references to papal supremacy, harbouring considerable liturgical innovation. Where old rituals remained outwardly unchanged the new teaching on them altered their meaning, which in turn greatly affected both people's understanding of traditional prayers and their approach to faith.[19] Worship in the Roman rite, in short, needed to be taught, more or less from scratch.

*

Pole's programme of combatting heresy has drawn particular criticism focused on an allegation that he neglected preaching in favour of archaic ceremonial and rituals[20] and eschewed modern methods of evangelisation espoused by new vigorous groups like the Society of Jesus (Jesuits).[21] Pogson goes as far as to claim that Pole did not have 'his own plan for a vigorous attack on the heretical doctrine which still corrupted the English church' seemingly ignoring 'the chance of bringing the dynamic preaching of the Counter-Reformation to England' and discouraging preaching in general.[22] If proven the allegation would go a long way to reinforce claims that he was an unsuitable manager of the recatholicisation of England. Close examination of Pole's methods, however, reveals a varied approach that strove to maximise the usefulness of each method.

Pole's prioritisation, for instance, of emphasising God's grace over personal knowledge of Scripture as a means of restoring faith was not done to the exclusion of catechesis and preaching.[23] Perhaps the most probable reason that has coloured perceptions about Pole's attitude towards preaching has been a mistranslation and misreading of crucial sources. A case in point is a 'catastrophic misreading' of a letter Pole sent to the influential theologian, Bartolomé Carranza, the archbishop of Toledo on 20 June 1558, which Duffy argues went on to generate the myth that Pole downplayed the value of preaching. Duffy particularly takes issue with Pogson's interpretation of the letter which has Pole declaring that 'it is better to check the preaching of the Word of God rather than to proclaim it, unless the discipline of the Church has been fully restored'.[24] Here, Duffy claims, the all too important context of the letter is missing from the analysis, which in turn, he argues, has led to a misinterpretation of Pole's intentions. It should also be noted that Pole's tone in the letter is defensive as it is a reply to a formal complaint that Carranza had lodged against him based on accusations of absenteeism and prolonged residence at court.[25] Dermot Fenlon suggests a twist in the tail that further broadens the context of Pole's letter. Pole, as noted, had long-standing enemies in Rome who suspected his theology, suspicions that would in fact plague him for the rest of his life. Carranza himself was not free from suspicions, having frequently collaborated with Pole on a number of projects. Fenlon suggests that having been asked to question Pole, Carranza was in fact inadvertently partaking in a conspiracy that was supposed to bring both clerics into the spotlight that in turn could trigger cases against them.[26] The fact that both would face high-level investigations, Pole in Rome and Carranza in Spain, perhaps suggests that there is something in this.

Taken out of context, the extract from Pole's letter does indeed appear to show Pole's aversion to preaching. Pole's concern in his reply, however, is not about preaching *per se* but its inappropriateness at that particular time in certain parts of the country, especially London. Although Pole stresses that it would indeed be fitting for proper Catholic ritual to be restored and sacraments adhered to before there could be any benefit from preaching the Word of God for those who heard it, no-where does he suggest that preaching should be 'checked', a term, Duffy attributes to a mistranslation from Latin.[27] 'Of course I don't [. . .] deny the necessity of preaching the Word', Pole writes, 'but I do say that the Word can be more of a hindrance than a help unless it is proceeded or at the same time accompanied by the establishment of Church discipline, because carnal men turn [preaching] into an empty ear-tickling entertainment, rather than a health-giving discipline and food for the soul.'[28] As far as Pole's absenteeism was concerned, he stressed that his presence was frequently needed in the country's administrative centre and that this in no way hampered the welfare of any of the parishes that were under his care as all were provided for and he could visit them at any time.[29]

Notwithstanding Pole's own noteworthy preaching record, he actively encouraged others to preach, but only those who were competent enough to do so. Decrees on preaching and teaching dominated the legatine synod of 1555 which led to the publication of several significant works, Thomas Watson's collection of homilies, *Holesome and Catholyke Doctryne*, referred to above, being just one. The synod emphatically highlighted the importance of preaching, though stressed that it was not to be performed by heretical or unqualified men.

Pole himself in fact preached often, delivering at least thirteen sermons during his short stay in England, in contrast to his Protestant successor, Matthew Parker who preached merely nine sermons in twenty-five years.[30] His most notable sermon was delivered in Whitehall on St Andrew's Day 1557, in the presence of the queen, the court and London's dignitaries to commemorate England's reconciliation with Rome. The sermon was skilfully composed, raising several of the key topics of the day. It not only reveals much about Pole's thinking behind his programme of restoration but also undermines accusations against him of being out of touch with contemporary realities in England. In outlining his vision for the future, he focused on the social calamities and spiritual ruin brought on by the Reformation. He contrasted the humility and courage that the martyrs More and Fisher had exhibited with the 'develyche pertynacye' of the 'pseudo martyrs' who, like the crucified wicked thief, showed neither fear nor humility in death.[31] In lamenting the stubborn resistance of Protestantism, a faith manufactured from selected texts 'that were not harde of in our fathers dayes', he admonished those who had profited from the ill-gotten gains and who ignored the interests of the poor.

The search for appropriate context is similarly important when assessing claims that Pole's reservations in employing Jesuits were based on some aversion towards 'modern' continental reform. Here again a misinterpretation of source material has perhaps coloured judgements of the Cardinal ever since.[32] A letter from the Spanish ambassador, Count Feria, to the leading Spanish Jesuit, Pedro Ribadeneira, on 22 March 1558, in which Feria expressed concern about Pole's 'lukewarm' approach in refusing to countenance Jesuit assistance in recatholicising England,[33] has been seized upon by several historians, even those who are otherwise inclined to offer positive assessments of the Marian policies, as evidence of Pole's imprudence. Loades, for instance, claimed that Pole

> simply did not want men with the fire of the counter-reformation in their bellies trying to implant in his flock a vision of the Church and its doctrines which he did not share. He belonged to an older generation. His spirituality had been formed by the [. . .] Carthusians, with whom he lodged on several occasions in his youth [. . .] He certainly did not shirk his responsibility in England, but his gifts were not those of an inspiring leader.[34]

Yet given Pole's work and achievements, it is a curious conclusion to arrive at. Pole knew Ignatius Loyola for many years; he was nine years his junior. He corresponded with him regularly while in England and the letters between them reveal a warm and friendly relationship. What the letters also indicate is that Loyola was prepared at best to use the Society's 'slender resources' to train English students for work in England rather than to send a cohort of ready-made Jesuits on a mission to the country.[35] It is a scenario much apart from the one depicted by Pole's critics of a backward thinking Cardinal refusing the eager assistance of the most dynamic Catholic group of the time. Moreover, historians who have criticised Pole for his unenthusiastic approach towards the Jesuits of course had the benefit of centuries of Jesuit work and achievement to base their judgement on. At the time, the Jesuits were somewhat of an unknown quantity and Pole was certainly not the only bishop in contemporary Europe to have declined assistance from them. Moreover, it was highly likely that Feria's criticism of Pole reflected his own frustration that he had 'so far been unable to move the queen or the Cardinal (Pole) towards letting members of the Company come [to England]',[36] rather than it being a reaction to the Cardinal's purported short-sightedness and lack of zeal in declining Jesuit assistance. Pole's reservations about the effectiveness of a Jesuit mission in England need to be understood also in the context of the confidence he had in his own extensive and creative programme which actually did include many aspects of Jesuit teaching.[37] It is likely, given his friendship with Loyola and the financial support that he provided the Jesuit missions in Italy, that he would have invited the Society to England at some stage. For the time being, however, he opted to pursue his own programme[38] without having to deal with competition and overlapping interests.[39]

The rituals and colourful ceremonies, especially the Mass, which Pole reintroduced into worship became very popular. This stood in stark contrast to the colourless Protestant services of recent years. Reinforcing the vigour of these rituals was a revival of England's choral and instrumental traditions of worship that had been so gravely undermined by the austerity of Edwardian religious reforms that starved most churches, including the Chapel Royal, of funds for musical and choral development. For radical reformers of the time, such as Thomas Becon, music was akin to idolatry, obscuring the path to God and distracting people from serious study and worship.[40] Here too, Mary's ideas chimed with those of the Tridentine programme. In the same way as the Council of Trent Church so keenly patronised some of the most eminent musicians of the time like Giovanni Pierluigi da Palestrina and Orlando de Lasso, so Mary, a keen musician and aficionado of sacred music, celebrated England's great composers like Thomas Tallis, Christopher Tye and William Byrd. She demonstrated her commitment by providing large funds to develop orchestral and choral music. Cathedral choirs were particular beneficiaries of Mary's strategy, managing to build a tradition that survived Elizabethan attacks on sacred music. Composers like Byrd were able to continue producing hymnal music, albeit for Protestant worshippers, that survives to this very day. Mary's policy attracted musicians from overseas to collaborate with their English counterparts as well as to perform at various festivities, notably at Mary's and Philip's nuptial Mass at Winchester Cathedral on 25 July 1554.[41] 'By the death of Mary', noted Jonathan P. Willis, 'the process of Catholic musical and liturgical restoration was largely complete.'[42] William Wizeman adds, 'Having been almost annihilated during Edward's reformation, England's ancient musical heritage rose from the ashes during Mary's Counter-Reformation, to be preserved under Elizabeth I and after', albeit with its original purpose, that of reinforcing Catholic worship, severely compromised.[43] In an attempt to preserve recent achievements, Byrd, at least, continued to compose quintessentially Catholic music, much of it being performed at recusant

Masses. But in doing so he sailed close to the wind in an atmosphere that was increasingly hostile to the old faith. The popularity of traditional worship was an indication that traditional piety, at least among the lower classes, had not drastically declined.[44] It was inevitable, however, that religiosity among those who coveted the material fruits that the Reformation offered would be compromised; and it certainly was, as noted. Yet there still remained even among the upper classes, which had benefited most out of the loot-fest, a degree of social responsibility. Although the number of benefactions fell, alms that otherwise would have been destined for the Church were in many instances being diverted towards alleviating the distress of the poor during these harsh times, acts of charity that Archbishop Bonner encouraged. With the funds that the Church did have available, however, much work was done to make good the losses that churches had suffered during the Reformation. Roods, altars and tabernacles were reconstructed and new wall decorations created. And in this much innovation was evident that reflected the cultural vibrancy of the continental Renaissance. A notable example is the arcaded wooden canopy crowning the shrine of St Edward the Confessor in Westminster Abbey, which was reconstructed by Benedictine monks after its destruction by the Edwardian regime. Duffy writes, 'there is nothing the least backward looking or "gothicising" about this confident renaissance woodwork'.[45] The reconstructed choir of Worcester Cathedral offers similar insight into the modern styles deployed by Marian craftsmen.[46]

Attempts to restore monastic life were less successful than restoring decorative craftsmanship to churches. With ex-monastic land having been sold off and ex-religious having settled into secular lives on pensions received from the Crown following the Dissolution, chances of restoring monastic life to anything like its pre-Reformation state were slim. The six religious houses that had been established by the summer of 1557, which housed merely a hundred religious were a fraction of the former size of the monastic infrastructure. This indeed would suggest that there was little enthusiasm for the development of what Dickens called backward looking 'retreats from the world'.[47] And though endowed and supported by the Crown, the new houses had been restored in response to petitions of former religious rather than as a result of a determined government initiative.[48] It is true that the initiative to restore religious houses was 'little more than a gesture',[49] but one which could have developed into something much more profound had time allowed. We will never know.

What we do know is that the claim that the government was 'incompetent' in its use of the printing press to counter subversive Protestant literature has no substance to it.[50] Pioneering work by Jennifer Loach in the 1980s on the Marian press,[51] augmented thereafter by further scholarship, sheds new light on the matter. A government policy that may have appeared as underdeveloped actually represented a very subtle approach to the issue that skilfully navigated the potentially perilous terrain of barrack room politics. The government figured that to confront scurrilous Protestant polemic with something similarly defamatory was not conducive either to instill truth or to calm religious emotions. In recognising the dangers of such texts, Mary, in her proclamation on 'freedom of conscience', prohibited the publication of 'false fond books, ballads, rhymes and other lewd treatises' that could 'stir up unquietness in her people'.[52] The injunction of March 1554 and subsequent proclamations reinforced bans on printing and possession of proscribed material. 'It was the Protestants', noted Duffy, 'who needed to make an impression, and who sought to deploy the belly-laugh and the jeer to make their point.'[53] For the administration, conversely, the dignity and holiness of ritual rather than ale-house polemic was the best way to foster doctrinal truth.

That said, however, the government's literary output compared favourably to that of the underground Protestant press, both quantitatively and qualitatively.[54] It may be true that quantitatively Protestants had the edge over the administration. But this should not surprise given that the clandestine printing press was the only means through which they could disseminate their views given that all official channels had been closed to them after 1553.[55] What is also noteworthy is that far fewer Catholic texts than Protestant texts of the period have survived, so many having fallen victim to Elizabethan purges against Catholic culture. What any analysis of Marian printing strategy also needs to take into consideration is the fact that many printers continued to harbour evangelical sympathies, having been at the forefront of the Edwardian assault on the old faith and therefore were now disinclined to take on Catholic work. The consolidation of the entire printing industry under the control of the London Stationers' Company in June 1557, in an effort to overcome this problem, came rather late and had a limited effect.

There is, nevertheless, much of literary value that has been passed down to us and which reveals a programme that was not only broad but full of innovative counsel that evoked Tridentine as well as reformist trends of recent years. Bishop Edmund Bonner's *Profitable and Necessarye Doctryne*, published in 1555, for instance, offered the clergy, as well as educated laity, a comprehensive catechetical programme. Although its stylistic similarity to the 1543 'King's Book' (*Necessarye Doctryne and Erudician for a Chrysten Man*) may have raised eyebrows among some who had become fatigued by diktats from on high, which in turn may have limited its effectiveness, its quality is unmistaken. The accompanying *Homilies* by John Pendleton and John Harpsfield offered readers inspirational salvific theology in contrast to doom-laden Protestant tracts. Bonner's guidance on children's education, *An Honest Godlye Instruction and Information for the Tradynge, and Bringinge up of Children* similarly was a competent attempt to reverse the teaching of Protestant radicals. Protestant propagandists, who went on to blacken Bonner's name, would downplay his literary work. 'Bonner the oppressor' was a more convenient conclusion in their narrative than 'Bonner the scholar'.

Other catechetical works soon followed in an ambitious plan set out by Pole to create a catalogue of catechetical literary material. Bartolomé Carranza's *Commentaries on the Christian Catechism*, for instance, was a sophisticated work of catechetical instruction that would not only make an important contribution to the catechising of England's laity but also provide the basis for the Roman catechism of 1556. It would in fact go on to become a major source of instruction for clergy for centuries to come. Though composed by a Spaniard, the spiritual roots of the *Commentaries* lay in Mary's Counter-Reformation, 'born in the heat of the English synod begun at the end of 1555' noted José Ignacio Tellechea Idígoras.[56] Another immensely popular work was Thomas Watson's collection of sermons, *Holsome and Catholyke Doctryne* that ran through three official editions. A pirated edition was also produced to meet demand.[57] Numerous primers were also produced such as reprints of the traditional Sarum primers as well as more modern primers such as those published by John Wayland. Though traditional in context, the Wayland primers were unique in that they were written in English, with Latin confined to margins. What is more, these, as well as other Marian primers, omitted reference to many of the old superstitions that pervaded their pre-Reformation counterparts. 'The wonder of charm, pardon and promise', Duffy noted, 'in the older primers had gone for ever.'[58] This blend of old and new that characterised Marian primers was a progressive move by the Catholic Church in recognition of the need to purge worship of superfluous traditions. As such there was little about these trends that can be described as reactionary. Rather they were consistent with the Tridentine initiatives and those of the Catholic (Counter-)Reformation in general.

It is important to add here that the trend of using the vernacular in religious publications was not a Marian novelty, forced upon the administration by Protestants. It is true that the Church had been reluctant to use the vernacular in religious publications lest it encourage among the laity misinterpretations, division and quarrels, all of which were characteristic features of the Protestant Reformation.[59] This did not, however, mean that Rome was universally hostile to vernacular Scripture. A rich, albeit limited, tradition of vernacular writing had existed for centuries, though the invention of the printing press undoubtedly 'democratised God's Word to a degree that had never been possible in a culture of scribal publication'.[60] It should also be remembered that in 1543 Henry VIII himself restricted the reading of Scripture to certain educated quarters of society as noted above, having acknowledged that universal access to the Word of God provoked social unrest. Mary herself may have eschewed the English liturgy for its heretical deviations, but neither she nor Pole was hostile to vernacular Scripture nor was either averse to the translation of the Bible. This they demonstrated by not prohibiting the Great Bible that was prepared by Myles Coverdale in 1539, who worked under commission from Thomas Cromwell. The Marian Church did in fact approve preparation for a new translation of the Bible, though this project never properly got off the ground amidst justifiable fears, akin to those that Henry VIII had, that such a text could provoke quarrels and polemic if held by the wrong hands. John Standish would argue in his work *A discourse wherein is debated whether it be expedient that the Scripture should be in English for al men to reade that wyll*, published in 1554, shortly after Mary's accession, that such texts were unsettling not only for the Church, as the judge of scriptural truth, but also for society in general. He argued that 'teachers in corners and conventicles' would encourage disputes 'betwene man and man, man and wife, maister and servant'.[61] Standish's self-serving doctrinal flip-flopping over the course of the Reformation should not serve to diminish the relevance of his point.[62]

It was not only catechetical works that the Marian administration produced. While the priority, as noted, was to re-establish the dignity of ritual rather than to produce literature to counter scurrilous and satirical Protestant propaganda, production of propagandistic works was not neglected. The leitmotif of contemporary Catholic polemic was to explore both the doctrinal confusion and social destruction that the Reformation had wrought. And there was certainly no shortage of episodes that Catholic writers could cite as consequences of Protestant heresy. In November 1553 the bishop of Gloucester, James Brookes, preaching at St Paul's Cross, rebuked those who had engaged in 'chaunge upon chaunge and lyke never to have lefte chaungyng, til al the hole world had cleane been changed'.[63] Miles Hoggard, in his populist pamphlet, *Displaying of the Protestants*, published in 1556, attributed the indecision and inconsistencies of Protestant theology to the vanities of 'these bunglers' who presumptuously saw fit to contravene the guidance of the Holy Spirit in the formulation of the Mass.[64] Several works highlighted social unrest as the most destructive consequence of heresy. In this respect, the duke of Northumberland's pre-execution address itself was to perform a great service. He confessed that he, as well as others, whom he did not name, had been seduced by 'false and seditious preachers, that have erred from the Catholic faith and the true doctrines of Christ. The doctrine, I mean, which hath continued thro' all Christendom since Christ. For, good people, there is, and hath been ever since Christ, one Catholic church'. He went on to exhort those present 'to take you all example of me, and forsake this new doctrine', not least because of the 'misery that we have been brought; what open rebellion, what open sedition, what great division hath been throughout the whole realm'.[65] John Christopherson developed this theme further, attributing familial, social and political disputes where 'the son hated his own father, the sister her brother, the wife her husband, the servant his master, the subject the ruler', to the work of 'false preachers', 'wicked blasphemy', and the work of the Antichrist.[66]

The range of Marian polemic and apologia was broad in scope and was qualitatively comparable to any Protestant equivalent. Their writers were skilled at choosing themes that chimed most with contemporary popular feelings. Their strong focus on Protestant distortions of the Mass, for instance, was particularly fitting given that the confusion and continual change in church services must have provoked considerable anxiety among a population which was still either largely attached to old rituals or willing to embrace them.

*

Harnessing the intellectual elite to the cause of recatholicisation became a crucial element of the restoration programme. Much work needed to be done here to reorientate both of the universities (Oxford and Cambridge) to their pre-schism theological outlook,[67] conservatives having been steadily rooted out and replaced with evangelicals. Even before the most radical Edwardian attacks on the old faith had occurred, many Zwinglian and Calvinist refugees from the Continent had gained a foothold in both institutions. Most notable among these was Peter Martyr Vermigli, who took the chair of divinity at Cambridge in 1548. By then Stephen Gardiner, the former Chancellor as well as bishop of Winchester, was already languishing in the Tower for his conservative sympathies. With the duke of Northumberland as its chancellor, Cambridge was staunchly supportive of Jane Grey, having been quick to declare the marriage of Mary's parents void and Mary a bastard. Oxford was less radical under its most recent more conservative Chancellor, Sir John Mason, but it too had declared for the split from Rome. After Mary's accession Mason, together with Gardiner, who resumed his old post in Cambridge, was charged with the task of reinstating Catholicism in both institutions. But when Gardiner died in 1555 and Mason stepped aside a year later, suspicions of Protestanism hanging over him, Pole assumed the chancellorship of both universities.

During the short period that had been available, much work was done, especially under Pole's oversight. Several colleges were founded and refounded. In Cambridge Trinity was refounded from scratch, Magdalene College was founded on the site of Buckingham College, a former Benedictine institution, and Gonville Hall was reformed along

Catholic lines under the patronage of John Caius, the College to be known henceforth as Gonville and Caius. In Oxford, St John the Baptist College was founded on the former site of the dissolved monastic college of St Bernard's while the College of the Most Holy Trinity was founded on the remains of the Benedictine Durham College. The subsequent visitations to both universities enacted a purge of some 130 evangelicals who were exiled and replaced by a new conservative cohort. Masses were restored to chapels,[68] old rituals were revived and traditional theology was once again taught. Additionally, those Cambridge academics who remained in their posts but were suspected of harbouring evangelical sympathies were compelled to swear a public oath of allegiance to the restored faith. The reforms of the universities represented major progress after their neglect under Edward during whose reign much of Oxford's library, for instance, had been destroyed and colleges in both universities had been deprived of their choral foundations.[69] So comprehensive was the work of Marian visitations that 'by the spring of 1557', noted Claire Cross, 'Pole could realistically presume that his officers had extirpated all outward signs of heresy from both universities [. . .] As with the strength of committed Protestantism in the universities at the end of Edward VI's reign, the extent of Catholic reconversion only became apparent with the change of government on the queen's death'.[70]

The seminaries and academic foundations that the Marian Church established were to be chiefly responsible for the widespread recusancy of the early to mid-Elizabethan period.[71] The seminary missions of the Jesuits and others, conversely, which Dickens, for instance, claimed had a formative impact on Elizabethan Catholicism offered in fact little more than a supportive role to an already flourishing Catholic community which played host to a large body of priests.[72] Seminary priests did become important for the preservation of post-Reformation Catholicism but not until the death of Marian recusant clergy. 'Even if we adopt the strict test of organic unity with and obedience to the see of Rome', argued Haigh, 'the continuity of English Catholicism was fractured only briefly.' In 1564, a year after the end of the Council of Trent, Rome began to issue directives to English Catholics, forbidding them to comply with Elizabethan religious laws, most notably prohibiting them to attend Protestant services.[73] As such, 'the early part of the reign of Elizabeth should not be seen as an unfortunate gap in the history of English Catholicism but as a period in which the constituency from which later recusants could be recruited was substantially maintained'.[74] Considerable Catholic resistance to Elizabethan Protestantism was made possible not only because of the strong foundations that the Marian administration had laid but also because of the Elizabethan regime's slow progress to Protestantise England. Even during the last two decades of Elizabeth's reign, state visitations to parishes were reporting a high level of Catholic practice.[75] Haigh concluded that, although there were practical adjustments to the way Catholics worshipped, that was brought about by the 'disestablishment in 1559, but there was no breach in the continuity of English Catholicism'.[76] Tridentine reforms did penetrate English Catholicism through missionaries, but they did not create a 'new' Church devoid of Marian roots. The recusant Church was already imbued with the spirit of the Counter-Reformation, chiefly because of the work of the Marian administration. Suffice it to note that resistance to Elizabethan reforms among the clergy came overwhelmingly from Marian appointees, which, according to Duffy, 'is a remarkable testimony to the [Marian] regime's ability to recognise or to inspire men with a principled commitment to Catholicism'.[77]

Like Mary, Elizabeth moved quickly to purge the universities of non-conformers, but as the Protestant exiles returned they were astounded by the level of restoration that had been achieved at the universities. It is crucial not to view Elizabeth's reversals of these achievements as a failure of Marian academic strategy. In fact Marian policies were to have a lasting impact. For instance, the Catholic humanism that was instilled in Oxford by Pole attracted many Catholic students. The most notable of these was Edmund Campion, who would leave the University for Douai in 1569 to return to England as a Jesuit in 1579 to try to convince Elizabeth's Council of the truth of Catholicism. For his efforts he was found guilty of treason and executed in 1581. So rather than there being any particular flaw in the Marian strategy, it was the shortage of time, more than any other single factor, argued Cross, that 'frustrated the plans of Mary and Pole for Catholic higher education in England'.[78] Despite this impediment the survival of Catholicism in England owes much to Marian education policy.

*

The Dickensian idea that Mary 'failed to discover the Counter-Reformation',[79] however, continues to appeal to modern historians. 'Even her reunion with Rome', Guy argued, 'lacked the fire of true Counter-Reformation.'[80] Dickens certainly had nothing positive to say about Marian religious policy. He saw her restoration of religious houses as particularly reactionary, a throwback to a 'medieval past' when what was needed, he argued, was an imaginative drive towards a 'seminarist future'. The Catholic cause, he continued, 'needed training colleges, not retreats from the world'. The few monks in the restored houses could never provide the vigour and swiftness that 'the parlous situation of English Catholicism demanded'. Or be a substitute for Jesuit missionary work, which, he claimed, Pole so opposed.[81] So obsessed was the Marian administration with repealing Protestant legislation, Dickens contended, that it forgot that in the last resort proper religious instruction mattered infinitely more than ecclesiastical legislation and endless rituals.[82] In short, he concludes, both Mary and Pole 'displayed the tragedy of the doctrinarians called to practical leadership, yet lacking the instinct toward human beings, that sense of possible in a real world, which have always proved more useful in English affairs than high principles and strict logic based on narrow premises'.[83] And, he concluded, it would have made no difference to the state of Catholicism had the Marian administration lasted longer. The components to make it work were simply not present.

The achievements of the Marian administration in restoring Catholicism run contrary to the claims of anti-Marian historiography, Protestant or otherwise, which prevailed up to the 1960s and to a lesser extent, beyond. Layers of prejudice, myth and misrepresentation have now been peeled away to reveal a picture that is at odds with the old assumptions. Critics of Marian religious policy tend to overlook the task that confronted the regime. So weakened was the Church by successive reformations, its property purloined and desecrated, its independence eradicated, its clergy cowed into submission and believers terrorised by treason laws, that it is in fact surprising just how much of the old faith was restored during Mary's brief rule. And much that was subsequently achieved became part of mainstream post-Trent Catholicism.

The brevity of Mary's reign, however, does not fully explain why there remained gaps. Here it is unhelpful and altogether inaccurate to look for blame exclusively towards Mary herself or her bishops and advisors, although some blame can certainly be attributed to them all. The legacy of the previous twenty years together with inclement weather conditions, poor harvests, high mortality, especially among priests, inherited financial burdens and continuous economic woes all had a significant bearing on the ability of the government to implement its programme of restoration. Notwithstanding the continued reverence for the old ways among the English population, there was no getting away from the fact that the two decades since the break from Rome had nurtured a sense of apathy towards religious observance in varying degrees among the population at large. There was also a feeling of uncertainty about the prospect of the survival of Mary's legacy. As long as she remained childless and Elizabeth remained coy about the religious direction that she would take once on the throne, many who would have otherwise invested financially in the Marian programme of restoration held off.[84]

The Continent as yet did not offer anything radically new to emulate given that most of the work of the Council of Trent was to occur after both Mary and Pole had died. This is a significant point when addressing the accusation that the Marian regime failed to discover the Counter-Reformation.[85] If the Marian Church had been detached from continental developments[86] it was only to the extent that the schism that had lasted for over two decades had allowed it to be. Many gaps of course by now had been filled. It has already been noted that Mary's restoration programme was based on both pragmatism and caution. 'Far from pursuing a programme of blind reaction', noted Duffy, 'the Marian authorities consistently sought to promote a version of traditional Christianity which had absorbed whatever they saw as positive in the Edwardian and Henrician reforms, and which was subtly but distinctively different from the Catholicism of the 1520s.'[87] As such, it would be reasonable to claim that Mary's was a programme not of reaction but of creative reconstruction.[88]

Ideally Mary would have liked a hastier pace of reform, but the politician in her urged caution. The level-headedness of her proclamation on 'freedom of conscience', which prohibited both written and verbal religious disputes whilst allowing freedom of conscience pending parliamentary legislation to the contrary,[89] reflected her realisation that the reconstruction of Catholic England was not going to be as easy as either she or Pole had thought. Thomas Mayer stressed Pole's legation as a success both in terms of the administration of the Church and in the restoration of theological order. By 1558, Mayer noted, 'a good deal had been done and an administrative and legal framework put in place that would have allowed a good deal more, to say nothing of the progress of Christian instruction and restoration of Catholic ceremonial [...] together with reserves of traditional piety and practice [... and] the Marians' success in grasping the value of the printing press'.[90] The fact 'that England did not remain a Catholic country', he concluded, 'must be seen much more as an accident that we have been readily prepared to admit'.[91]

*

The contrast between Dickens's or Elton's view that Mary failed to discover the Counter-Reformation and that of William Wizeman's that 'the Marian church invented what is often called the Counter-Reformation'[92] could not be more striking. Yet what traditionalists like Dickens claimed, which was held up for so long as received wisdom on the subject, has been shown to have been mostly wrong. In fact it would not be unreasonable to claim that the traditional view of Marian religious policy was one of the most erroneously held opinions in British history, given the successes of the Marian administration in implementing so much of its programme of renewal and its anticipation of so much of Tridentine theology. In the Tridentine spirit, the Marian Church remained rooted in tradition, in prayers for the dead, in the doctrine of Purgatory, in the veneration of saints, yet it did not eschew innovations, many of which, such as vernacular worship and new models of preaching, were central to Protestant reformers. That the Church survived only for the lifetime of its key patron, Mary, is no aspersion on its achievements, especially in view of the survival of much of its substance within recusant spheres and of its organic connection with the subsequent reforms in mainstream Counter-Reformation Catholicism.

Yet at this point the reader may be forgiven for posing the question 'what about the burnings?' And indeed, he would be justified in posing it, for no amount of talk about the successes of Marian religious policy can serve to whitewash the suppression of Protestants. Nor should it be allowed to do so. But that is not to say that the policy cannot be explained and even justified. Even suggesting this may shock some readers in today's hypersensitive world. But to avoid a classic historian's fallacy it is essential to set one's enquiry within proper context so that motives can be understood, if not necessarily sympathised with. It is to this issue, therefore, that the final chapter of this study will now turn.

NOTES

[1] 'Simon Renard to the Emperor, 19 October 1553', CSPS, vol. 11.

[2] 'Cardinal Pole to the Cardinal of Lorraine, 5 January 1555, 4', CSPV, vol. 6.

[3] Edwards, *Mary I*, p. 223.

[4] T. F. Mayer, 'Cardinal Pole's Concept of *Reformatio*: The *Reformatio Angliae* and Bartelome Carranza', in Edwards and R. Truman, eds., *Reforming Catholicism in the England of Mary Tudor*, pp. 65–6.

[5] Cited in J. Edwards, 'Fray Bartolomé Carranza's blueprint for a reformed Catholic Church in England', in T. F. Mayer, ed., *Reforming Reformation* (Farnham: Ashgate, 2012), p. 144.

[6] L. F. Solt, *Church and State in Early Modern England, 1509–1640* (Oxford: Oxford University Press, 1990), pp. 61–2; Also, 'Brief Summary of what took place concerning Church Property, 20 January 1555?', CSPV, vol. 6.

[7] D. Loades, 'The Marian Episcopate', in Duffy and Loades eds., *The Church of Mary Tudor*, p. 33.

[8] Ibid., p. 46.

[9] Ibid., p. 50.

[10] E. Duffy, *Fires of Faith: Catholic England under Mary Tudor* (New Haven: Yale University Press, 2009), p. 25.

[11] Ibid., p. 23, p. 99.

[12] C. Haigh, 'The Continuity of Catholicism in the English Reformation', in Haigh, ed., *The English Reformation Revised*, p. 177.

[13] Duffy, *Fires of Faith*, p. 25.

[14] See for instance R. Pogson, 'Revival and Reform in Mary Tudor's Church: A Question of Money', in Haigh, ed., *The English Reformation Revised*, p. 141.

[15] Ibid., p. 155.

[16] T. F. Mayer, *Reginald Pole: Prince and Prophet* (Cambridge: Cambridge University Press, 2000), pp. 256–66.

[17] W. Wizeman, *The Theology and Spirituality of Mary Tudor's Church* (Aldershot and Burlington: Ashgate Publishing, 2006), p. 20.

[18] Ibid., p. 20.

[19] See A. de Mezerac-Zanetti, 'Reforming the Liturgy under Henry VIII: The

Instructions of John Clerk, Bishop of Bath and Wells', *Journal of Ecclesiastical History*, 64 (2013), 96–111; see also Duffy, *Stripping of the Altars*, ch. 11, 12, 13 and 14.

[20] Elton, *Reform and Reformation: England*, p. 385.

[21] Dickens, *English Reformation*, p. 383.

[22] R. Pogson, 'Reginald Pole and the Priorities of Government in Mary Tudor's Church', *The Historical Journal*, 18, 1975, p. 6.

[23] Loades, *The Reign of Mary Tudor: politics*, p. 293.

[24] E. Duffy, 'Cardinal Pole Preaching: St Andrew's Day 1557', in Duffy and Loades, ed., *The Church of Mary Tudor*, pp. 177–8; For details of controversy and translation of crucial passage in the letter see J. Edwards, *Archbishop Pole* (Farnham and Burlington: Ashgate Publishing, 2014), chapter 8.

[25] D. Fenlon, 'Pole, Carranza and the Pulpit', in Edwards and R. Truman, eds., *Reforming Catholicism in the England of Mary Tudor*, p. 85.

[26] Ibid.

[27] Duffy, 'Cardinal Pole Preaching', p. 181.

[28] Ibid. John Edwards's translation is slightly different but the gist of what Pole is writing remains the same. See Edwards, *Archbishop Pole*, p. 215.

[29] Fenlon, 'Pole, Carranza and the Pulpit', p. 86.

[30] Edwards, *Mary I*, p. 243.

[31] For a discussion of this theme see Wizeman, 'Martyrs and Anti-martyrs and Mary Tudor's Church'.

[32] Duffy, 'Cardinal Pole Preaching', p. 176.

[33] 'Count Feria to Father Ribadeneyra, 22 March 1558, 415', CSPS, vol. 13.

[34] Loades, *The Reign of Mary Tudor*, pp. 293–4.

[35] 'Letter to the whole Society', July 23 and 7 August 1553, 'Letter to Cardinal Pole', January 24, 1555, *Letters of St. Ignatius Loyola*, ed. W. J. Young (Chicago: Loyola University Press, 1959), pp. 300–1, 361–2. See also 'Letter form Ignatius Loyola to Pole', 2 July 1555 in which Loyola again offers the society's services to 'send two or three students here of to the German College', T. F. Mayer, *The Correspondence of Reginald Pole, A Calendar, 1555–1558, Restoring the English Church*. 3 vols. (Aldershot: Ashgate, 2004), vol. 3, p. 119.

[36] 'Count Feria to Father Ribadeneyra, 22 March 1558, 415', CSPS, vol. 13.

[37] Duffy, *Fires of Faith*, p. 31.

[38] Duffy, 'Cardinal Pole Preaching', p. 176.

[39] Fenlon, 'Pole, Carranza and the Pulpit', p. 94.

[40] J. P. Willis, *Church Music and Protestantism in Post-Reformation England: Discourses, Sites and Identities* (Farnham and Burlington: Ashgate, 2010), p. 53.

[41] Wizeman, 'The Religious Policy of Mary I', p. 165.

[42] Willis, *Church Music and Protestantism in Post-Reformation England*, p. 108.

[43] Wizeman 'The Religious Policy of Mary', p. 166.

[44] Loades, *The Reign of Mary Tudor*, p. 298.

[45] Duffy, *Fires of Faith*, p. 6.

[46] Ibid., p. 6.

[47] Dickens, *English Reformation*, p. 383.

[48] Loades, 'The English Church during the Reign of Mary I', p. 41.

[49] Loades, *The Reign of Mary Tudor*, p. 301.

[50] Elton, *Reform and Reformation*, p. 383.

[51] J. Loach, 'The Marian Establishment and the Printing Press', *English Historical Review*, 101/398, 1986, pp. 135–48.

[52] Hughes and Larkin, *Tudor Royal Proclamations*, vol. 2, p. 6.

[53] Duffy, *The Stripping of the Altars*, p. 529.

54 Duffy, *Fires of Faith*, pp. 59–60.

55 Ibid., p. 60.

56 Cited in Edwards, *Fray Bartolomé Caranza*, p. 144.

57 Duffy, *Fires of Faith*, p. 69.

58 Duffy, *The Stripping of the Altars*, p. 541.

59 A. Walsham, 'Unclasping the Book? Post-Reformation English Catholicism and the Vernacular Bible', *Journal of British Studies*, 42/2, 2003, p. 147.

60 Ibid., p. 160.

61 Martin, *Religious Radicals*, p. 81.

62 Duffy, 'Fires of Faith', p. 63.

63 Duffy, *Fires of Faith*, p. 73.

64 Ibid., p. 78.

65 Cited in, P. F. Tytler, *England under the reigns of Edward VI and Mary: With the Contemporary History of Europe* (London: Richard Bently, 1839). 2 vols., vol. 2, pp. 230–3.

66 Cited in Duffy, *Fires of Faith*, pp. 71–2.

67 For discussion of this theme see C. Cross, 'The English Universities 1553–1558', in Duffy and Loades, eds., *The Church of Mary Tudor*; also, Edwards, *Mary I*, pp. 242–5.

68 Cross in ibid., p. 64.

69 Wizeman, 'The Religious Policy of Mary I', pp. 160–1.

70 Cross, 'The English Universities 1553–1558', pp. 72–3.

71 Haigh, 'The Continuity of Catholicism in the English Reformation', p. 207.

72 Ibid., pp. 187, 196.

73 Ibid., p. 185.

74 Ibid., p. 179.

75 Ibid., p. 206; for a discussion see Duffy, *The Stripping of the Altars*, pp. 570–84.

76 Haigh, 'The Continuity of Catholicism in the English Reformation', p. 204.

77 Duffy, *Fires of Faith*, p. 197.

78 Cross, 'The English Universities 1553–1558', p. 76.

79 Dickens, *English Reformation*, p. 384.

80 Guy, *Tudor England*, p. 227.

81 Dickens, *English Reformation*, p. 383.

82 Ibid., p. 384.

83 Ibid., p. 385.

84 Wizeman, *The Theology and Spirituality of Mary Tudor's Church*, p. 22.

85 Duffy, *The Stripping of the Altars*, p. 525.

86 L. Wooding, *Rethinking Catholicism in Marian England*. Oxford Historical Monographs (Oxford: Clarendon Press, 2000), pp. 115–51.

87 Duffy, *The Stripping of the Altars*, p. 525.

88 Ibid., p. 526.

89 Hughes and Larkin, *Tudor Royal Proclamations*, pp. 5–6.

90 T. F. Mayer, 'The Success of Cardinal Pole's Final Legation', in Duffy and Loades, eds., *The Church of Mary Tudor*, p. 174.

91 Ibid., pp. 174–5.

92 Wizeman, *The Theology And Spirituality*, p. 251.

✣ 12 ✣

Defending the Indefensible

T HE NATURE OF THE SUPPRESSION of recalcitrant Protestants remains
the most difficult aspect of the Marian reign to justify or defend and
which overshadows the government's numerous achievements. It is its most
maligned and best-remembered policy. 'The madness of a system', wrote
Dickens, 'which would burn a virtuous human being for his inability to
accept a metaphysical theory of the Eucharist must stagger even a generation
well accustomed to institutional and doctrinaire crimes.'[1] The image of Mary
as 'that horrible monster Jezebel of England' was made famous by John
Knox in his *The first blast of the trumpet against the monstruous regiment of
women* published in 1559 while the cruelties of her regime were enshrined
for posterity by John Foxe's *Book of Martyrs*, which according to Elton
'did not (as apologists would have it) create a legend; it commemorated a
truth'.[2] But even allowing for partisan hyperbole that for too long passed
for scholarship, the burning of nearly three hundred men and women,
mostly from lower social strata, argued Duffy, presents the 'greatest barrier
to a positive assessment of the Marian restoration'.[3] It is this aspect of her
reign that ushers in charges against the regime of fanaticism and bigotry.

As we have seen, recent scholarship has done much to ensure that the
burnings, as horrific as they were, should no longer be regarded as the only
benchmark by which to assess the Marian administration. It is important
to note that most of the criticism of both Mary and her administration
was compiled from a confessional perspective and as such was deliberately
designed to give the impression that Mary was the inventor of the practice
of the burning of heretics, or at the very least, that she was enthusiastic
about it. As a concept, however, martyrdom was as familiar to the early
Church as it was to the pencraft of Foxe. To be a martyr, the term deriving
from the Greek word (*martys*) meaning witness, was to assert an unyielding
adherence to one's faith, even to the point of death. Martyrdom had become,
noted Edwards, 'fully part of the religious life and the procedures of the
Church long before Mary's time'.[4] The early Church had no shortage of
martyrs who had been condemned by pagan authorities. But with the onset
of successive schisms in the Roman Church during the Middle Ages the

number of those falling foul of any given doctrinal orthodoxy grew as too did the number of those being called martyrs by their co-religionists and heretics by their persecutors.

Foxe was to initiate a trend in Protestant historiography that conventionally was to regard the Marian 'martyrs' as victims of persecution. He neither acknowledged the political and social context of the burnings nor assessed positively the due process of the law that the accused were subjected to.[5] Taken out of context, the process of condemning heretics may be seen to have been outright persecution, but in reality the hearings and executions were not determined by hatred of the condemned.[6] In fact, as Dodd wrote, 'great moderation was used', and execution of those charged with heresy was the final part of a meticulous process that offered the accused earthly, as well as spiritual salvation and the chance of last minute conversions. The bishops, Dodd continued, 'were persons of great compassion, and no friends of persecution'.[7] The Marian Church was clear that the role of tribunals was to save souls and as such any burning of heretics was deemed by the authorities to be a failure.

'Neither Mary nor Pole', as Whitelock noted, 'expected to burn so many; they wanted the heretics to be reconciled rather than die, and for the burnings to be carried out judiciously and without vindictiveness.'[8] Writing to Cardinal Pole in December 1555, Mary stressed that although she believed 'it would be well to inflict punishment at this beginning', it had to be done so 'without much cruelty or passion'. Moreover, while it was important not to omit 'to do such justice on those who choose by their false doctrine to deceive simple persons', it was similarly important 'that the people may clearly comprehend that they have not been condemned without just cause, whereby others will be brought to know the truth, and will beware of letting themselves be induced to relapse into such new and false opinions'. She stressed her desire for the burnings ultimately to act not only as a deterrent, but as a means of converting souls by insisting that any burnings in London should be conducted 'in the presence of some member of the Council; and that during such executions, both here and elsewhere, some good and pious sermons be preached'.[9]

Foxe's own records of the lengthy and meticulous exchanges between the accused and their interrogators indicate that the administration and its ecclesiastical officials sought primarily to redeem rather than condemn the accused, though Foxe's intention here is to illustrate the anxiety and traumas to which the accused were subjected to. Foxe noted that:

> The bishop of Winchester, in the name of him selfe and the rest moued Maister Hooper earnestly, to forsake the euyll & corrupt doctrine (as he termed it) preached in the dayes of king Edward. 6. Gardiner exhorteth M. Hooper to returne to the Popes church.and to returne to the vnitie

of the catholicke church, and to acknowledge the Popes holynes to
be the head of the same Church, according to the determination of
the whole Parlament, promising that as he hym selfe, wyth other hys
brethren had receyued the Popes blessing and the Queenes mercy:
euen so mercy was ready to be shewed to hym and others, if he would
arise with them, and condescend to the Popes holynes.[10]

Not quite the process of unadulterated cruelty that Foxe intended to portray.
The burnings, therefore, were intended as a last resort to serve not only as
punishment but also as a source of purification of the condemned as well
as a deterrent against those intending to lapse into doctrinal error. Every
burning, however, was considered by the Church as a failure on its part to
reclaim souls for the faith.

What crucially needs to be remembered here is that every European
state in the sixteenth century considered heresy to be a grave sin that
required purging not only for the sake of the guilty individual but also
for the general good of society itself. Heresy was as much associated by
the Marian administration with sedition as it would be by Protestant
administrations that followed.[11] Mary believed that heresy 'had ruined her
mother's marriage and her own early life. When it took hold, it destroyed the
immortal souls of those whom it afflicted, and the most extreme steps were
justified in eliminating it and thus protecting the realm'.[12] As such, it did
not matter from which background or social standing heretics came from,
whether they were genuine in their heretical beliefs, or opportunist, male
or female. If they did not recant, they would burn 'like an infected animal
to protect the rest of the flock'.[13] Mary's proclamation on the 'freedom of
conscience', as well as her proclamation of 26 May 1555 on the enforcement
of the statutes on public order, declared that 'sedition and false rumours
have been nourished and maintained in this realm by the subtlety and
malice of some evil-disposed persons which take it upon them without
sufficient authority to preach and to interpret the word of God'[14] and that
'heresy and Lollardy, reading and expounding of scripture and matters of
religion in secret corners by persons not authorized' was as menacing as
such seditious behaviour as 'counterfeiting of coin' and 'unlawful assemblies
and conventicles'.[15]

The punishments meted out to heretics in England were never arbitrary,
but followed a carefully structured process based on parliamentary statute,
with the acquiescence, it should be noted, of the political class.[16] Mary's
heresy legislation was no exception given that the 'majority of Christians
of all shades of opinion believed that the death penalty was appropriate
for obstinate heretics'.[17] Indeed, it is not mere Marian apologia to argue,
as Lingard pointed out, that it 'was the lot of Mary to live in an age of
religious intolerance, when to punish the professors of erroneous doctrine

was inculcated as a duty, no less by those who rejected, than by those who asserted the papal authority'.[18] It is a point that Thomas Freeman reiterated. 'Toleration of all religious opinions', he argued, 'was in sixteenth-century eyes not a realistic option. No English government had ever practised it and the only European governments that accepted the existence of dissident religious minorities did so out of necessity, because they were too weak to crush them.'[19]

Belief in the necessity of the suppression of heresy spanned the denominational divide, though it varied in both brutality and intensity. Modern commentators may regard such a situation with indignation, albeit often hypocritically as an indignation about one persecution often accompanies acceptance of another, but to inhabitants of the medieval world such treatment of heretics was not only acceptable but essential. To have chosen to adhere to a particular variant of Christianity as opposed to another, a heretic, a term derived from Greek *hairein*, 'to choose', had both transgressed against God and threatened the integrity of society itself. John Fisher's view that heresy was 'a perilous weed' that corrupted hearts, quenched faith and murdered men's souls was not that of a religious fanatic, but of a bishop concerned about the devastating social and political consequences of men deviating from orthodox teaching for personal gain or from ill-thought out or erroneous interpretation of Scripture.[20] With religion being at the core of political and social life, as well as defining people's view of personal salvation, the state saw the suppression of a creed, which it perceived to be distorted or alien, to be as necessary as states see the suppression of terrorism today. The fate of dynasties, of social and political order and the welfare of millions, both spiritual and material, could be disturbed by heretical views, which is why such a hard line was taken against them. The Marian burnings from a political perspective were regarded necessary both to stem the tide of heresy and to suppress the possibility of a Protestant plot akin to Wyatt's rebellion. There was, moreover, to recall once more, a genuine concern over the souls of the heretics, which is why every opportunity was given to the accused to recant.

By the time of the Reformation a complex set of laws to deal with heresy prevailed across Europe, notably in Spain with the Inquisition but latterly in Protestant areas. England itself enacted legislation to deal with the growing heresy of Lollardy, notably during the reigns of Richard II in 1382, Henry IV in 1401 and Henry V in 1414. Under Edward VI, 'no sooner had the Protestants obtained ascendancy', wrote Lingard, 'than they displayed the same persecuting spirit which they had formally condemned; burning the Anabaptists, and preparing to burn the catholic at the stake, for no other crime than adherence to religious opinion'.[21] Though Edward's regime repealed heresy legislation, it sanctioned under treason laws the burning of at least two Anabaptists.[22] Similar legislation was used against More and Fisher and which would be used against many of Elizabeth's religious opponents. John Rogers, Edward VI's royal chaplain, had been a fervent supporter of the need to burn heretics. When asked by Foxe, one of the few evangelical opponents of the practice, to intervene on behalf of Joan Bocher, one of the Anabaptists, he refused, commenting that burning was 'sufficiently mild' for a crime as serious as heresy.[23] Cranmer, with the highest profile of the Marian victims, was in the process of codifying a reformed version of canon law, the *Reformatio mobilis ecclesiasticarum*, which enshrined execution as the ultimate penalty for heresy. Whether or not this would have involved burning is uncertain,[24] but given Cranmer's central role in sending the Anabaptists to the fire during Edward's reign it is certain that he would have been more than willing to prescribe death to heretics when persuasion failed. Given that he had virtually bullied 'a reluctant Edward VI into signing Joan (Bocher's) death warrant',[25] burning as the method of execution cannot be discounted from Cranmer's prescriptions. Whatever the case, had the code ever been enacted then 'a type of Protestant inquisition' was certainly on the cards.[26]

The consensus, therefore, which prevailed across the denominational divide was that society needed to be purged of heresy and that the most effective way to do this was to burn recalcitrant heretics at the stake. Mary's view, in this respect, as Richards noted, was that of 'a thoroughly conventional person'.[27] Mary's pursuit of doctrinal orthodoxy totally reflected the sixteenth-century value system in which contrary religious views were regarded as error and treasonous. She was no more a religious fanatic than any other ruler of the time, while in terms of a numbers game, as Guy argued, 'in the European context her "inquisition" was small scale'.[28]

Gruesome torture, especially public executions, was nothing new in either medieval England or Europe. Nor was it infrequent, or for that matter, socially disapproved of. Huge bloodthirsty crowds would gather wherever the latest hanging, pressing, boiling, ducking, flogging, burning, decapitation or quartering was being staged. Specifically during the reign of Henry VIII, tens of thousands in England (excluding Wales) alone,[29] including every surviving member of the Plantagenet dynasty, were executed for a variety of crimes. As well as More and Fisher, Henry had over thirty people executed for non-compliance with prevailing religious doctrine. In total, eighty-one people were burnt at the stake during his reign. The execution of Friar John Forest on 22 May 1538, the only Catholic to be executed for heresy (as opposed to treason), was particularly gruesome. After spending four years in prison, he was dragged to the place of his execution in Smithfield, his hands and feet tied to a hurdle. Having listened to an hour of lecturing from Bishop Hugh Latimer on the virtues of the royal supremacy in front of a baying crowd, he had chains wrapped around his waist and under his armpits before being suspended above a fire to die an excruciating, lingering death. The Edwardian regime, as noted, continued to burn heretics, while Elizabeth, though more lenient than her father, was responsible for around 2500 executions, among which five were by burning. Particularly severe was her persecution of Catholic recusants during the latter half of her reign, during which her leniency became exhausted after the discovery of a number of plots to depose her. Between 1577 and 1603, 183 Catholics were executed. These cases, however, have been viewed by historians more as objectionable details than as reign-defining events. For instance, Foxe gives cursive attention in a rather prosaic style to the religious executions perpetuated by the Henrician regime in stark contrast to the emotion ridden, detailed narrative he accords to the Marian executions. The Elizabethan religious executions are omitted altogether from his accounts. For pursuing those who refused to accept her laws, Elizabeth has been commended for her shrewdness and competence in the face of adversity. Mary for her part has been demonised as bloodthirsty for doing the same during her reign.

Hundreds of Catholics continued to be executed during the seventeenth century under the treason laws while in Ireland during the 1640s to 1650s the anti-Catholic purges and deliberate policies of crop-burning and starvation were responsible for the majority of the estimated 600,000 deaths out of a population of 1.4 million.[30] Following the final defeat of the Jacobite (Catholic) cause during the late seventeenth century Catholics in the United Kingdom officially became second-class subjects until their emancipation in 1829, though unofficially long after that.[31] Is the morbid fascination for blood and gore any less prevalent in the twenty-first century than it was in centuries past? An overview of internet sites offering footage of gruesome executions suggests not. The modern and medieval mindsets in this respect perhaps are not that far apart after all.

It was always expected that there would be some executions in the wake of Mary's accession, Northumberland and Cranmer leading the list of dead men walking. In the end, 'however enlightened its thinking and however broad its support base, Mary's Church conducted one of the fiercest and most concentrated persecutions in Christian history'.[32] The search for moral equivalents and the exaggerated and hyperbolic accounts by Foxe and other Protestant polemicists can neither underplay nor disguise the fact that the number of burnings occurring on Mary's watch was exceptionally high, in English history at least, if not by European standards as a whole. In 1556 in the Netherlands alone some 1300 heretics had been executed by burning, hanging or drowning.[33] Determining the reasons for the level of burnings that occurred during the Marian reign is complex, but apportioning blame to one or two individuals serves little purpose other than that of propaganda.

To expect the authorities to have overlooked such dangerous threats from heretics is to miss the point completely. The victims were fully aware of the potential consequences of their actions. As Richards noted, 'By the legal and doctrinal criteria of the time, they were indeed "heretics"'[34] and not, as Loades claimed, 'perfectly innocuous people' because they would not accept transubstantiation.[35] By openly transgressing against both ecclesiastical and temporal law, they willfully went to the fire, refusing even to accept the mercy that was extended to them up to the point of death in return for their recantations.[36] Heretics, as defined by the contemporary legal code, were simultaneously criminals and as such needed to be treated accordingly. Denying transubstantiation was not merely a religious act but an act of political defiance. Consequently, Richards's exoneration of the victims as blameless because they were merely making a 'choice to witness to their faith by dying for it and in it'[37] does not offer a consistent argument; they either were heretics and with it guilty of a heinous crime for the time or they were not. They were to blame in the sense that they chose to engage in a criminal act by the standards of the mid-sixteenth century, and a serious one at that. Nevertheless, apportioning blame to the victims is not wholly satisfactory; someone still had to light the pyre.

Everything was done in strict accordance with the law, which secular authority – Crown, Parliament and Privy Council – endorsed. But in the past heresy legislation was applied sparingly, which raises the question, why not so under Mary? To ask, however, 'what turned this humane well-read humanist Christian [. . .] into the most ruthless persecutor'[38] is to enquire with a modern mind and to ignore the contemporary moral order and political necessities as well as the meticulous legal process that accompanied heresy trials. With confessional identity entwined with national identity, a heretic could plausibly be identified as a traitor as he would be under Elizabeth as much as under Mary. But if stamping out sedition was a key motive for the burnings then the chosen victims, most of whom were from lower social strata – artisans, husbandmen, men and women – were hardly the stuff that political rebels and leaders were made of.[39] More fitting targets from the gentry and nobility suffered mere exile, from where they continued to campaign against the regime. One could, however, speculate whether focusing on heretics from lower strata did in fact deter sedition among heretics from higher strata. Indeed, contrary to long-received scholarly opinion,[40] there were clear signs that the tide of heresy was being checked and with this too the chances of a Protestant plot (see below).

It is unlikely that letters from the Privy Council dating from July 1557 to several local sheriffs and bailiffs requesting explanations as to 'what hath moved them to staye suche personnes as have byn condempned for heresye from execucion'[41] is evidence of scepticism among some local authorities about the effectiveness of the burnings. It was most probably procedural and administrative obstacles rather than any doubts or scruples on the part of local officials that were responsible for the delay in the executions of a few condemned people. The execution of Agnes Bongeor, for instance, scheduled for 2 August 1557, was stayed because, as Foxe records, 'her name was wrong writtē within the writ'. Once the paperwork had been sorted out, she was executed on 17 September.[42] There may well have been one or two cases in which local officials delayed procedures to save the lives of the condemned. The events surrounding the Wiltshire pair John Hunt and Richard White in 1557–8 is a case in point. The two key officials involved, Henry Clifford, the justice of the peace, and his father-in-law, Sir Anthony Hungerford, the under-sheriff of Wiltshire, seem to have found a procedural error in the writ concerning the two men and deferred their execution until amendments could be made. The motive of the under-sheriff may well have been to stall the execution for as long as possible in the knowledge that Mary was seriously ill, so much so that when he received the new writ he burnt it and denied that he had ever received it. The death on 28 August 1558 of William Geffrie, the chancellor of the diocese of Salisbury and arch-suppressor of heretics, as well as the trial judge in the case, doubtless emboldened the under-sheriff to act as he did.[43] His act in fact saved both Hunt and White from the fire as Mary died before their case could be resolved. Scruple might well have played a part only in a few isolated cases, and even here there is simply insufficient evidence to be certain if it had placed a spanner in an otherwise well-oiled machine of suppression that carried on right through to the end of Mary's reign. And apart from the Hunt and White case, all that the stays gained for the condemned were temporary reprieves.

The claims that the Church 'had come no-where near destroying its heretics'[44] or that the stream 'of ordinary men and women who were prepared to die for their faith showed no sign of drying up'[45] are unconvincing. The evidence indicates that the burnings were in fact tailing off by the summer of 1558 not because the authorities and local magistrates were having second thoughts about the effectiveness of the policy, or that the machinery of state was breaking down, but because the 'Protestant hydra' was being finally decapitated. The reduction in the number of defiant activists to execute would suggest so.[46] It needs to be remembered that those who were burnt were the most radical of the evangelicals. To most of their co-religionists death by burning did not appeal and certainly such a gruesome prospect persuaded many waverers to conform to the new religious order,[47] reducing defiance to a minimum. The recantation of so many, from high-profile personalities like Sir John Cheke, Edward VI's former tutor,[48] to ordinary people, was sufficient to galvanise evangelical exiles into reinforcing their campaign so as to stiffen the resolve of the co-religionists back home. Perhaps, as Duffy argued, the increase in the volume of clandestine publications in circulation during 1555–6 was a mark not of Protestant strength but of profound anxiety among Protestants about the number of recantations that were being made by their co-religionists.[49] It is all but certain that had the Marian administration lasted longer the burnings would have ceased and the restored Church would have developed its authority unchallenged. It is difficult, therefore, to identify the conditions for 'a religious civil war on the French model' which Loades suggests could have potentially occurred had Mary remained queen for longer.[50]

If the outcome of the campaign against heresy is viewed in this light then the accusation of abject cruelty levelled against the Marian administration, that it perpetrated in five years what other regimes perpetrated in decades, loses much of its ability to shock. By ridding the country of the most radical Protestants, either through execution or exile, 'one by one, the conventicles were being uprooted and destroyed', and the restoration could continue more or less unhindered.[51] This was only made possible, however, because of the intensity of the campaign to track down heretics.

Protestant martyrologists have vehemently asserted that the burnings were acts of an evil and vengeful Church. But, as has been argued, this view does not sit well with either the nature of the restored Church or the personalities of Mary and her bishops. Why the painstaking interrogations of suspects and the determination to save souls if vengeance was the motive of the interrogators? Not only were thousands of those who had been subjected to investigations subsequently released, the vast majority of reported cases were local and in most of these religion was used as cover for other allegations levied by accusers against their targets. Indeed, the unsettled religious climate offered much scope for denunciation and accusation. The settling of old scores provided ample motive for accusers, especially if the punishment of the accused resulted in some material benefit for the accuser in these economically challenging times. Husbands reported wives because they were tired of them, fathers reported sons over inheritance issues, and neighbour informed on neighbour to avenge some dispute or another.[52] In fact, the policy of the administration could not have functioned without the complicity of local officials and priests. Central administrators like Archdeacon Nicholas Harpsfield may have provided firm supervision of local affairs, but there was no shortage of newly appointed orthodox clergy to collaborate willingly in the hunt for heretics. Similar zeal was evident among newly appointed officials whom Mary had rewarded for their rallying to her cause during Edward's reign and after her brother's death. Conservative by nature, gentlemen like John and Edmund Tyrell, and men of humbler origins like Philip Williams of Ipswich, merchant-cum-social climber under Mary's patronage, were only too willing to apprehend those who defied the new political and religious order.[53]

For all the enthusiasm of officials, there was little to suggest, apart from the pursuit of Cranmer to the stake, that vengeance played any significant part in the proceedings to hunt down heretics. At times, the campaign was intense, but this was not due to vengeance but to strategic necessity when the authorities had discovered that the lenient approach that had been pursued at the start of Mary's reign had proved to have been ineffective. Many of those who had been released after they had recanted relapsed to provoke the government anew. Of the twenty-two in Essex, for instance, who had been released after they had recanted, seven were burned a few months later and an eighth was awaiting execution.[54] The case of the Munt Family is most illustrative. Having been released after initial investigations, they continued to meet in secret, abstain from Mass and publicly mock the host. They were rearrested and duly executed, having rejected further opportunities to recant.[55] Mocking the host to a twenty-first-century Catholic, let alone to a sixteenth-century one, is tantamount to abject blasphemy. For this to have gone unpunished would have shown weakness that could well have undermined the entire programme of restoration.

Mary's role in the pursuit of heretics has been inevitably subjected to the greatest scrutiny. What is crucial here, however, is not to allow centuries of anti-Marian invective to cloud an assessment of her motives. Mary, as sovereign monarch, has to bear ultimate responsibility for the policy of burning heretics. To recall, however, Mary's view was wholly in keeping with the conventional view of the time in how to deal with heretics; heresy was an infectious and dangerous disease that had to be urgently stamped out to ensure not only religious heterodoxy but also political and social stability. The potential for heresy to provoke rebellion was something that no state could ignore. However, it was the sheer numbers of recalcitrant heretics willing to endure such horrific deaths that overwhelmed the authorities. The government may have been at fault for not finding an alternative way of dealing with heresy, which in this respect would have been a radical departure for the time, but once it embarked on its chosen course it is difficult to see how it could have abandoned it without having to concede defeat to its enemies.[56] In pursuing heresy as she did, Mary did not act on 'hysterical' impulses or in reaction to phantom pregnancies, as has been so often claimed. Her decision was very much rational and in keeping with prevailing political fashion. The numerous opportunities that heretics were given to recant and save themselves up to the point of death offers further testament to the judiciousness of her policy. It is true, of course, that she was directly involved in restoring the heresy laws but like her father she was not an absolute monarch and had to work through consensus, especially when such a sensitive policy was involved. It was a consensus, as noted, that stretched from the very apex of the administration to its lowest levels as well as to the willing informers eager to avenge a wrong.

There is no evidence that could paint a picture of Mary as an unprincipled persecutor of heretics. She is said to have rebuked both Edmund Bonner in May 1555 for procrastinating in his prosecution of cases brought before him and the sheriff of Hampshire in August 1558 for having stayed the execution of a heretic who had recanted upon encountering the flames.[57] Both of these cases, however, are not as straightforward as has been suggested. In the first, it is likely that it was Philip, not she, who rebuked Bonner, Mary having withdrawn to Hampton Court and from state business a few weeks earlier in expectation of the birth of her child. The second case is perhaps less easy to defend though her age, intense misery and illness could be advanced in mitigation.[58] And it would be the only case which could be cited, apart from Cranmer's, of her eagerness to send people to the fire (see below). Even Foxe acknowledges this, and notwithstanding the invective that he levels against her, she emerges from his text much less of an odious monster than others do. Though he unreservedly believes that her reign was cruel, he almost views her as a victim herself of iniquitous priests. It was as if she, as a lawful and anointed queen and head of the Church, was acting as an agent of God who had permitted the evil to happen, for whatever reason, only to allow subsequent redemption. To be sure, much of Foxe's restraint was due to prevailing political conditions. He could challenge neither female rule, given that Elizabeth sat on the throne, nor Mary's legitimacy as that would question Elizabeth's own position. There was also the more pressing need for the anti-Catholic campaign of his day to focus its ire more on the leading clerics of the Catholic Church than on their secular kindred spirits. Nevertheless, a propagandist of Foxe's ilk could not ignore certain inalienable facts. Even if it is assumed that Mary did intervene in a few cases, there is little doubt that the vast majority of cases were initiated by officials within her administration.[59] A case can certainly be made from both moral and political standpoints against Mary's determined pursuit of Cranmer, as personal to her as this was, but the image of her as a 'neurotic' and 'embittered' woman, motivated by hatred in encouraging ever greater severity to be meted out to the condemned,[60] does not bear up to serious scrutiny.

Adding further to such an image of her has been the suggestion that had she heeded the advice of wiser counsel, things would not have got out of hand. Renard, for instance, though no defender of heresy, regarded the burnings as a tactical error.[61] A day after the execution of the first victim, John Rogers, on 4 February 1555, he communicated his concerns to Philip about the discomfort among the people 'about the cruel enforcement of the recent acts of Parliament on heresy, which now begins' and which 'may well cause a revolt'. He subsequently advised against further burnings 'unless the reasons are overwhelmingly strong and the offences committed have been so scandalous as to render this course justifiable in the eyes of the people'.[62] Renard reiterated his concerns to Emperor Charles a few weeks later, noting that the daily burnings pursued by the 'rashness' of the bishops 'have hardened many hearts [and] may cause the people to rise in arms this spring'.[63] As historical documents go, however, Renard's dispatches need to be approached with caution. Voiced during the start of the burnings, they were primarily concerned with political stability. Once it became clear that the burnings would not provoke any major social disturbance the dispatches ceased. It was also clear that they did not have much influence on the recipients.

Foxe's attempt to attribute to Philip a desire to restrain the prosecutors of the burnings is a deliberate ploy to isolate his chosen targets for his vitriol. He cites a sermon preached in February 1555 by Philip's Franciscan confessor, Alfonso de Castro, shortly after the burnings began, in which Castro denounced the wickedness of burning men for their religion. The abatement in the burnings the following month was evidence for Foxe of Philip's intervention, a claim that continues to be made by scholars. Loades, in his latest work on Mary, notes that Mary's 'hatred of heresy was a consuming passion, and in her strength of will she ignored everyone, including Philip, who tried to persuade her to take a more dispassionate approach'.[64] That she passionately hated heresy is not in doubt, but that she operated as a lone crusader acting against the advice of moderate counsel is difficult to substantiate. Philip for one generally did not interfere in this or any other domestic policy while his own intolerance of heresy renders him an unlikely force for moderation. Indeed, where Philip has been said to have intervened, he was to have done so to urge greater severity, as noted above regarding his probable rebuke of Bonner for going soft on heretics. This would be in keeping with the way he treated heresy in his own lands. The edict issued in the Netherlands in 1550 against heresy provided for particularly harsh punishment. 'Men [were to be executed] with the sword and the women to be buried alive, if they do not persist in their errors; if they do persist in them, then they are to be executed with fire; all their property in both cases being confiscated to the crown.' As has been noted, some 1300 Dutch heretics were executed in 1556 alone. Only a few months after Renard had expressed his concerns to him, Philip wrote to Ruy Gómez de Silva, one of his principal advisors, that MPs 'should take great care in their districts to punish offences against religion, from now on'.[65] Moreover, Castro's stated position in his sermon was out of step with his own uncompromising orthodoxy in dealing with heresy which included censorship of suspect books and the execution of recalcitrant heretics (though he probably did not support execution by burning).[66]

From the Lord Chancellor, Stephen Gardiner, Mary received little encouragement for restraint. Gardiner held heretics in utter contempt. He believed 'from his own experience [. . .] that the so-called "Reformed Faith" was no more than an ideological smokescreen behind which ambitious politicians manoeuvred to plunder the Church and secure control of the government'.[67] He was not, however, the merciless killer of Foxian legend. He ultimately believed that determined threats would be sufficient to either deter further heresy or drive heretics into exile.[68] Once the leaders were killed, he argued, heresy would wither away. Only when his strategy failed did Gardiner opt for more radical measures, albeit unenthusiastically. 'His *frightfulness* was largely a pose, but because people like John Rogers and John Hooper refused to be intimidated, his bluff was called and he was forced to burn them.'[69] As Lord Chancellor, his complicity in the burnings is undeniable while his hypocrisy, having been a supporter of Henry's supremacy, provoked the chagrin of Protestant polemicists. But even Foxe was compelled to acknowledge, albeit with gritted teeth, that this 'man hated of God and all good men', was motivated more by political calculation than natural sadism.[70]

Foxe reserved his greatest ire for Edmund Bonner, the bishop of London and chief overseer of the suppression. 'This Cannibal in three yeares space three hundred Martirs slew. They were his food, he loued so blood, he spared none he knew.'[71] It was an accusation repeated by John Bale, a former friar and bishop of Ossory, Ireland, who wrote of Bonner from exile in Basle in 1554, some time before the main wave of assaults had occurred, as 'the bloody sheep-bite of London'.[72] Such invective was to set the tone for the assessment of Bonner and his work for centuries to come.

By his own admission Bonner was a tempestuous man, not one to ingratiate himself easily with others. At face value, his reputation does indeed appear irredeemable. Notwithstanding his character flaws, he was to oversee between a third and a half of all burnings. Yet despite such seemingly damnable evidence against him, his reputation for sadism is not convincing. For one, given the high concentration of Protestants in London, it was inevitable that his jurisdiction would oversee the largest number of executions, especially as forty of the victims had been sent to him from Essex, which had a similarly high Protestant presence. 'It may be said in his behalf', wrote Dodd, 'that, London, being the stage where most of the offenders were to make their appearance, 'tis a thing not to be wondered at, if we find the bishop of that see more active, than any of the rest, in seeing the laws executed.'[73] Furthermore, the disproportionate number of victims that he dealt with does not reveal the meticulousness of Bonner's interrogations, which he designed primarily to secure recantations. His notorious bluster was thus more a reflection of his frustration of failing in this task than an expression of satisfaction with the duties that he was compelled to perform. It was such laborious methods that earned him a rebuke from the highest quarters, as noted above. In any case, he had little choice in the process, which was being ultimately directed from above.[74]

It is understandable why it was difficult to believe Bonner's claim that he pursued heretics to the stake out of Christian charity and love which demanded 'those that be evil, of love, we ought to procure unto them theyr corrections'.[75] His penchant for flogging those whom he deemed deserving of such treatment gave his detractors further grist for the mill. But here too he was adamant that his motive was a sincere desire to correct errant behaviour rather than to exercise malice.[76] Even if Foxe had understood his motives, he was not going to pass over an opportunity to secure for his cause such an arch-villain.[77]

There was more to Bonner than crude persecution. His countrywide visitations revealed to him the extent of the apathy towards Christian observance that had crept in in many areas among both the laity and clergy and he understood that the restoration of the old faith could not rely on the suppression of heresy alone, but on a widespread re-education programme. As noted, his writings stand out as worthy contributions to this process. Perhaps his flawed character together with a general lack of both resources and men of high calibre needed for such an ambitious programme played against him.[78] Though he was central in the hunt for heretics, he was not the sadistic villain whom Foxe portrayed, but a functionary in a system which was based on much more than vengeance.

Mary was thus surrounded by like-minded people, who shared her zeal for the uncompromising suppression of heresy, with the possible exception, according to some accounts, of Reginald Pole. These depict Pole as a reluctant participant in the policy of suppression, who goes along with it but is unconvinced about its effectiveness.[79] Foxe himself viewed Pole as different from 'the bloudy and cruell sort of papists'.[80] Gentle and noble in disposition and once harbouring reformist sympathies himself on issues such as justification, Pole, for Foxe, simply did not fit into the world inhabited by turncoats like Gardiner and brutes like Bonner.[81] Pole's alleged leniency in dealing with heretics was sufficient to attract concerns from Carranza who subsequently raised the issue in Rome.[82] A closer look, however, at Pole's approach to the matter reveals that in essence it differed little from that of any of his contemporaries in power

Pole, it is true, was a mild-mannered, saintly individual. 'As a pastor', Fenlon noted, he was 'at once paternal and patrician. He believed in the "fear of law", leniently applied, as a means of persuading people to come to church.' For him, applying the harshness of the law in the absence of any heartfelt persuasion would merely lead to outward conversion and not to the inward salvation of souls, which for Pole was of central importance.[83] Pole's spirituality drove him to prioritise conversion over punishment. 'If there were only a way, or means, or fashion', he despairingly wrote to Cranmer, 'that I might fynd to remove you from errour, bryngeng you to the knowledge of the treuth for your salvation.'[84] The spectacular reconversion of Sir John Cheke was Pole's greatest coup. But in his vision of reform there was nothing significant to distinguish him from any other leading figure of his time.[85] What Foxe and other commentators failed to appreciate was that promoting leniency did not preclude advocating execution of recalcitrant heretics. Pole did clash with Bonner over the bishop's handling in June 1556 of the Essex heretics, but this was over procedure, not principle. Pole was in no doubt about the importance of vigorously pursuing heresy, having admonished Cranmer and other reformist clergy for having misled the laity. Those who refused to recant he likened to 'the blasphemer, whatsoever their words be in honour of Christ', like the wicked thief on Calvary who showed no fear in the face of death.[86] His circular of September 1555 to bishops in preparation for the synod of that year closely reflected Mary's earlier directions to the episcopate which advocated a balance between instructing the ignorant and punishing the guilty.[87]

Pole's close relationship with Mary was something that she treasured and on matters of religion she took her cues from him. The burning of Cranmer was the only significant exception to this rule, her hunger for vengeance overriding his appeals for moderation. In November 1558, shortly before his and the queen's death, Pole assumed a direct role in the burnings, signing orders for the burning of five unrepentant heretics in his own diocese of Canterbury that hosted some of the highest levels of suppression. Suggestions of divergence of opinion between Mary and Pole on matters of religion are overshadowed by a convergence in their actions. In this respect assessment of Pole's role in the burnings is closer to that of Froude than of Foxe.

*

Foxe's accounts taken at face value paint a picture of contemporary communal solidarity with those burnt. His over-dramatised, though gruesome, accounts of 'fat, water, and bloud dropp(ing) out at his fingers endes',[88] in reference to the execution of John Hooper, the Anglican bishop of Gloucester and Worcester, and of protracted deaths certainly evoked sympathy among onlookers. Many, according to Renard, 'wept, others prayed God to give him (John Rogers, burnt at the stake on 4 February 1555) strength, perseverance and patience to bear the pain and not to recant, others gathered the ashes and bones and wrapped them up in paper to preserve them, yet others threatening the bishops'.[89] Commenting on the execution of Thomas Hawkes, who was sentenced to be burnt for refusing to allow his son to become a Catholic, Foxe noted how

> with no smal multitude of people on euery side compassing him about. Vnto whom after he had spoken many things [...], & poured out vnto God, þe fier was set vnto him [...] hys skynne also drawen together, and hys fingers consumed with the fier, so that now all men thought certainly he had bene gone, sodainly and contrary to all expectation reached vp hys hands burning on a lyght fier (which was marueilous to behold) ouer his head to the liuing God, and wyth great reioysing, as seemed, strooke or clapped thē three times together,

having promised earlier that in the midst of the flames he should show them some token, whether the pains of burning were so great that a man might not collectedly endure it. Foxe continued:

> At the sight whereof there followed such applause and outcry of the people, and especially of them which vnderstoode the matter, that the lyke hath not commonly bene heard: And so þe blessed Martyr of Christ, straight way sincking downe into the fier, gaue vp hys spirite, 10, June 1555.[90]

Yet as horrific as these burnings were of undoubtedly brave men and women, sympathy towards the victims was by no means widespread, universal or necessarily motivated by confessional solidarity. Residents in areas other than London, Canterbury or Colchester, where most of the executions occurred, were unlikely to have witnessed a burning. And even in these areas the burnings would have eluded most people. It is understandable why Protestant historiography should focus so much on the burnings, but what was familiar to people who read it was unfamiliar to the vast majority of people during Mary's reign. The burnings in fact frequently offered opportunities to settle scores with heretics, which counters the view that the burnings were initiated solely from above. For instance, Foxe's portrayal of John Bland, a former Catholic priest turned Anglican vicar, who was burnt at Canterbury on 12 July 1555 as 'a man so litle borne for his own commoditye, that no part of his lyfe was separated from the common and publike vtility of al men',[91] is at odds with local feeling towards him and his radical preaching.[92] Foxe's hyperbole, however, prevailed to paint a picture that deviated significantly from reality.

Foxe again 'is pulling the wool over our eyes, or attempting to do so' in his account of the execution of the 'Maidstone Seven' in 1557.[93] In order not to undermine the appearance of confessional homogeneity that he tried to portray among the martyrs, he concealed evidence available to him that threatened to do so. The evidence took the form of a letter of complaint from Roger Hall to Pole's successor as archbishop of Canterbury, Matthew Parker, against the local vicar, John Day, who had been present at the execution of Hall's sister, Alice Benden. In his letter, Hall arraigns Day for claiming that not only did Alice deny the Catholic doctrine of the real presence, which alone would have been sufficient to condemn her, but also that she denied the doctrine of the Holy Trinity. This latter accusation would have been totally unacceptable to Protestants and Catholics alike. Although Alice's denial of the Holy Trinity may have been concocted by Day so as to exonerate himself in the eyes of the post-Marian regime, it was an uncomfortable piece of evidence to which Foxe should have at least referred, if only to discredit it. However, knowing fully that even the slightest suspicion that any of the 'Maidstone Seven' had denied the doctrine of the Holy Trinity could have challenged his carefully cultivated image of confessional homogeneity, he chose not to do so.[94]

Disturbances were often provoked by the burnings, but never to the point of threatening the general peace of the realm. Empathy expressed at the pyres by onlookers towards the victims may well suggest the persistence of Protestant sympathies, but it does not offer evidence either of widespread national disillusionment with the burnings or of burgeoning Protestant support.[95] In Colchester, for instance, the burnings did provoke some ill-feeling. The rebels here were apparently 'stout', as reported to Bonner by a local priest, Sir Thomas Tye. Alarmed, he wrote in December 1557 that:

> The ministers of the Church are hemd at in the open streets, and called knaues. The blessed Sacrament of the aultar is blasphemed and rayled vpon in euery Alehouse and Tauerne. Prayer and fasting is not regarded. Seditious talkes and newes are rife, both in towne and countrey.[96]

Colchester, however, was an anomaly. Around half of the twenty-three people who were burned there were residents, whose burning understandably stirred emotions, more so as the suppression was particularly ruthlessly enforced by Edmund Tyrell. But despite the tensions that existed there, they never provoked any major disturbances. In London too, where around half of the forty-four victims were also residents, tensions were evident. The execution of the first victim, the preacher John Rogers, for instance, drew a huge crowd. Foxe dramatically describes 'all the people wonderfully reioycing at his constancie' for not having succumbed to attempts of his interrogators to recant, and 'with great prayses and thankes to God'[97] France's ambassador Antoine de Noailles concurred, noting that in 'persisting in his opinions [...] the greatest part of the people took such pleasure that they were not afraid to make him many exclamations to strengthen his courage'.[98] The assembled crowd greeted the steadfastness of the popular vicar, John Cardmaker, before his execution on 30 May 1555 at Smithfield in a similar way,[99] something which the Venetian ambassador, Giovanni Michieli, verified. Cardmaker and his fellow condemned, John Warne, were executed, he noted, 'to the displeasure as usual of the population here [as] he was held in great esteem'. Generally, he concludes, 'such sudden severity is odious to many people'.[100]

Such outburts of sympathy for the victims were sufficiently common to compel the authorities to manipulate the timing of the executions and limit the size of the crowds. Winter executions, for instance, were preferred to summer ones as it was expected by the authorities that the cold would attract fewer spectators. In January 1556 a prohibition was issued on the eve of the burning of seven at Smithfield on the attendance at the executions of young people.[101] Orders were sent by the Privy Council to householders that they should not allow any of their 'apprentices or other servants to be abrode, other thenne suche as their maisters will aunswere for'.[102] A similar directive was dispatched to 'Lord Maior and Shiriefes' of London to ensure the presence at executions in London of 'a goode nombre of officers and other men' to apprehend any 'who may be charged to see suche as shall misuse themselfes either by comforting, aiding or paying the offenders, or otherwise use themselfes to the ill example of others'.[103] The impact of the orders, however, had limited effect as large crowds continued to gather at executions. Yet any hopes held by protestors that their demonstrations might weaken the resolve of London's authorities to carry on with burnings were misplaced as the executions continued up until the summer of 1558.

In fact none of the protests ever came close to threatening the stability of the government itself. Not only were they relatively small, but they were local. Apart from London and Colchester, the response towards the burnings elsewhere, which Dickens argues was 'both hostile and immediate',[104] was in fact muted to say the least. What also needs to be stressed is that even in Protestant hotspots like London the burnings were occurring against a backdrop of a revival of Catholic practice and against considerable hostility towards Protestantism, which even Foxe was compelled to acknowledge. John Lithall, who avoided execution only because Mary died, noted in his testimony, as recorded by Foxe, that 'when they coulde not make me to kneele before the roode, neither to see their Masse, there gathered a great company about us, and all against me. Some spit on me, and sayd: Fie on thee hereticke, and other said it was pitie I was not burned already'.[105] Another, Thomas Benbridge, reports Foxe, was heckled at the stake, by 'one that stoode by: Sir, cut out his tongue, & an other beyng a temporall man, rayled on hym worse'.[106] Even if, as Dickens states, there 'is no reason to suppose that the majority of English Catholics relished the spectacle of a persecution along these lines',[107] there is no evidence that Catholics campaigned against it. Humanitarian expressions of sympathy by Catholics towards the victims was not analogous with rebellion against the authorities. There was no universal opprobrium towards the burnings and so it must follow that claims that the burnings severely damaged the standing of the Marian administration are exaggerated.[108]

So did the burnings damage it at all? On balance, the answer to this question, despite the nuances of the issue, is not really. Loades argued that the burnings were a 'catastrophic mistake'[109] and had Mary's 'policy of coercive uniformity been more politic and sensitive there would have been less anger, and the cry that England was under judgement for murdering the saints of God would have had no resonance'.[110] This view, however, seems valid only within the context of the myth-making of Protestant propagandists in the aftermath of the Marian reign. Talk of damage, therefore, should be confined to that which was inflicted on the memory of the administration rather than on the administration itself. To recall, the Marian programme of religious restoration was designed for the long haul. Had the administration survived for longer, subsequent generations would have regarded its policy of burning heretics with little amazement, particularly as these generations would have been Catholic and which would not have been subjected to incessant Protestant propaganda which the likes of Foxe purveyed.

The Marian pursuit of heretics was counter-productive for Catholicism only in the context of the short-lived nature of Mary's administration. In an otherwise different world in which Mary had lived to see the fruits of her actions more fully, the contrast that the administration had highlighted between the seditiousness of the Protestant victims and the virtuousness of Catholic martyrs like More and Fisher would have held good in subsequent histories of the period, as it did at the time among most of the people. The mythology later invented by Protestant propagandists that not only depicted the perpetrators of the burnings as the epitome of evil but also dignified a cause that otherwise would have had little to commemorate would not have transpired. In reference to the campaign of burnings in Kent, second only to London in its intensity, Patrick Collinson asks 'if there had been no Foxe, no *Acts and Monuments*, would the martyrs have lived on in folk memory as they seem to have done in Sussex, where the Pope is still burned in effigy in Lewes every 5 November?'[111] Collinson concludes that in spite of local memories, 'by and large [...] the Kentish martyrs would not have existed, in a manner of speaking, but for Foxe',[112] whose book was to reappear several times down the centuries, offering successive generations insight into his propaganda. History here was exclusively written by the victors.

There is no denying that a degree of inept management of the process surrounding the burnings made things much easier for Protestant propagandists. For instance, allowing victims to communicate with the public shortly before their death added to the drama, which polemicists like Foxe could later embellish. Cardinal Pole as well as Alfonso de Castro expressed concern about the dangers of public executions of determined heretics.[113] Though designed to deter others, such executions had the potential to have the opposite effect. Similar poor judgement accompanied the government's failure to make more capital from Cranmer's recantations. Here Mary's judgement was clouded by her desire to avenge her mother's treatment, for which she held Cranmer responsible to a large extent. The prolonged period of grace that he was given after Mary's accession was only so that he could die a heretic's death, Mary having foregone the opportunity of having him executed under common law as a traitor. For this to happen he needed to be stripped of the see of Canterbury, of which, in strict accordance to canon law, he had as yet not been.[114] As things stood, the orders conferred on him by Pope Clement VII remained valid and as such only the pope could strip him of his office. Mary, therefore, had to wait for England to be restored to Roman obedience before she could act against Cranmer. In the end, however, the opportunity that Cranmer's recantations presented for a public relations coup was not taken. So complete was his capitulation to the faith that he had so recently scorned that it should have served as the crowning victory over heresy for the Marian administration.[115] At the point of having expressed elation at having been rejoined to the Catholic faith and asking and receiving sacramental absolution, his life should have been spared under the normal practice of canon law.

Doubtless he would have retired as a living symbol of the prodigal son, returning from error to the bosom of the merciful Catholic Church. Instead, spurious reasons were given as to why Cranmer should die a heretic's death.[116] Cornered and with nothing to lose, he recanted his previously made recantations in dramatic form. 'Forasmuch as my hand offended writing contrary to my heart', he declared from the place of his execution as the fire was being stoked, 'my hand shall first be punished therefore.'[117] Then, in theatrical fashion, he stretched his right hand into the fire and while he still could, uttered the dying words of Stephen, the first martyr, 'Lord Jesus, receive my Spirit [. . .] I see the heavens open and Jesus standing at the right hand of God'.[118] With this, noted Diarmaid MacCulloch, the 'Catholic Church's publicity coup lay in ruins'.[119] Well, not quite. The authorities did have Cranmer's recantations, which they duly published, and his transgressions were subsequently hammered home across the country by preachers. But the campaign to limit the damage caused by Cranmer's last-minute 'reconversion' was not all that convincing. By the time a pamphlet with his recantations was published, the revised version of events was being peddled by Protestant sympathisers, the truth of the drama surrounding his death having already become common knowledge both at home and abroad.[120]

*

The suffering of those who went to the stake should by no means be demeaned, but once the burnings are placed in their proper historical context and stripped of the hyperbole that has been built up around them, and which has determined how they have been perceived, they lose much of their ability to shock. 'While in no way seeking to condone the horrors of the Marian persecution', wrote Lingard, 'it is well to remember that those responsible for them should be judged, not by our standards of tolerance, but by the ethics then accepted as guides for man's conduct.'[121] Appropriate contextualisation in turn contributes to a reappraisal of the Marian administration, which for so long has been primarily associated with cruel persecution. Given the way that events unfolded since Mary's death, the burning of Protestants, concluded Freeman, 'was a policy that ultimately failed, and in its failure it did enormous damage to English Catholicism', but the 'persecution failed for the same reasons that the restoration of Catholicism failed: the sudden deaths of Mary and the accession of a Protestant successor'.[122]

NOTES

[1] Dickens, *English Reformation*, p. 371.
[2] Elton, *Reform and Reformation*, p. 386.
[3] Duffy, *Fires of Faith*, p. 7.
[4] Edwards, *Mary I*, p. 255.
[5] Richards *Mary Tudor*, p. 195.
[6] Elton, *Reform and Reformation* p. 387.
[7] Tootell (Charles Dodd), *Church History of England*, p. 463.
[8] Whitelock, *Mary Tudor, England's First Queen*, p. 265.
[9] 'Opinion of the most Serene Queen of England, which she wrote with her own hand and gave to his Right Reverend Lordship the Legate [Cardinal Pole] at the time when the Synod was held. (Translated from the English tongue.), December 1555', CSPV, 136, vol. 6.
[10] 'An other examination of Maister Hooper', *Acts*, book 11, 1570, p. 1718.
[11] Loades, 'The English Church during the Reign of Mary I', p. 36.
[12] Ibid., 2005, pp. 38–9.
[13] Ibid., 2005, p. 39.
[14] Hughes and Larkin, Hughes and J. F. Larkin, *Tudor Royal Proclamations*, p. 6.
[15] Ibid., pp. 52–5.
[16] Richards, *Mary Tudor*, p. 196.
[17] Loades, 'The English Church during the Reign of Mary I', p. 34.
[18] *Lingard's History of England: Newly Abridged and Brought Down to the Accession of King George V*, ed. H. Norbert (London: G. Bell and Sons, 1918, first published, 1819–30), p. 354.
[19] T. S. Freeman, 'Burning Zeal: Mary Tudor and the Marian Persecution', in Doran

and Freeman, eds., *Mary Tudor, Old and New Perspectives*, p. 203.

[20] H. C. Porter, 'Fisher and Erasmus', in Brendon Bradshaw, ed., *Humanism, Reform and the Reformation: The Career of Bishop John Fisher* (Cambridge: University of Cambridge, 1989), p. 93.

[21] Norbert ed., *Lingard's History of England*, p. 354.

[22] MacCulloch, *Thomas Cranmer*, p. 474.

[23] Duffy, *Fires of Faith*, p. 87.

[24] MacCulloch, *Thomas Cranmer*, p. 501.

[25] Ibid., p. 476.

[26] Edwards, *Mary I*, p. 257.

[27] Richards, *Mary Tudor*, p. 193.

[28] Guy, *Tudor England*, p. 227.

[29] Jasper Ridley puts the number of Henry's victims at 60,000. He bases this figure on various sources from judges and officials which document the number of executed from six or eight to twelve to fourteen per quarter session. An average of ten hangings per session would amount to forty per year in every county or 1600 per year in England's forty counties. This in short would amount to 60,000 executions in Henry's thirty-eight-year reign. Ridley, *Henry VIII*, p. 281.

[30] Cited in D. Keen, 'The Political Economy of War', in F. Stewart and V. Fitzgerald, eds., *War and Underdevelopment: Economic and Social Consequences of Conflict*. 2 vols. Queen Elizabeth House Series in Development Studies (Oxford: Oxford University Press, 2000), vol. 1, p. 51.

[31] There are restrictions on Catholics even today. The monarch, for instance, is not permitted to marry a Catholic while someone who is in the succession to the Crown may marry a Catholic on the condition he/she renounce the right to succeed. Moreover, although there is no constitutional reason why a Catholic cannot become Prime Minister, there is a legal bar under the Roman Catholic Relief Act of 1829, sect. 17, for a Roman Catholic to advise the sovereign on ecclesiastical matters, which is one of the Prime Minister's roles. Hence a Catholic Prime Minister would be constitutionally awkward.

[32] Loades, 'The English Church during the Reign of Mary I', p. 34.

[33] Richards, *Mary Tudor*, pp. 194–5.

[34] Ibid., p. 201.

[35] Loades, 'The English Church during the Reign of Mary I', p. 48.

[36] Ibid., p. 37.

[37] Richards, *Mary Tudor*, p. 201.

[38] Loades, 'Introduction: The Personal Religion of Mary I', p. 28.

[39] Loades, 'The English Church during the Reign of Mary I', p. 37.

[40] Elton, *Reform and Reformation*, p. 387; D. Loades, *Oxford Martyrs* (New York: Stein and Day, 1970), p. 157; Dickens, *English Reformation*, pp. 362–9, and others.

[41] APCE, vol. 6, p. 135.

[42] 'Q. Mary. 4. Martirs burned at Islyngtō. Marg. Thurstō, Agn.Bngeor', *Acts*, book 12, 1576, p. 1939.

[43] 'Queene Mary. The story and condemnation of John Hunt, and Richard White Martyrs', *Acts*, book 12, 1583, p. 2078.

[44] Loades, *Mary Tudor*, pp. 202.

[45] Ibid., p. 263.

[46] Duffy, *Fires of Faith*, p. 7. See also Freeman, 'Inventing Bloody Mary', p. 179.

[47] Duffy, *Fires of Faith*, pp. 162–3.

[48] For details of Cheke's conversion see ibid., pp. 147–8.

[49] Ibid., p. 163.

[50] Loades, *Mary Tudor*, p. 263.

[51] Freeman, 'Inventing Bloody Mary', p. 203.

[52] Loades, 'The English Church during the Reign of Mary I', p. 46.

[53] Freeman, 'Inventing Bloody Mary', pp. 181–90.

[54] Ibid., p. 178.

[55] 'Queene Mary. The burning of Rose Allins hand by Ed. Tyrrell persecutour. Anno 1557 August A Letter sent to Boner Byshop of London, from Syr Thomas Tye Priest', *Acts*, book 12, 1583, p. 2030; 'Queene Mary. The story apprehension, and examination of George Eagles Martyr', *Acts*, book 12, 1583, p. 2033.

[56] Richards, *Mary Tudor*, p. 198.

[57] Prescott, *Mary Tudor*, p. 387.

[58] Ibid.

[59] Richards *Mary Tudor*, p. 202.

[60] Dickens *English Reformation*, p. 363, *Reform and Reformation*, p. 387.

[61] Loades, 'The English Church during the Reign of Mary', p. 43.

[62] 'Simon Renard to Philip, 5 February 1555, 148', CSPS, vol. 13.

[63] 'Simon Renard to Emperor Charles, 27 March 1555', CSPS, vol. 13.

[64] Loades, *Mary Tudor*, p. 10.

[65] 'Philip to Ruy Gómez de Silva, 2 August, 1555, 229', CSPS, vol. 13.

[66] Duffy *Fires of Faith*, pp. 113–14. Edwards, *Mary I*, p. 261.

[67] Loades 'The Marian Episcopate', p. 37.

[68] D. Loades, 'Foxe and Queen Mary: Stephen Gardiner: Edmund Bonner', in John Foxe's *Acts and Monuments* online, http://www.johnfoxe.org/index.php?realm=more&gototype=modern&type=essay&book=essay19&anchor, accessed 21 September, 2013.

[69] Ibid.

[70] 'The death and ende of Stephen Gardiner Bishop of Winchester', *Acts*, book 11, 1576, p. 1704.

[71] 'A letter written by Richard Roth, vnto certayne brethren, and sistren in Christ, condempned at Colchester, and redy to be burned for the testimony of the truth', *Acts*, book 5, 1563 edition, p. 1712.; 'In effigiem Boneri, carmen', *Acts*, 1563, book 5, p. 1770.

[72] Cited in C. G. Herbermann, *The Catholic Encyclopedia: An International Work of Reference on the Constitution, Coctrine, Ciscipline, and History of the Catholic Church* (Appleton: University of Michigan, 1907), p. 676.

[73] Tootell (Charles Dodd), *Church History of England*, p. 463.

[74] G. Alexander, 'Bonner and the Marian Persecutions', in Haigh ed., *The English Reformation Revised*, p. 160.

[75] Cited ibid.

[76] Loades, 'Foxe and Queen Mary'.

[77] Ibid.

[78] Alexander, 'Bonner and the Marian Persecutions', p. 172.

[79] Loades, *The Reign of Mary Tudor*, pp. 271–2. Fenlon, 'Pole, Carranza and the Pulpit', p. 87; Loades, *Mary Tudor*, pp. 179–80.

[80] 'Q. Mary. XXij. Prisoners. The maner of their bringing vp to London', *Acts*, book 12, 1576, p. 1891.

[81] 'The Articles which were fyrst of all preasented vnto Poope Ihon the xxiii. by Michaell de Causis, for the condemnation of master Ihon Hus, after he was newly imprisoned', *Acts*, book 2, 1563 edition, p. 253 (On several occasions Foxe refers to Pole's gentleness and nobility).

[82] Fenlon, 'Pole, Carranza and the Pulpit', p. 88.

[83] Ibid.

[84] J. Strype, 'Pole Cardinal Legate, to Archbishop Cranmer, in answer to the letter he had sent to the queene', *Memorials of the Most Reverend Father in God Thomas Cranmer, Sometime Lord Archbishop of Canterbury. Wherein the history of the church and the reformation of it, during the primacy of the said Archbishop* (Oxford: Clarendon Press, 1812), vol. 2 , p. 972.

[85] Fenlon, 'Pole, Carranza and the Pulpit', p. 94.

[86] Duffy, 'Cardinal Pole Preaching', p. 197.

[87] Edwards, *Mary I*, p. 265.

[88] 'The Martyrdome of M. Hooper, Byshop and Martyr', *Acts*, book 11, 1570, p. 1723.

[89] 'Simon Renard to Philip, 5 February 1555, 148', CSPS, vol. 13.

[90] 'The death and Martyrdome of Thomas Haukes', *Acts*, book 11, 1570, p. 1806.

[91] 'The hystorye of Mayster Iohn Blande, Preacher, and Martyr, constantlye sufferyng for the word of Iesus Christ', *Acts*, book 5, 1563, p. 1287.

[92] Duffy, *The Stripping of the Altars*, p. 435.

[93] P. Collinson, 'The Persecution in Kent', in Duffy and Loades, eds., *The Church of Mary Tudor*, p. 331.

[94] For discussion of this see ibid., pp. 327–31.

[95] Duffy, *Fires of Faith*, p. 161.

[96] 'A Letter sent to Boner Byshop of London, from Syr Thomas tye Priest', *Acts*, book 12, 1570, p. 2238.

[97] 'The cruell Martyrdome of M. Rogers Martyr. The history of M. Saunders', *Acts*, book 11, 1583, p. 1517.

[98] Sidney Lee ed., *Dictionary of National Biography*, Smith elder and co., London, 1897, 63 vols., First series, vol. 49, pp. 128–9.

[99] 'The Martyrdome of Iohn cardmaker, and Iohn Warne Martyrs', *Acts*, book 11, 1583, p. 1604.

[100] 'Giovanni Michieli, Venetian ambassador in England, to the Doge and Senate, 1 June 1555, 116', CSPV, vol. 6.

[101] *The Diary of Henry Machyn*, pp. 99–109.

[102] APCE, vol. 5, p. 224.

[103] Ibid.

[104] Dickens, *English Reformation*, p. 368.

[105] 'The trouble and deliueraunce of Iohn Lithall' *Acts*, book 12, 1583, p. 2088.

[106] 'Queene Mary. The burning of Thomas Benbrige Martyr. Foure burned at S Edmondsbury', *Acts*, book 12, 1583, p. 2071.

[107] Dickens, *English Reformation*, p. 367.

[108] Freeman, 'Burning Zeal', p. 202.

[109] Loades, 'Introduction: The Personal Religion of Mary I', p. 28.

[110] Loades, 'The English Church during the Reign of Mary', p. 48.

[111] Collinson, 'The Persecution in Kent', p. 332.

[112] Ibid., p. 333.

[113] Edwards, *Mary I*, p. 261, Richards, *Mary Tudor*, p. 200.

[114] MacCulloch, *Thomas Cranmer*, p. 571.

[115] For details of Cranmer's hearing and recantations see ibid., chapter 13.

[116] Ibid., pp. 600–1.

[117] Ibid., p. 603.

[118] Ibid.,

[119] Ibid.

120 Ibid., p. 607.
121 *Lingard's History of England*, ed. Norbert, p. 354.
122 Freeman, 'Burning Zeal', p. 204.

CONCLUSION

MARY DIED ON 17 NOVEMBER 1558 at the age of forty-two after suffering a range of illnesses for several months. The abandonment of her by her husband Philip, who had long departed England for the last time, and the death on 21 September 1558 of Charles V, her long-time mentor and supporter, compounded her mental depression. Conceding that she would never bear a Catholic heir, Mary reluctantly recognised Elizabeth as her successor after Parliament had rejected her attempts to exclude her half-sister. In her will Mary stipulated that England should remain united with the Holy See,[1] though the chances of this happening were slim, given that Elizabeth had no intention of honouring Mary's religious settlement despite giving her assurances to the contrary. Twelve hours after Mary's death a frail Reginald Pole died, his death doubtless hastened by news of his queen's passing.

All formal obsequies were observed. For three weeks Mary's body lay in state in the Privy Chamber of St James's Palace after which it was processed to Westminster Abbey for burial.[2] A sung Catholic funeral Mass was celebrated by the bishop of Winchester, John White, whose exaggerated praise for the dead queen, as well as his less than enthusiastic endorsement of her successor got him into deep water. Mary's coffin was lowered into a vault in the chapel of her grandfather, Henry VII. An era had come to an end.

The site of her burial may well tell a story of its own. For forty years or so before the erection by James I (James VI of Scotland) of the elaborate tomb marking Elizabeth I's grave (Fig. 3), in which Elizabeth's coffin was placed above that of her half-sister, Mary's place of rest had no memorial or inscribed gravestone or even a marker. Its only distinguishing feature was a mound consisting of fragments of the altars that Mary had re-erected in the abbey and which had been smashed up on 16 April 1561 and deposited over the place where she had been put to rest (Fig. 4).[3] It is not known whether the pile was neatly arranged or a heap of rubble. Either way, the appearance of the site must have been that of neglect. Over the next four decades, during which Mary fell victim to a campaign of misrepresentation and character assassination, there was little scope of commemorating her. Even the day of her death was to be annually overshadowed by the commemoration of Elizabeth's accession.

James's motives for the erection of the joint tomb are uncertain. We may

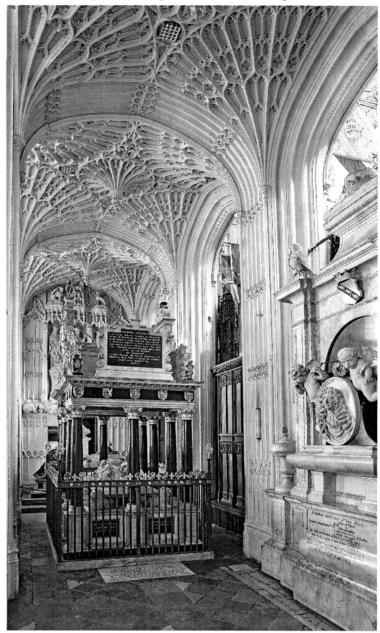

Fig 3. The tomb of Elizabeth I (and Mary I). A Latin inscription reads: 'Partners in throne and grave, here we sleep, Elizabeth and Mary, sisters, in hope of the Resurrection'.
Courtesy of The Library, Westminster Abbey.

Fig. 4. Artist's impression of Queen Mary's place of rest, 1561–1606, based on a description by Henry Machyn. Additional information provided by Christine Reynolds, Assistant Keeper of Muniments, The Library, Westminster Abbey, London. Sketch by Stephen Grant.

speculate that his priority was to commemorate his mother, Mary, Queen of Scots, who had been executed by Elizabeth, by erecting an elaborate commemorative tomb for her. Such an act would have been imprudent without simultaneously appeasing English national sentiments by erecting a similarly grandiose monument to Elizabeth. It is interesting to note, however, that his mother's tomb is slightly larger than Elizabeth's, which may indeed betray his true feelings towards the English queen. Such subtle diplomacy may also have been behind his intention for Mary to share a tomb with her half-sister, his way perhaps of commemorating his mother's faith. He never, however, had an effigy of Mary erected on the tomb to match that of Elizabeth but merely had an inscription carved on it that implied a sepulchral reconciliation. Perhaps an even more subtle political game was being played out here. Royal tombs were not only a means by which to commemorate the life of a monarch but were also political statements. Perhaps the promotion of Mary's resting place from an unidentified grave to an almost anonymous adjunct to Elizabeth's imposing edifice was coded confirmation that explicit celebration of Mary was not the done-thing, even for ruling monarchs. But this is all speculation.

Elizabeth's personal animosity towards her deceased half-sister played a pivotal, albeit subtle role in the denunciation of her reign, whose policies and legacy were hastily depicted as having been harmful to the country. The emergent legends formed the basis of the narrative on the Marian administration for the next four and a half centuries, which despite recent scholarly reappraisals, continue to feed popular imaginations. The begrudging acknowledgement by Mary's detractors of her triumphant accession descended quickly into a scathing assessment of her legacy – her domestic policy plunged the country into chaos, her foreign policy reduced it to a dependency of Spain while her religious policy failed in its ultimate aim of restoring Catholicism to England. This position now of course is rigorously challenged. Mary was conscientious and hardworking, steadfast in her principles, generous to her allies and merciful to her foes. She was no religious fanatic, but a conservative on faith, who was at the same time open to doctrinal innovation. And it was a faith that was showing 'many signs of broad acceptance before she died'.[4]

Mary's unflinching loyalty to her husband did draw England into unprofitable wars, though she, unlike her brother and father, avoided a bloody and costly war with Scotland, despite continual French provocations there. The loss of Calais may have been a setback, but it was far from the disaster that it was portrayed later as having been. The fact that her successor made no attempt to reclaim it attests to this. In the less dramatic domestic arena, she oversaw an administration that was sufficiently creative to procure financial, administrative and naval reforms that were to pave the way for

Elizabeth's successes in these areas. In the cultural sphere, Mary was an even greater innovator, sponsoring many long-lasting achievements. And all this despite inherited financial and economic problems, recurrent plagues and epidemics and weather inflicted famines. All this indeed, as Smith noted, makes 'nonsense of Pollard's cruel and too celebrated epigram that "sterility was the conclusive note of Mary's reign"'.[5]

The Marian administration of course had weaknesses. The frequent divisions in the Council often made decision-making difficult. But there is little to indicate that either the Council or Mary was unable to govern effectively in most situations. In all ordinary aspects the country was as well and as fully governed as at any time during the century.[6] Elizabeth inherited neither a distraught nor an ungovernable country, but 'a fully functioning polity',[7] that was of great importance for the survival of her own administration,[8] altogether a far cry from the bleak imagery contrived by the likes of Dickens and Elton. In any case, to compare the reign of Mary with that of Elizabeth is unfair and ultimately unproductive. Though a competent ruler in her own right, Elizabeth experienced her fair share of crises, which could easily in any assessment of her rule, be lost among her many triumphs in a reign that lasted nine times as long as that of Mary. It seems, moreover, somewhat perverse to negate one monarch's achievements with the triumphs of another. The campaign against Mary, however, was motivated by the necessity to demonise Catholicism and all those associated with it, which was made all too urgent amidst the triumphalism of the Protestant state and empire that began to emerge in the late sixteenth century. Pope Benedict XVI, when asked by journalists to comment on the opposition from secularists and atheists to his state visit to Britain in September 2010, ventured to say that Britain had a 'great history of anti-Catholicism', adding diplomatically, 'but it is also a country with a great history of tolerance'.[9] In surveying post-Reformation history, it is possible to see that little of this tolerance has been extended to Catholics.

In the context of England's and later Britain's state Protestantism, the reasons for the blackening of Mary's name and her administration are clear. It has only been with the reassessment of Britain's own national identity since the mid-twentieth century that a reassessment of the Marian period assumed new momentum and acquired growing historical interest. The twin pillars of Britishness – Protestantism and national sovereignty – began to be challenged, the former by secularism, the latter by membership of various international and supra-national bodies, especially the European Union. This in turn created a cultural identity vacuum which made a reappraisal of the Marian period possible. This should not only be seen as a belated exercise in scholarly revisionism but also as long-overdue justice for a monarch and a human being who had been maligned unfairly for centuries. Where once in every textbook Mary was depicted as a villain and chief architect of the 'mid-Tudor crisis', now titles of textbook chapters on the Marian years are put as questions – 'Was there a mid-Tudor crisis?'[10] – implying that past historians got it wrong.

But there is another important consequence of the scholarly revision of the Marian period. By slaying legends about Mary, an entire edifice of myths about Catholicism in general, as well as the origins and nature of the Reformation, has been disturbed. Peter Ackroyd is the most recent commentator to aptly cut through the sentimental evangelical mush and anti-Catholic fables that had been propagated by Protestant polemicists down the ages. The reformation of the English Church, he noted, was 'from the beginning, a political and dynastic matter', having 'no roots in popular protest or the principles of humanist reform [...] and entirely under the direction of the king'.[11] It worked not because of some popular will, but because:

> the king carried out the work of change piece by piece so that no one could contemplate or guess the finished design. Henry himself may not have known where he was going. Those who supported the king's cause were, in large part, of a practical persuasion; they wanted the lands and revenues of the Church for themselves [...] Only for a few scholars and divines was the theology of the Reformation important.[12]

The people in turn were dragged along. Apathy and indifference became entrenched in their attitudes towards the whole thing and where persuasion failed terror prevailed, ensuring passivity if not acquiescence. Those who actively objected were too few to make a difference. And so England became a Protestant nation, the old faith steadily forgotten amidst ridicule and scorn. 'The passage of time', concludes Ackryod, 'had accomplished what the will of men could not work.'[13] The ratchet effect is an effective method in the pursuit of revolutionary change. Christopher Haigh's conclusion is also worth revisiting here:

> The late medieval Church was not a corrupt and repressive institution whose abuses demanded radical reforms. There was very little popular demand for Reformation, so official changes were implemented without enthusiasm and Protestantism spread only slowly. The reign of Mary saw a vigorous and quite imaginative programme of restoration, and, despite difficulties, the prospects for an established Catholic Church seemed good. Widespread attachment to Catholic beliefs and rituals survived both State repression and Protestant evangelism, and popular conservatism remained strong well into the reign of Elizabeth I. The English Reformation, therefore, was not a joyous national rejection of outmoded superstition: it was a long drawn-out struggle between

reformist minorities and a reluctant majority, and the victory of the reformers was late and limited. Only in the 1570s and after did the officially Protestant Church of England acquire the missionary manpower and organisation for a campaign of conversion, and even then its impact was restricted. Conscious Catholic commitment remained entrenched in many parts of England, and there was stubborn resistance to some central Protestant tenets. The Reformation did not produce a Protestant England: it produced a divided England.[14]

In short, the English Reformation was engineered by powerful and influential minorities which harboured vested interests. There were genuine reformers, who sought an alternative way to heaven, there were common lawyers who coveted the Church's juridical authority, there were parliamentary reformers who sought their share of sovereignty, there was Henry VIII who sought a new wife, there was Anne Boleyn who tempted him into getting one and there were Thomas Cromwell and Thomas Cranmer who facilitated all of this. It was in the interests of these minorities and their successors to blacken the name of anyone who sought to overthrow the new order. And in the midst of this turmoil was Mary, upon whose shoulders the consequences of their actions, for which she bore no responsibility, eventually rested.

*

By any standard, whether contemporary or modern, Mary Tudor was an extraordinary human being. From a very early age she endured frequent tragedies in her personal life and as queen she confronted numerous trials, some for sure of her own making, but most no more so than any confronted by other monarchs, including her father and half-sister. Yet she confronted adversity, whether in her private or public life, with great fortitude and resoluteness. 'For not only is she brave and valiant, unlike other spiritless women', declared Giovanni Michieli in 1557, 'but so courageous and resolute, that neither in adversity nor peril did she ever display or commit any act of cowardice or pusillanimity, maintaining always, on the contrary, a wonderful grandeur and dignity'.[15] Strength of character, of course, is no guarantor of political success; but it certainly helps. To dismiss the Marian reign as a failure or to claim that had it lasted longer it would have yielded few triumphs is at odds with its key signposts – the achievements of Cardinal Pole's restoration programme, the successes in trade policy, the financial and military reforms, to name but a few. All this suggested that further progress in these and other areas would undoubtedly have been made had time allowed. The historical revision of the Marian reign and of the characters and achievements of its protagonists has now formed a scholarly, if not as yet popular consensus, replacing the prejudices, misrepresentations and outright lies that were passed off as truth for over four and a half centuries.

The motto that Mary adopted upon her succession – *Veritas Temporis Filia* ('Truth is the daughter of time') or put simply 'Truth will out' – has never appeared more apposite. It seems that Mary, England's first queen regnant, is having the last laugh.

NOTES

1 'The Will of Mary I', http://tudorhistory.org/primary/will.html, accessed August 12 2013.

2 *The Diary of Henry Machyn*, pp. 169–84.

3 Ibid., pp. 247–62.

4 Whitelock, *Mary Tudor*, p. 309.

5 Ibid., p. 86.

6 Loades, *The Reign of Mary Tudor*, p. 395.

7 Smith, *The Emergence of a Nation-State*, p. 86.

8 Loades, *The Reign of Mary Tudor*, p. 395.

9 'Apostolic journey to the United Kingdom, September, 16–19, 2010, Interview of the Holy Father Benedict XVI with the journalists during the flight to the United Kingdom, papal flight', Thursday, 16 September 2010, website of the Holy See, http://www.vatican.va/holy_father/benedict_xvi/speeches/2010/september/documents/hf_ben-xvi_spe_20100916_interv-regno-unito_en.html, accessed 12 June 2013.

10 See for instance, 'A Mid-Tudor Crisis? The Reign of Mary I, 1553–1558' (chapter 8), in D. Murphy, P. Walsh-Atkins and A. Keen, *England 1485–1603* (London: Collins, 1999), pp. 197–212.

11 P. Ackroyd, *The History of England: Tudors* (London: Macmillan, 2012), vol. 2 , p. 467.

12 Ibid., pp. 467–8.

13 Ibid., p. 468.

14 Haigh, ed., *The English Reformation Revised*, p. 209.

15 This description of Queen Mary I was written by Giovanni Michieli, the Venetian ambassador to her court, http://englishhistory.net/tudor/marydesc.html, accessed 12 June 2012.

BIBLIOGRAPHY

PRINTED SOURCES

A collection of scarce and valuable tracts, on the most interesting and entertaining subjects; but chiefly such as relate to the history and constitution of the three kingdoms, selected from an infinite number in print and manuscript; in the royal Cotton, Sion and other public libraries, particularly that of the late Lord Somers, 2nd edition, revised, augmented and arranged by Walter Scott, 8 vols., vol. 8. London: T. Cadell, 1812.

A Necessary Doctrine and Erudition for Any Christian Man Set forth by the King's Majesty of England, &c. 1543. Introduction by the Reverend T. A. Lacey. London: R. Browning, 1895.

Ackroyd, P., *The History of England: Tudors*, 2 vols. London: Macmillan, 2012.

Alexander, G., 'Bonner and the Marian Persecutions', in C. Haigh, ed., *The English Reformation Revised*. Cambridge: Cambridge University Press, 1992.

Ansgar Kelly, H., *The Matrimonial Trials of Henry VIII*. Redwood City: Stanford University Press, 1976.

Bancroft, R., *Dangerous Positions and Proceedings: Published and Practised within this Island of Britain under Pretence of Reformation and for the Presbyterial Discipline*. London: A. and J. Churchill, 1712.

Berglar, P., *Thomas More: A Lonely Voice against the Power of the State*. New York: Sceptre, 1999.

Bernard, G. W., *Anne Boleyn: Fatal Attractions*. New Haven: Yale University Press, 2011.

Burnet, G., *History of the Reformation of the Church of England*, ed. N. Pocock. Oxford: Oxford University Press, 1865.

Carte, T., *A General History of England*, 4 vols. London: printed by William Bowyer, 1752.

Challis, E., *The Tudor Coinage*. Manchester: Manchester University Press, 1978.

Chamberlain, R., *The Bad Popes*. Oxford: Sutton Publishing, 2004.

Chrimes, S. B., *Henry VII*. Berkley and Los Angeles: University of California Press, 1972.

Clapham, J., *Elizabeth of England: Certain Observations on the Life and Reign of Queen Elizabeth*, ed. E. Plummer Read and C. Read. Philadelphia: University of Philadelphia Press, 1951.

Cogswell, T., *The Blessed Revolution: English Politics and the Coming of War, 1621–1624*. Cambridge: Cambridge University Press, 2005.

Collcott, M., *Little Arthur's History of England*. London: John Murray, 1866.

Colley, L., *Britons: Forging the Nation, 1707–1837*. New Haven and London: Yale University Press, 1992.

Collier, J., *Ecclesiastical History of Great Britain, Chiefly of England from the first Planting of Christianity in this Island*, 2 vols., vol. 2. London: Samuel Keble and Benjamin Tooke, 1714.

Collinson, P., 'The Persecution in Kent', in E. Duffy and D. Loades, eds., *The Church of Mary Tudor*. Aldershot and Burlington: Ashgate, 2006.

The Coronation of Queen Elizabeth, with the restauration of the Protestant religion, or, The downfal of the Pope: being a most excellent play, as it was acted both at Bartholomew and Southwark fairs, this present year, 1680, with great applause and approved of and highly commended by all the Protestant nobility, gentry and commonalty of England, who came to be spectators of the same. London, 1680.

Coulton, G. G., *The Monastic Legend: A Criticism of Abbot Gasquet's 'Henry VIII and the English Monasteries'*. London: Simpkin, Marshall, Hamilton, Kent & Co., 1905

Cross, C., 'The English Universities 1553–1558', in E. Duffy and D. Loades, eds., *The Church of Mary Tudor*. Aldershot and Burlington: Ashgate, 2006.

Davies, C. S. L., 'England and the French Wars', in Jennifer Loach and Robert Tittler, *The Mid-Tudor Polity, 1540–60*. London: Palgrave Macmillan, 1980.

de Mezerac-Zanetti, A., 'Reforming the Liturgy under Henry VIII: The Instructions of John Clerk, Bishop of Bath and Wells', *Journal of Ecclesiastical History*, 64 (2013), 96–111.

de Souza, Raymond, 'Confronting the Church's Past: An Interview with Eamon Duffy', *Commonweal* 127/1, January 2000.

Dickens, A. G., *English Reformation*, Fontana Press, 13th impr. 1983 [1964].

Dodds, G. D., *Exploiting Erasmus: The Erasmian Legacy and Religious Change in Early Modern England*. Toronto, Buffalo and London: University of Toronto Press, 2009.

Doran, S., 'A "Sharp Rod" of Chastisement: Mary I through Protestant Eyes during the Reign of Elizabeth I', in S. Doran and T. S. Freeman, eds., *Mary Tudor, Old and New Perspectives*. Basingstoke: Palgrave Macmillan, 2011.

——and T. S. Freeman, eds., *Mary Tudor, Old and New Perspectives*. Basingstoke: Palgrave Macmillan, 2011.

Duffy, E., 'Cardinal Pole preaching: St Andrew's Day 1557', in E. Duffy and D. Loades, eds., *The Church of Mary Tudor*. Aldershot and Burlington: Ashgate, 2006.

—— *Fires of Faith: Catholic England under Mary Tudor*. New Haven: Yale University Press, 2009.

——*Saints, Sacrilege and Sedition: Religion and Conflict in the Tudor Reformations*. London, Berlin, New York and Sydney: Bloomsbury Publications, 2012.

Duffy, E., *The Stripping of the Altars: Traditional Religion in England, 1400–1580*. New Haven and London: Yale University Press, 2nd edn, 2005 [1992].

—— and D. Loades, eds., *The Church of Mary Tudor*. Aldershot and Burlington: Ashgate, 2006.

Echard, L., *The History of England, from the First Entrance of Julius Caesar and the Romans to the End of the Reign of James the First*, 3 vols. London: Jacob Tonson, 1707.

Edwards, J., *Archbishop Pole*. Farnham and Burlington: Ashgate Publishing, 2014.

—— *Mary I: England's Catholic Queen*. New Haven: Yale University Press, 2011.

—— 'Fray Bartolomé Carranza's blueprint for a reformed Catholic Church in England', in T. F. Mayer, ed., *Reforming Reformation*. Farnham: Ashgate, 2012.

—— and Ronald Truman, eds., *Reforming Catholicism in the England of Mary Tudor: The Achievements of Friar Bartolomē Carranza*. Aldershot and Burlington: Ashgate, 2005.

Elton, G. R., *Policy and Police: The Enforcement of the Reformation in the Age of Thomas Cromwell*. Cambridge: Cambridge University Press, 1972.

—— *Reform and Reformation: England 1509–1558*. London: Edward Arnold, 1977.

—— *The Practice of History*. Oxford: Wiley-Blackwell, 2002.

Fenlon, D., 'Pole, Carranza and the Pulpit', in J. Edwards and Ronald Truman, eds., *Reforming Catholicism in the England of Mary Tudor: The Achievements of Friar Bartolomē Carranza*. Aldershot and Burlington: Ashgate, 2005.

Fish, S., 'A Supplycacion for the Beggars', 1559, in Gerald L. Carroll and Joseph B. Murray, eds., The Yale Edition of *The Complete Works of St. Thomas More*. 15 vols., vol. 7. New Haven: Yale University Press, 1990.

Fletcher, C., *The Divorce of Henry VIII: The Untold Story from inside the Vatican*. Basingstoke: Palgrave Macmillan, 2012.

[Foxe, John], *Fox's Original and Complete Book of Martyrs: Or, an Universal History of Martyrdom. Containing Accounts of the Lives, Sufferings & Deaths of the Protestant Martyrs in the Reign of Queen Mary the First . . . Originally Composed by the Rev'd. John Fox. M. A. Now Revised and Corrected by a Minister of the Gosple.*, Paul Wright. London: R. Balfe, 1782.

Freeman, T. S., 'Burning Zeal: Mary Tudor and the Marian Persecution', in S. Doran and T. S. Freeman, eds., *Mary Tudor, Old and New Perspectives*. Basingstoke: Palgrave Macmillan, 2011.

—— 'Inventing Bloody Mary: Perceptions of Mary Tudor', in S. Doran and T. S. Freeman, eds., *Mary Tudor, Old and New Perspectives*. Basingstoke: Palgrave Macmillan, 2011.

Froude, J. A., *History of England from the Fall of Wolsey to the Defeat of the Spanish Armada*. London: Longman, Green and Co., London, 1870, new edn 1893.

—— *The Reign of Mary Tudor*, selected and introduced by E. Duffy. London and New York: Continuum, 2009.

Fuller, T., *The Church History of Britain, from the Birth of Jesus Christ to the year MDCXLVIII*, new edition in 6 volumes, rev. J. S. Brewer, vol. 6. Oxford: Oxford University Press, 1845.

Gasquet, A., *Henry VIII and the English Monasteries: An Attempt to Illustrate the History of their Suppression*, 2 vols. London: John Hodges, 1888.

—— *The Eve of the Reformation: Studies in the Religious Life and Thought of the English People in the Period Preceeding the Rejection of the Roman Jurisdiction by Henry VIII*. London: G Bell and Sons, 1923.

Grafton, R., *A Chronicle at Large and Meere History of the Affayres of Englande and Kinges of the Same, Deduced from the Creation of the World, unto the First Habitation of thys Islande: And so by Contynuance unto the First Yere of the Reigne of Our Most Deere and Soureigne Lady Queen Elizabeth*. 2 vols. London: J. Johnson, 1809. ('Grafton's Chronicle')

Grant, T., '"Thus like a nun, not like a princess born": Dramatic Representations of Mary Tudor in the Early Years of the Seventeenth Century', in S. Doran and T. S. Freeman, eds., *Mary Tudor, Old and New Perspectives*. Basingstoke: Palgrave Macmillan, 2011.

Gregory, B. S., *Salvation at Stake Christian Martyrdom in Early Modern Europe*. Cambridge, Mass: Harvard University Press, 1999.

Guy, J., *Tudor England*. Oxford: Oxford University Press, 1998.

Haigh, C., 'Anti-clericalism and the English Reformation', in C. Haigh, ed., *The English Reformation Revised*. Cambridge: Cambridge University Press, 1992.

—— 'Introduction', in C. Haigh, ed., *The English Reformation Revised*. Cambridge: Cambridge University Press, 1992.

—— 'The continuity of Catholicism in the English Reformation', in C. Haigh, ed., *The English Reformation Revised*. Cambridge: Cambridge University Press, 1992.

—— 'The recent historiography of the English Reformation', in C. Haigh, ed., *The English Reformation Revised*. Cambridge: Cambridge University Press, 1992.

——, ed., *The English Reformation Revised*. Cambridge: Cambridge University Press, 1992.

—— *Elizabeth I*. London, Longman, 2001.

Hale, J. R., *Renaissance Europe: The Individual and Society, 1480–1520*. Los Angeles and London: University of California Press, 1971.

Harbison, E. H., *Rival Ambassadors at the Court of Queen Mary*. Princeton: Princeton University Press, 1940.

Haydon, C., *Anti-Catholicism in Eighteenth-Century England, c. 1714–1780: A Political and Social Study*. Manchester: Manchester University Press, 1993.

Herbermann, C. G., *The Catholic Encyclopedia: An International Work of Reference on the Constitution, Doctrine, Discipline, and History of the Catholic Church*. Appleton: University of Michigan Press, 1907.

Holmes, D. L., *A Brief History of the Episcopal Chur*ch. London: T. and T. Clark, 1993.

Houliston, V., '"Her majesty, who is now in heaven": Mary Tudor and the Elizabethan Catholics', in S. Doran and T. S. Freeman, eds., *Mary Tudor, Old and New Perspectives*. Basingstoke: Palgrave Macmillan, 2011.

—— *Catholic Resistance in Elizabethan England: Robert Persons's Jesuit Polemic*. Aldershot and Burlington: Ashgate, 2007.

Howes, E., *Annales or a General Chronicle of England Begun by John Stow, Continued and Augmented by Matters Foraign and Domestique, Modern, unto the End of the Present Year, 1631*. London: Richardi Meighen, 1631.

Hughes, P., *The Reformation in England. The King's Proceedings*. 2 vols. London: Hollis and Carter, 1956.

Hughes, P. L., and J. F. Larkin, *Tudor Royal Proclamations: The Later Tudors (1553–1587)*. 3 vols.. New Haven and London: Yale University Press, 1969.

Hume, D., *The History of England from the Invasion of Julius Caesar to the Revolution of 1688*. 8 vols. Dublin: United Company of Book Sellers, 1775.

Ignatius Loyola, *Letters of St. Ignatius Loyola*, ed. W. J. Young. Chicago: Loyola University Press, 1959.

Ives, E., *Lady Jane Grey: A Tudor Mystery*. Chichester: Wiley-Blackwell, 2009.

James, S., *Kateryn Parr*. Aldershot and Burlington: Ashgate Publishing, 1999.

Jansson, M., ed., *Proceedings in the Opening Session of the Long Parliament: House of Commons, 3 November to 19 December 1540*. 2 vols. Rochester, New York, and Woodbridge, Suffolk: University of Rochester Press, 2000.

Jones, E., *John Lingard and the Pursuit of Historical Truth*. Brighton and Portland: Sussex Academic Press, 2001.

Kaufman, P. I., 'Henry VII and Sanctuary Church History', *Church History: Studies in Christianity and Culture*, 53/4, December 1984.

Keen, D., 'The Political Economy of War', in F. Stewart and V. Fitzgerald, eds., *War and Underdevelopment: Economic and Social Consequences of Conflict*. 2 vols. Queen Elizabeth House Series in Development Studies. Oxford: Oxford University Press, 2000.

Kewes, P., 'The Exclusion Crisis of 1553 and the Elizabethan Succession', in S. Doran and T. S. Freeman, eds., *Mary Tudor, Old and New Perspectives*. Basingstoke: Palgrave Macmillan, 2011.

Knowles, D., *Cardinal Gasquet as an Historian*. Creighton lecture. London: Athlone Press, 1957.

Lanquet, T., T. Cooper and R. Crowley, *An epitome of chronicles Conteyninge the whole discourse of the histories as well of this realme of England, as al other countreys, with the succession of their kinges, the time of their reigne, and what notable actes they did ... gathered out of most probable auctours. Firste by Thomas Lanquet, from the beginning of the worlde to the incarnacion of Christe, secondely to the reigne of our soueraigne lord king Edward the sixt by Thomas Cooper,* and thirdly to the reigne of our soueraigne Ladye Quene Elizabeth, by Robert Crowley*. London: Printed by William Seres *in ædibus* Thomæ Marshe, 1559.

Lee, S., ed., *Dictionary of National Biography*. Smith elder and co., London, 1897, 63 vols., First series.

Lehmberg, S. E., *The Reformation Parliament 1529–1536*, Cambridge: Cambridge University Press, 2008.

Lerins, V., *The waie home to Christ and truth leadinge from Antichrist and errour*, trans., J. Proctor. Ann Arbor, Michigan: University of Michigan Press, 2011.

Lingard, J., *A History of England from the First Invasion by the Romans*. 14 vols., 4th edition. Paris: L. Baudry, 1819–30.

—— *Lingard's History of England Abridged: With a Continuation, from 1688 to 1854*. 3rd enlarged edition. Baltimore: John Murphy & Co., 1875.

—— *Lingard's History of England: Newly Abridged and Brought Down to the Accession of King George V*, ed. H. Norbert. London: G. Bell and Sons, 1918, first published, 1819–30.

Loach, J., 'The Marian Establishment and the Printing Press', *English Historical Review*, 101, 1986.

—— *Parliament under the Tudors*. Oxford: Clarendon Press, 1991.

Loades, D., 'Introduction: The Personal Religion of Mary I', in E. Duffy and D. Loades, eds., *The Church of Mary Tudor*. Aldershot and Burlington: Ashgate, 2006.

—— 'The English Church during the Reign of Mary I', in J. Edwards and Ronald Truman, eds., *Reforming Catholicism in the England of Mary Tudor: The Achievements of Friar Bartolomé Carranza*. Aldershot and Burlington: Ashgate, 2005.

—— 'The Marian Episcopate', in E. Duffy and D. Loades, eds., *The Church of Mary Tudor*. Aldershot and Burlington: Ashgate, 2006.

—— *John Dudley Duke of Northumberland 1504–1553*. Oxford: Clarendon Press, 1996.

—— *Mary Tudor*. Stroud: Amberley Publishing, 2012.

—— *The Reign of Mary Tudor: Politics, Government and Religion in England, 1553–1558*. London and New York: Longman, 1991.

—— *Two Tudor Conspiracies*. Cambridge: Cambridge University Press, 1965.

Macaulay, T. B., *The History of England from the Accession of James the Second*. 5 vols. London: Longman, Brown, Green and Longman, 1849.

MacCulloch, D., *Thomas Cranmer: A Life*. New Haven and London: Yale University Press, 1996.

The Diary of Henry Machyn: Citizen and Merchant-Taylor of London (1550–1563), ed. J. G. Nichols. London: Camden Society, 1848.

Marshall, P., *The Catholic Priesthood and the English Reformation*. New York and Oxford: Oxford University Press, 1994.

Martin, J. W., *Religious Radicals in Tudor England*. London and Roncerverte: Hambledon, 1989.

Mayer, T. F., 'Cardinal Pole's Concept of *Reformatio*: The *Reformatio Angliae* and Bartelome Carranza', in J. Edwards and Ronald Truman, eds., *Reforming Catholicism in the England of Mary Tudor: The Achievements of Friar Bartolomē Carranza*. Aldershot and Burlington: Ashgate, 2005.

—— *Reginald Pole: Prince and Prophet*. Cambridge: Cambridge University Press, 2000.

—— *The Correspondence of Reginald Pole, A Calendar, 1555–1558, Restoring the English Church*. 3 vols. Aldershot: Ashgate, 2004.

—— 'The Success of Cardinal Pole's Final Legation', in E. Duffy and D. Loades, eds., *The Church of Mary Tudor*. Aldershot and Burlington: Ashgate, 2006.

More, T., 'The Supplycatyon of Soulys 1529', in Gerald L. Carroll and Joseph B. Murray, The Yale Edition of *The Complete Works of St. Thomas More*. 15 vols., vol. 7. New Haven: Yale University Press, 1990.

Morice, R., 'Anecdotes and Character of Archbishop Cranmer', in J. G. Nichols, ed., *Narratives of the Days of the Reformation*. London: Camden Society, 1859.

Motley, J. L., *The Rise of the Dutch Republic*. New York: Cosimo Books, 2005 [1856].

Murphy, D., P. Walsh-Atkins and A. Keen, *England 1485–1603*. London: Collins, 1999.

Nichols, J. G., ed., *Literary Remains of Kind Edward the Sixth*. 2 vols. London: J. B. Nichols and Sons, 1857.

Oldmixon, J., *The History of England: During the Reigns of Henry VIII. Edward VI. Queen Mary. Queen Elizabeth. Including the History of the Reformation of the Churches of England and Scotland . . . Also Including a History of Mary, Queen of Scots*. London: T. Cox and R. Hett, 1739.

Original Letters Relative to the English Reformation Written during the Reigns of King Henry VIII, King Edward VI and Queen Mary, Chiefly from Authenticated Copies of the Autographs and Edited for the Rev. Hasting Robinson. Cambridge: Cambridge University Press, 1846.

Palliser, D. M., 'Popular Reactions to the Reformation during the Years of Uncertainty, 1530–1570', in C. Haigh, ed., *The English Reformation Revised*. Cambridge: Cambridge University Press, 1992.

Persons, R., *A Treatise of Three Conversions of England from Paganisme to Christian Religion*. St Omer, 1603.

Plucknett, T. F. T., and J. L. Barton, eds., *St. German's Doctor and Student*. London: Selden Society, 1974.

Pogson, R., 'Revival and Reform in Mary Tudor's Church: A Question of Money', in C. Haigh, ed., *The English Reformation Revised*. Cambridge: Cambridge University Press, 1992.

Pogson, R., 'Reginald Pole and the Priorities of Government in Mary Tudor's Church', *The Historical Journal*, 18, 1975.

Pole, R., *Pole's Defence of the Unity of the Church*, translated with introduction by Joseph G Dwyer. Westminster, Maryland: The Newman Press, 1965.

—— 'Pole Cardinal Legate, to Archbishop Cranmer, in Answer to the Letter he had Sent to the Queene', in *Memorials of the Most Reverend Father in God Thomas Cranmer, Sometime Lord Archbishop of Canterbury*, ed. J. Strype. 2 vols. Oxford: Clarendon Press, 1812.

Pollard, A. F., *Henry VII*. London: Longman, Green and Co., 1919.

—— *The History of England: From the Accession of Edward VI to the Death of Elizabeth*. London: Longman, Green and Co., 1910.

Pollnitz, A., 'Religion and Translation at the Court of Henry VIII', in S. Doran and T. S. Freeman, eds., *Mary Tudor, Old and New Perspectives*. Basingstoke: Palgrave Macmillan, 2011.

Porter, H. C., 'Fisher and Erasmus', in Brendon Bradshaw, ed., *Humanism, Reform and the Reformation: The Career of Bishop John Fisher*. Cambridge: Cambridge University Press, 1989.

Porter, L., *Mary Tudor, the First Queen*. London: Piakus, 2009.

Prescott, H. F. M., *Mary Tudor: The Spanish Tudor*. London: Phoenix, 2003 [1940, rev. edn 1952].

Rex, R., *The Theology of John Fisher*. Cambridge: Cambridge University Press, 1991.

Richards, J. M., 'Reassessing Mary Tudor: Some Concluding Points', in S. Doran and T. S. Freeman, eds., *Mary Tudor, Old and New Perspectives*. Basingstoke: Palgrave Macmillan, 2011.

—— *Mary Tudor*. Abingdon and New York: Routledge, 2008.

Ridley, J., *Henry VIII*. London: Penguin Books, 1984.

Salzman, P., *Literary Culture in Jacobean England: Reading 1621*. Basingstoke: Palgrave Macmillan, 2002.

Sanders, N., *The Rise and Growth of the Anglican Schism*, trans. David Lewis. London: Burns and Oates, 1877.

Sansom, C. J., *Lamentation*. Basingstoke and Oxford: Mantle, 2014.

Scarisbrick, J. J., *Henry VIII*. London: Methuen, 1991 [1968].

Schama, S., *History of Britain: At the Edge of the World? 3000BC–AD1603*. London: BBC Worldwide Ltd, 2000.

—— *History of Britain*, episode 6: *Burning Convictions*. London: BBC production, 2002.

Sharpe, K., *Selling the Tudor Monarchy: Authority and Image in Sixteenth Century England*. New Haven and London: Yale University Press, 2009.

Skidmore, C., *Edward VI: The Lost King of England*. London: Weidenfeld & Nicolson, 2007.

Smith, A. G. R., *The Emergence of a Nation-State: The Commonwealth of England 1529–1660*. London: Longman, 1997.

Solt, L. F., *Church and State in Early Modern England, 1509–1640*. Oxford: Oxford University Press, 1990.

Standish, J., *A discourse wherein is debated whether it be expedient that the Scripture should be in English for al men to reade that wyll*. London: Robery Caly, 1554.

Stewart, F., and V. Fitzgerald, eds., *War and Underdevelopment: Economic and Social Consequences of Conflict*. 2 vols. Queen Elizabeth House Series in Development Studies. Oxford: Oxford University Press, 2000.

Strickland, A., and E. Strickland, *Lives of the Queens of England: From the Norman Conquest*. London: Colburn & Co., 1851–2.

Taylor, A. W., 'Ad Omne Virtutum Genus"? Mary between Piety, Pedagogy and Praise in Early Tudor Humanism', in S. Doran and T. S. Freeman, eds., *Mary Tudor, Old and New Perspectives*. Basingstoke: Palgrave Macmillan, 2011.

Thompson, A. C., *Britain, Hanover and the Protestant Interest, 1688–1756*. Woodbridge: Boydell & Brewer, 2005.

Tittler, R., 'The Emergence of Urban Policy, 1536–58', in J. Loach and R. Tittler, eds., *The Mid-Tudor Polity, 1540–60*. Problems in Focus. London and Basingstoke: Palgrave Macmillan, 1980.

Tootell, H. (Charles Dodd), *Church History of England from the Year 1500 to the Year 1688*. Brussels, 1737; republished Westmead, Farnborough: Gregg International Publishers, England, 1970.

Tytler, P. F., *England under the Reigns of Edward VI and Mary: With the Contemporary History of Europe*. 2 vols. London: Richard Bentley, 1839.

Vidmar, J., *English Catholic Historians and the English Reformation, 1585–1954*. Brighton and Portland: Sussex Academic Press, 2005.

Vox populi, Vox Dei; or England's general lamentation for the dissolution of the Parliament, 1681.

Walsham, A., 'Unclasping the Book? Post-Reformation English Catholicism and the Vernacular Bible', *Journal of British Studies*, 42/2, 2003.

Warner, W., *Albion's England, the third time corrected and augmented*. London 1592.

Weir, A., *Henry VIII: King and Court*. London: Random House, 2011.

—— *Six Wives of Henry VIII*. London: Vintage, 2007.

Whitelock, A., *Mary Tudor, England's First Queen*. London, Berlin, New York, Sydney, Bloomsbury Publications. 2009.

Willis, J. P., *Church Music and Protestantism in Post-Reformation England: Discourses, Sites and Identities*. Farnham and Burlington: Ashgate, 2010.

Wilson, F., 'The Sunday Times Christmas Books', *The Sunday Times*, 29 November, 2009 (online at: http://www.thesundaytimes.co.uk/sto/culture/books/non_fiction/article191236.ece).

Wizeman, W., 'Martyrs and Anti-martyrs and Mary Tudor's Church', in T. S. Freeman and T. F. Mayer, eds., *Martyrs and Martyrdom in England c. 1400–1700*. Woodbridge: The Boydell Press, 2007.

Wizeman, W., 'The Religious Policy of Mary I', in S. Doran and T. S. Freeman, eds., *Mary Tudor, Old and New Perspectives*. Basingstoke: Palgrave Macmillan, 2011.

——— *The Theology and Spirituality of Mary Tudor's Church*. Aldershot and Burllington: Ashgate, 2006.

Wooding, L., 'The Marian Restoration and the Language of Catholic Reform', in J. Edwards and Ronald Truman, eds., *Reforming Catholicism in the England of Mary Tudor: The Achievements of Friar Bartolomē Carranza*. Aldershot and Burlington: Ashgate, 2005.

——— 'The Marian Restoration and the Mass', in E. Duffy and D. Loades, eds., *The Church of Mary Tudor*. Aldershot and Burlington: Ashgate, 2006.

——— 'The Restoration and Language of Catholic Reform', in J. Edwards and R. Truman, eds., *Reforming Catholicism in the England of Mary Tudor: The Achievements of Friar Bartolomē Carranza*. Aldershot and Burlington: Ashgate Press, 2005.

——— *Rethinking Catholicism in Marian England*. Oxford Historical Monographs. Oxford: Clarendon Press, 2000.

Wriothesley, C., *A Chronicle of England during the Reign of the Tudors from 1485 to 1559*, ed., W. D. Hamilton. 2 vols. London: Camden Society, 1777.

SOURCES FOUND ON THE INTERNET

The first Act of Succession, 1534, *Luminarium: Encyclopaedia Project – England under the Tudors*: http://www.luminarium.org/encyclopedia/firstactofsuccession.htm.

Acts of the Privy Council of England: http://www.british-history.ac.uk/catalogue.aspx?type=3&gid=156

'Apostolic journey to the United Kingdom, September, 16–19, 2010, Interview of the Holy Father Benedict XVI with the journalists during the flight to the United Kingdom, papal flight', Thursday, 16 September 2010, website of the Holy See: http://www.vatican.va/holy_father/benedict_xvi/speeches/2010/september/documents/hf_ben-xvi_spe_20100916_interv-regno-unito_en.html

'Banned Bloody Mary Zombie Advert for London Dungeon'. http://www.youtube.com/watch?v=09WtEmTLp1Y.

Calendar of State Papers relating to English Affairs in the Archives of Venice: http://www.britishhistory.ac.uk/catalogue.aspx?gid=140

Calendar of State Papers, Spain: http://www.british-history.ac.uk/catalogue.aspx?gid=136

John Foxe's *Acts and Monuments* online: http://www.johnfoxe.org/

Guy, J., 'Elizabeth I and Politics: The Views of Historians': http://www.tudors.org/asa2-level/59-elizabeth-i-and-politics-the-views-of-historians.html, accessed 12 June 2012.

Bibliography

Knox, J., *The first blast of the trumpet against the monstruous regiment of women* (The English Scholar's Library, 2.1558, ed. E. Arber, Cambridge, Massachusetts: Harvard University Press, 1878), p. 1. Digitised version: Project Gutenberg: http://www.gutenberg.org/files/9660/9660-h/9660-h.htm.

Letters and Papers, Foreign and Domestic, Henry VIII: http://www.british-history.ac.uk/catalogue.aspx?gid=126

Loades, D., 'Foxe and Queen Mary: Stephen Gardiner: Edmund Bonner': http://www.johnfoxe.org/index.php?realm=more&gototype=modern&type=essay&book=essay19&anchor.

London Dungeon, Mary Tudor promotional poster: http://www.londonnet.co.uk/competition/the-london-dungeon.php.

Mary I, 'The Will of Mary I': http://tudorhistory.org/primary/will.html.

Micheli. G., '1557, A Contemporary Description of Mary I': http://englishhistory.net/tudor/marydesc.html.

Pope Pius V's Bull against Elizabeth, 1570, *Regnans in Excelsis*: http://tudorhistory.org/primary/papalbull.html.

'The Six Articles'. *Luminarium: Encyclopaedia Project – England under the Tudors*: http://www.luminarium.org/encyclopedia/sixarticles.htm.

'The Ten Articles'. *Luminarium: Encyclopaedia Project – England under the Tudors*: http://www.luminarium.org/encyclopedia/tenarticles.htm.

'The 24 Articles of the Pilgrimage of Grace rebels', *Luminarium: Encyclopaedia Project – England under the Tudors*: http://www.luminarium.org/encyclopedia/24articles.htm.

INDEX

Acton, lord 36
Ackroyd, Peter 204
Albert, prince, consort to Queen
    Victoria 116
Aske, Robert 85
Alexander VI, pope 67, 68
Anne of Cleves, queen of England 87,
    88
Alice Lady Cleve 80
Angel, John 63 149
Angelo, Michael 68
Anne, duchess of Brittany 67
Anne, queen 22, 23
Aquinas, St Thomas 70
Arthur Tudor, prince 60, 70, 71, 72, 79
Augustine, St (of Hippo) 63, 69, 70
Aylmer, John 12

Baker, John 25
Bale, John 186
Bancroft, Richard, archbishop of
    Canterbury 13
Bartolomé Carranza, archbishop of
    Toledo 158, 164, 159, 187
Batory, Elizabeth, countess 53
Becon, Thomas 161
Becket, St Thomas 11, 147
Bellarmine, St Robert, cardinal 70
Belloc, Hillaire 47
Benbridge, Thomas 190
Benden, Alice 190
Benedict XVI, pope 35, 203
Berrrington, Father Joseph 34
Berry Godfrey, Sir Edmund 20
Bland, John 189
Blount, Elizabeth 64
Bocher, Joan 178
Boleyn, Anne 2, 10, 65, 78, 79, 80, 89,
    92, 133, 136, 205
Bongeor, Agness 181

Borgia, Lucrezia 68
Borromeo, St Charles, cardinal 157
Bonner, Edmund, bishop of London
    13, 22, 23, 29, 33. 50, 84, 98, 148, 153,
    162, 163, 164, 184, 186, 188, 190
Brandon, Charles, duke of Suffolk 68
Brookes, James, bishop of Gloucester
    165
Bucer, Martin 138
Burnet, Gilbert 21, 22
Butler, Charles 34
Byrd, William 161

Cajetan, Tomaso, cardinal 70
Camden, William 3
Campeggio, Lorenzo, cardinal
    Protector of England 66, 73. 74
Campion, St Edmund 168
Cardmaker, John 191
Carte, Thomas 26
di Castro, Alfonso, cardinal 37, 185, 193
Chapuys, Eustace, Imperial
    ambassador to England 65, 80, 81,
    82, 83, 84, 93, 132
Charles I, king of England 20
Charles II, king of England 20
Charles V, Holy Roman emperor 26,
    61, 64, 65, 69, 72, 74, 80, 81, 84, 85, 93,
    94, 97, 99, 105, 107, 109, 111, 112, 113,
    114, 116, 117, 118 121, 132, 185, 199
Charles VIII, king of France 67
Cheke, John, Sir 181, 188
Christopherson, John 166
Clapham, John 113
Clarencius, Susan 107, 118
Clement VII, pope 66, 69, 72, 73, 80,
    193
Clifford, Henry, justice of the peace
    181
Collinson, Patrick 49, 192

Cranmer, Thomas, archbishop of
Canterbury 74, 79, 82, 83, 137, 151,
178, 179, 183, 184, 188, 193, 205
Cromwell, Thomas, Lord Chancellor
11, 75, 82, 83, 85, 87, 88, 134, 136, 165,
205
Cross, Claire 167, 168
Collcott, Maria 29
Collier, Jeremy 22, 23
Colley, Linda 23, 29
Coke, Edward 18, 19
Courtenay, Edward 110, 111, 113
Crowley, Robert 12, 13, 14

van der Delft, Francois, Imperial
ambassador to England 93, 94, 95, 117
Day, John 190
Dickens, Arthur Geoffrey 46, 47, 48,
49, 53, 104, 118, 133, 134, 135, 136, 138,
140, 162, 167, 168, 170, 174, 203
Dodd (Tootle), Charles 3, 33, 34. 36, 37,
175, 186
Dodds, Gregory 150
Douglas, archibald, earl of Angus 68
Dudley, John, earl of Warwick,
duke of Northumberland, Lord
President 94, 98, 99, 100, 104, 117,
118, 137, 153, 165, 166, 179
Dudley, Guildford 98, 104, 111
Duffy, Eamon 15, 30, 40, 45, 46, 51, 52,
129, 131, 139, 156, 158, 159, 162, 163,
164, 168, 170, 174, 182

Echard, Laurence 27
Edward VI, king 10, 13, 19, 21, 44, 46,
86, 87, 89, 90, 92, 93, 95, 96, 97, 98,
99, 104, 105, 107, 143, 144, 145, 146,
147, 149, 150, 153, 167, 175, 177, 178, 182
d'Egmont, count, Imperial
ambassador to the Netherlands 138
Englefield Sir Francis 97
Elizabeth I, princess, queen of
England 98, 103, 104, 107, 108, 109,
110, 111, 112, 116, 121, 128, 147, 156, 161,
167, 168, 169, 178, 179, 180, 184, 199,
201, 202, 203, 204

Elton, Geoffrey Rudolf 46, 47, 52, 62,
62, 83, 148, 170, 174, 203
Erasmus, Desiderius 9, 60, 63, 89, 143,
149, 150

Fawkes, Guy 24
Fenlon, Dermot 138,
Feria, count, Spain's ambassador to
England 11, 12, 14, 105, 160
Ferdinand, king of Aragon 59, 61, 113
Ferdinand, Holy Romane emperor 121
Fetherstone, Richard 63
Fisher, John, St, bishop 40, 66, 70, 71,
82, 115, 136, 160, 177, 178, 192
Fish, Simon 11, 1333
Fitzalan, Henry, earl of Arundel 100,
105
Fitzroy, Henry, earl of Richmond 64,
65
Forest, John, friar 179
Foxe, John 3, 13, 18, 19, 21, 25, 33, 34, 38,
48, 49, 50 53, 110, 112, 115, 147, 174, 175,
176, 178, 179, 181, 184, 185, 186, 187,
188, 189, 190, 191, 192, 193
Franciois, prince, dauphin of France 60
Francis, I, king of France 64, 66, 86,
90, 111
Freeman, Thomas 177, 194
Froude, James Anthony 4, 39, 40, 41,
47, 49, 188
Fuller, Thomas 20

Gasquet, Aidan, cardinal 3, 45, 46
George I, George Louis, elector of
Hanover, king of England 23
Gardiner, Stephen, bishop of
Winchester 21, 23, 29, 40, 63, 84, 93,
104, 105, 110, 137, 166, 175, 186, 187
Goldwell, Thomas, bishop of St Asaph
15
Grafton, Richard 13
Grant, Teresa 19
Gregory XIII, pope 15
Grey, Frances duchess of Suffolk 98
Grey, Jane, Lady, queen of England 12,
114, 98, 104, 111, 117, 166

Guy, John 34, 106, 109, 135, 140, 168, 178

Haigh, Christopher 2, 49, 128, 129, 132, 135
Hall, Roger 190
Harpsfield, John 163
Harpsfield, Nicholas, archdeacon of Canterbury 19, 182
Hastings, Sir Edward, Lord Privy Seal 12
Hawkes, Thomas 189
Henry Tudor, prince 59
Henry Stuart, prince 19
Henry V, king of England 177
Henry VII, king of England 98, 116
Henry VIII of England 1, 2, 3, 9, 11, 18, 19, 29, 44, 45, 47, 52, 74, 86, 108, 113, 116, 137, 144, 145, 153, 158, 165, 178, 199, 205,
Holbein, Hans 87
Hogarth, William 27, 28
Hoggard, Miles 165
Hooper, John, bishop of Gloucester and Worcester 155, 175, 186, 188
Howard, George, lord 100
Howard, Henry, 6th duke of Norfolk 20
Howard, Katherine, queen 88, 89, 92
Howard, Thomas, 3rd duke of Norfolk 29, 83, 88, 136,
Howard, William 105
Hughes, Father Philip 46, 47, 146
Hume, David 3, 27, 39, 50
Hungerford, Sir Anthony, the under-secretary sheriff of Wiltshire 181
Hunne, Richard 133, 134
Hunt, John 181

Innocent III, pope 171
Isabella of Castile, queen 59, 62, 113
Isabella, queen of Portugal 61

James I (VI), king of England and Scotland 19, 39, 199
James II, The duke of York, king of England and Scotland 20, 22

James IV, king of Scotland 68
Joan, St, princess of France 67, 68
Joanna, queen of Castile 59
John the Baptist, St 66, 167
Julius II, pope 66, 79, 154

Kapur, Shekhar 32
Katherine, (of Aragon) queen of England 40, 59, 60, 61, 62, 64, 65, 66, 67, 70, 71, 72, 73, 74, 78, 79, 80, 81, 83, 87, 116, 132, 153
Kett, Robert 94, 100
Kitchin, Anthony, bishop of Llandaff 156
Koch, Ilse 53
Knox, John 3, 12, 13, 18, 49, 50, 174
Knowles, David 46

de Lassus, Orlando 161
Latimer, Hugh, bishop of Worcester 178
Leo X, pope 74, 143
Lerins, Vincent, St 63
Linacre, Thomas 62
Lingard, John 3, 36, 37, 38, 40, 46, 176, 177, 194,
Lithall, John 191
Loach, Jenifer 49, 162
Loades, David 30, 48, 49, 53, 105, 106, 109, 144, 148, 147, 149, 160, 180, 182, 185, 192
Louis XI, king of France 67, 68
Louis XII, king of France 67
Loyola, St Ignatius 160, 161
Luiz, Don, prince of Portugal 85
Luther, Martin 128, 143

Macaulay, Thomas Babington 3, 39
MacCulloch, Diarmaid 53, 193
Machyn, Henry 115, 200
Margaret, Tudor, queen (of Scots) 68
de Marillac, Charles 90
Mary I, queen of England, Princess Mary, Lady Mary, Mary Tudor 1, 2, 3, 4, 5, 6, 9, 10, 11, 12, 13, 14, 15, 16, 18, 19, 20, 21, 22, 23, 24, 25, 26, 27, 28, 29,

30, 33, 34, 35, 35, 37, 38, 39, 40, 41, 43,
45, 46, 47, 48, 49, 50, 51, 52, 53, 54, 55,
56, 57, 58, 59, 60, 61, 62, 63, 64, 65, 66,
67, 68, 69, 70, 71, 72, 73, 74, 75, 78, 79,
80, 81, 82, 83, 83, 84, 85, 86, 86, 87, 88,
89, 90, 91, 92, 93, 94, 95, 95, 96, 96,
97, 98, 99, 100, 101, 102, 103, 104, 105,
106, 106, 107, 108, 109, 110, 111, 112,
113, 114, 115, 116, 117, 118, 119, 120, 121,
127, 128, 129, 130, 131, 132, 133, 134, 135,
136, 137, 138, 139, 140, 143, 144, 145,
146, 147, 148, 149, 150, 151, 152, 153, 154,
155, 156, 156, 157, 158, 159, 160, 161,
162, 163, 164, 165, 166, 167, 168, 169,
170, 172, 174, 175, 176, 177, 178, 179,
180, 181, 182, 183, 184, 186, 187, 188,
189, 190, 191, 192, 193, 194, 199, 200,
202, 203, 204, 205, 206.

Mary, queen (of Hungary), governor
of the Netherlands 84, 95, 97

Mary, queen of Scots 12, 202

Mason, Sir John 166,

Mayer, Thomas 170

Maximillian, Holy Roman emperor
69

Michieli, Giovanni, ambassador, 191,
205

Montagu, Geoffrey 87

Montagu, Henry 87

Montagu, Sir Edward, Lord Chief
Justice 99

More, St Sir Thomas 9, 40, 62, 75, 82,
115, 132, 136, 143, 160, 178, 192

Morice, Ralph 83

Murray, John 29

Neale, Sir John 3

Neville, Margaret 69

Newman, John Henry, cardinal 35

Nicodemus St 84

de Noailles, Antoine, duke, France's
ambassador to England 190

Oates, Titus 20, 21

Oldmixon, John 25, 26

Ormanetto, Niccolo 157

Ortiz, Pedro 73

Paget, William, Lord Privy Seal 100,
105

da Palestrina, Giovanni Pierluigi 161

Parker, Henry, Lord Morley 150

Parker, Matthew, archbishop of
Canterbury 159, 190

Parr, Katherine, queen of England 63,
89, 143, 140, 150, 151

Paul III, pope 84

Paul IV, pope, Giovanni Pietro Carafa
112, 118, 119, 121, 146

Pendleton, John 163

Persons, Robert 19

Peto, William 23, 120

Petre, Anne 106

Petre, Sir William 105, 106

Philip II, king of Spain and England
11, 14, 22, 26, 29, 37, 51, 105, 106, 108,
109, 110, 111, 112, 113, 114, 115, 116, 117,
118, 119, 120, 121, 138, 144, 146, 161,
184, 185, 199

Pius V, pope 10

Pius XII, pope 68

Pogson, Rex 157, 158

Pole, Margaret, countess of Salisbury
63, 87

Pole, Reginald, cardinal, archbishop of
Canterbury, papal legate 19, 21, 23,
41, 45, 50, 51, 63, 66, 87, 118, 119, 120,
121, 146, 147, 153, 154, 155, 157, 158, 159,
160, 161, 164, 165, 166, 167, 168, 169.
170, 175, 187, 188, 190, 193, 205

Pollard, Albert Frederick 4, 44, 45, 47,
48, 49, 50, 101, 202

Pollnitz, Aysha 150

Porter, Linda 4, 14, 105, 106, 109, 116

Prescott, Hilda 47, 48, 403, 138

Prior, William 24

Proctor, John 63

Pym, John 19

Renard, Simon, Spanish ambassador
to England 104, 105, 106, 111, 113,
114, 118, 153, 184, 188

Reynolds, Christine 200
Reynolds, John 19
Ribadeneira, Pedro 160
Richard II, king of England 177
Richards, Judith 41, 49, 115, 118, 146, 178, 180
Rich, Richard, Lord Chancellor 95
Ridley, Nicholas, bishop of London 98
Rishton, Edward 15
Rochester, Sir Robert 97, 105
Rogers, John 178, 184, 186, 188, 190

Sampson, Richard, bishop of Chichester 83
Sanders (Sander), Nicholas 3 15, 21
Savorgnano, Mario 63
Scarisbrick, John Joseph 49, 69, 71
Schama, Simon 52, 83
Scheyfve, Jehan, Imperial ambassador to England 117
Seymour, Edward, duke of Somerset, Lord Protector 92, 93, 94, 95, 137, 153
Seymour, Jane, queen of England 81, 85, 87
Sharpe, Kevin 2, 3
Shelton, Lady Anne 80
Sforza, Giovanni 68
de Silva, Ruy Gómez 185
Smith, A. G. R. 107, 203
Southwall, Henry 25
Standish, John 63, 165
Stapleton, Thomas 19
Stephen, St 193
St Germain, Christopher 11, 133
Stow, John 103
Strickland, Agnes 4, 36, 37, 38, 40
Strickland, Elizabeth 4, 36, 37, 38, 40
Stuart, Charles Edward, The Young Pretender (Bonnie Prince Charlie) 22, 24
Stuart, James Francis Edward, The Old Pretender 22, 24

Surian, Michiel, Venetian ambassador 118

Tallis, Thomas 161
Tellechea Idigoras, José Ignacio 155, 164
Tittler, Robert 108
Tonge, Israel 20
Tye, Sir Thomas 190
Tyre, Christopher 161
Tyrell, Edmund 182, 190
Tyrell, Sir John 182

Udall, Nicholas 150, 151

Vermigli, Peter Martyr 166
Vidmar, John 34
Virgil, Polydor 133, 134
Vives, Juan Luis 62, 143, 150

Waldegrave, Sir Edward 97
Warne, John 191
Warner, William 14
Watson, Thomas 148, 159, 164
Wayland, John 164
Webster, Thomas 18
Wentworth, Thomas, lord 117
White, John 14, 199
White, Richard 181
Whitelock, Anna 49, 175
Williams, Philip 183
Willis, Jonathan P. 161
Willoughby, Sir Anthony 71
Wizeman, William 161, 170
Wooding, Lucy 9, 149, 151
Wolsey, Thomas, cardinal, papal legate 22, 29, 60, 72, 74, 132, 133, 134
Wright, Paul 25
Wriothesley, Charles 82, 100, 115
Wyatt, Sir Thomas 13, 18, 23, 29, 104, 110, 111, 112, 116, 117, 177
Wycliffe, John 128

Lightning Source UK Ltd.
Milton Keynes UK
UKOW04f1707130915

258569UK00001B/109/P